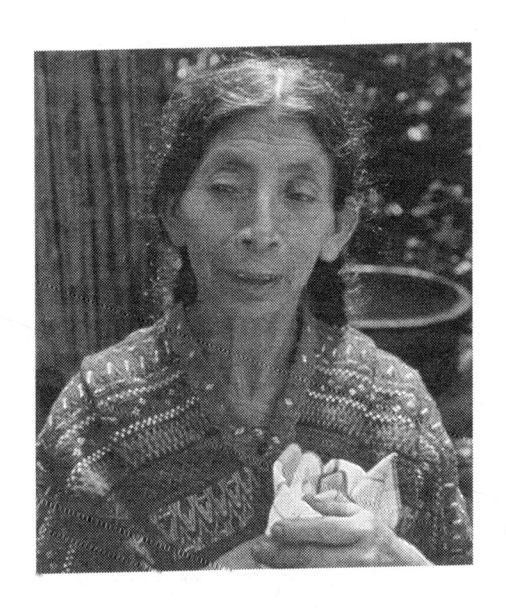

INDEX ON CENSORSHIP 3 1997

INDEX ON CENSORSHIP

Volume 26 No 3 May/June 1997 Issue 176

Editor & Chief Executive Ursula Owen
Deputy Editor Judith Vidal-Hall
News Editor Adam Newey
Production Editor Rose Bell
Eastern Europe Editor Irena Maryniak
Editorial Co-ordinator Nevine Mabro
Fundraising Manager Elizabeth Twining
Fundraising Executive Joe Hipgrave
Circulation & Marketing Director Louise Tyson
Subscriptions & Promotions Manager Lotte Pang
Marketing Assistant Dagmar Schlüter
Office Manager Gary Netherton
Website Manager Jules Nurrish
Volunteer Assistants
Jessie Banfield
Michaela Becker
Ann Chambers
Penny Dale
Victoria Millar
Syra Morley
Philippa Nugent
Bandele Olatunde Ologundudu
Esther Scott
Sarah Smith
Briony Stocker
Neil Tomlinson
Emily Walmsley
Tara Warren

Cover design by Senate

Back cover & title-page: Guatemala: Dona Dominga Yol Vala, the sole survivor of an army massacre in Guatemala, from the documentary *The Terror and the Truth* to be transmitted on BBC2 in June 1997 and distributed internationally by BBC Worldwide

Directors Louis Blom-Cooper, Ajay Chowdhury, Caroline Moorehead, Ursula Owen, Peter Palumbo, Jim Rose, Anthony Smith, Sue Woodford (Chair)

Council Ronald Dworkin, Amanda Foreman, Thomas Hammarberg, Clive Hollick, Geoffrey Hosking, Michael Ignatieff, Mark Littman, Pavel Litvinov, Robert McCrum, Uta Ruge, William Shawcross, Suriya Wickremasinghe

Patrons Chinua Achebe, David Astor, Robert L Bernstein, Harold Evans, Richard Hamilton, Stuart Hampshire, Yehudi Menuhin, Iris Murdoch, Philip Roth, Tom Stoppard, Michael Tippett, Morris West

Australian committee Phillip Adams, Blanche d'Alpuget, Bruce Dawe, Adele Horin, Angelo Loukakis, Ken Methold, Laurie Muller, Robert Pullan and David Williamson, c/o Ken Methold, PO Box 825, Glebe NSW 2037, Australia

Danish committee Paul Grosen, Niels Barfoed, Claus Sønderkøge, Herbert Pundik, Nils Thostrup, Toni Liversage and Björn Elmquist, c/o Claus Sønderkøge, Utkaervej 7, Ejerslev, DK-7900 Nykobing Mors, Denmark

Dutch committee Maarten Asscher, Gerlien van Dalen, Christel Jansen, Chris Keulemans, Wieke Rombach, Mineke Schipper and Steven de Winter, c/o Gerlien van Dalen and Chris Keulemans, De Balie, Kleine-Gartmanplantsoen 10, 1017 RR Amsterdam

Norwegian committee Trond Andreassen, Diis Bøhn, Helge Rønning and Sigmund Strømme, c/o Trond Andreassen, Tyrihansveren 8, N-0851 Oslo, Norway

Swedish committee Gunilla Abrandt and Ana L Valdés, c/o *Dagens Nyheter*, Kulturredaktionen, S-105 15 Stockholm, Sweden

USA committee Ariel Dorfman, Rea Hederman, Peter Jennings, Harvey J Kaye, Susan Kenny, Jane Kramer, Radha Kumar, Jeri Laber, Gara LaMarche, Anne Nelson, Faith Sale, Gay Salisbury, Michael Scammell, Vivienne Walt

---

Index on Censorship (ISSN 0306-4220) is published bi-monthly by a non-profit-making company: Writers & Scholars International Ltd, Lancaster House, 33 Islington High Street, London N1 9LH *Tel*: 0171-278 2313 *Fax*: 0171-278 1878 *Email*: indexoncenso@gn.apc.org http://www.oneworld.org/index_oc/ *Index on Censorship* is associated with Writers & Scholars Educational Trust, registered charity number 325003
Periodicals postage: (US subscribers only) paid at Newark, New Jersey. Postmaster: send US address changes to *Index on Censorship* c/o Mercury Airfreight Int/ Ltd Inc, 2323 Randolph Avenue, Avenel, NJ 07001, USA

Subscriptions 1997 (6 issues p.a.) Individuals: UK £38, US $50, rest of world £43
Institutions: UK £42, US $72, rest of world £48 Students: UK £25, US $35, rest of world £31

© This selection Writers & Scholars International Ltd, London 1997
© Contributors to this issue, except where otherwise indicated
Printed by Unwin Brothers Ltd, UK

Index on Censorship **and Writers and Scholars Educational Trust**
depend on donations to guarantee their independence and to fund research
The Trustees and Directors would like to thank all those whose
donations support Index and WSET, including

The late Baroness Birk
The Open Society Institute
The European Commission

Former Editors: Michael Scammell (1972-81); Hugh Lunghi (1981-83); George Theiner (1983-88); Sally Laird (1988-89); Andrew Graham-Yooll (1989-93)

EDITORIAL

Back to the future

'LET us drink to the success of our hopeless endeavour,' went the old toast of Soviet dissidents. Certainly for *Index* to have been truly successful it should have made itself redundant. The world being what it is, that is unthinkable. So thank God, alas, we are still in business, circulation rising, readership broader than ever. The geography of silencing may have altered since Stephen Spender founded the magazine in 1972, but there is still plenty of it (*see page 106*).

Writing this editorial, I am deeply conscious of the photographs on our office walls, the documents in the drawers, the range of talent and commitment among its writers, its editors, its staff over the years, the unique accumulated archive, of the fact that *Index* has published some of the best and most exciting contemporary writing over the past 25 years. What remain the most moving reassurances that we are doing something useful are the letters from silenced, exiled and marginalised writers, journalists, lawyers, teachers, saying that *Index* makes them feel visible, part of the human race, that their lives *matter*, that their writings have not disappeared 'into the dark'.

'The idea behind *Index* was that there should be the noise of publicity outside every detention centre and concentration camp, and a published record of every tyrannical denial of free expression,' wrote Stuart Hampshire when such denials were pretty brutal and fairly widespread. Then, in 1989, the world was turned upside down. As a result, maps have been redrawn and the world has had to cope with a strategic and intellectual cataclysm. Troubling questions have surfaced: religious extremism, relative values and cultural difference, nationalism, the rewriting of history, words that kill, pornography, violence on television, freedom on the Internet, the primacy of free expression itself are argued and anguished over. In this new world, *Index* has become the forum for these debates.

This anniversary issue of *Index* is about the future; we asked our contributors to be predictive, grapple with what is to come. They address the new age of uncertainty in unexpected ways and without a whiff of

URSULA OWEN

piety: Rushdie explains the lure of the nation for writers, Eco the primacy of the body as a measure of the universality of human rights, Buruma the argument over human rights imperialism. Malik warns us about the dangers of celebrating difference, Ballard and Cronenberg about fake morality and the panic of politicians, Chomsky about the manipulation of public opinion in a society run by business. More specifically, Irena Maryniak gives voice to some of those caught up in the rush of emigration from southern Europe, Aung San Sui Kyi reflects on the personal and philosophical origins of her non-violent protest movement in Burma, Wole Soyinka warns the West to abandon the language of accommodation and come to Nigeria's aid, while, in counterpoint, Chinweizu urges the Black world to remove itself from the ambit of the White. We juxtapose in our running chronicle Index Index the seminal documents and protests of the past 25 years with the all too familiar present day violations of free expression. And since we believe that it will be intolerance that dominates our agenda over the next 25 years, the story of Houria, a mother in Algeria where 'human life is not worth a rotten onion', is at the heart of our issue.

Ma Jian's story of fearful imaginings is perhaps a portent of Hong Kong's future. Stephen Spender once said that 'the opposite of censorship is self-expression, which we call literature', and from the very beginning *Index* ranged itself 'on the side of the scribblers'. That remains our task. But now, eight years after the fall of Communism, we have to address very different worlds at one and the same time. The end of tyranny turns out not, on the whole, to have led to a burst of creativity. We have to concern ourselves with how freedom is used as well as its suppression, and there are freedoms lost by us in the West, the 'spoilt brats of civilisation', when we allow ourselves to be dominated by the mediocrity of media moguls and the bottom line. But there are still plenty of dictatorships and fanaticisms, sacred as well as profane, which turn writers involuntarily into public heroes and martyrs. These writers know the price of *being forced* to abandon their real work — which is grappling with inwardness, with language itself.

Without the storytellers, Gunter Grass says, 'the history of humanity has not been fully told, but is at an end.' We at *Index* will continue to defend, everywhere, the right of the imagination to flourish. ❏

Right: Natalya Gorbanevskaya and her son

Index was founded in response to an open letter from Soviet dissidents Pavel Litvinov and Larisa Bogoraz Daniel published in *The Times*. They were protesting against political show trials taking place in Moscow. A group of western intellectuals including Stephen Spender, Cecil Day Lewis, Yehudi Menuhin, W H Auden and Igor Stravinsky sent the following telegram in response: 'We, a group of friends representing no organisation, support your statement, admire your courage, think of you and will help in any way possible.' The following poem by Natalya Gorbanevskaya, was published in the first issue of *Index* in May 1972.

I know them all by sight
in the conservatoire pack
but who'll send me one little word
one little letter from freedom

when I lie on my rough plank-bed
exhausted as a wolf
to whose lips shall I press mine
passionately tenderly

and whose hullo hullo my friend
shall I hear as I freeze
a huge light like a chandelier
and myself — such darkness

1967

Natalya Gorbanevskaya became active in the Soviet dissident movement in 1968, heading the petition drive on behalf of Yuri Galanskov and Alexander Ginzburg. In December 1969 she was arrested and committed to a psychiatric asylum in Kazan. She was released in February 1972. Among her collections are The Seacoast *(1972),* Flying across the Snowy Border *(1983),* Variable Clouds *and* When and When *(1985)*

contents

The vulnerable body — Umberto Eco discovers a universal ethic PAGE 12

'Beware the new Behalfism!' Salman Rushdie on writers and the lure of the nation PAGE 34

Algeria's plague of violence — Houria's story PAGE 40

3	**Editorial** URSULA OWEN Back to the future
5	NATALYA GORBANEVSKAYA Poem
8	**From the archive**

TOLERANCE
12	UMBERTO ECO The birth of ethics
20	ARIEL DORFMAN Language of survival
25	RONAN BENNETT Divided by the same language
30	NADINE GORDIMER Artful words
34	SALMAN RUSHDIE Notes on writing & the nation

INTOLERANCE
40	SELIM ZAOUI The terror that stalks the mountains
53	OLIVIER ROY Getting into the game

GLOBAL REACH
56	NOAM CHOMSKY Democracy lite
59	CHRISTOPHER HIRD The capable state

MEDIASCAPE
68	DAN SCHILLER O what a tangled web we weave
77	GABRIEL GARCIA MARQUEZ The best job in the world
81	JAY ROSEN In quest of journalism

THE IMAGE
90	DAVID CRONENBERG & JG BALLARD Set for collision
99	EDWARD LUCIE-SMITH Beyond fundamentalism

INDEX INDEX *25 years on the record*
106	ADAM NEWEY Witness in difficult times

141	**UNQUIET CITY: JERUSALEM**

ASIAN VALUES
148	RONALD DWORKIN Forked tongues, faked doctrines
152	YANG LIAN Poet without a nation
157	IAN BURUMA God bless America
162	AUNG SAN SUU KYI Voice of hope
169	URVASHI BUTALIA Voices of India

OUTSIDERS
172	CHINWEIZU Black redemption
183	KENAN MALIK The perils of pluralism
190	IRENA MARYNIAK Rights of passage

BODY POLITICS
198	WOLE SOYINKA A call for sanctions
203	CAROLINE MOOREHEAD All rights reserved
209	MICHAEL IGNATIEFF Varieties of experience
213	MA JIAN Darkness & light

From the archive
INDEX 1972-97

'The men who humiliate you must first humiliate the humanity within themselves' — George Mangakis on torture in 'Greece Today: Letter to Europeans' in the first issue of *Index* May 1972

1972
In its first year, *Index* reports the arrest or confinement of 76 poets, musicians, scientists, journalists in the Soviet Union

Glavlit, the Soviet censorship body, employs around 70,000 people

Over 300 Spanish intellectuals send a letter to the Ministry of Information protesting a ban on a proposed lecture to commemorate Picasso's 90th birthday

The State Publications Control Board of South Africa has vetted over 14,440 films since 1963. The 'official' cut of the movie *M.A.S.H* is reduced to 26 minutes

'Do you know how humiliating it is to hear that loud and vicious banging at the door, and watch helplessly as armed police pull blankets off sleeping children? Searching, scratching and stamping, until the whole damn house is filled with hatred and anger' — Don Mattera, South Africa 1980

1974
Following the military coup, *Index* reports that the Chilean government has forbidden newspapers to publish political news. In August it bans Marxist parties in perpetuity

A recording of *Snow White and the Seven Dwarfs* joins 1,000 other victims of cultural ostracism in Czechoslovakia

1975
Censorship in India is so strict under Indira Gandhi that newspapers are no longer allowed to print extracts from speeches by Nehru, Gandhi or Tagore which relate to freedom or touch upon the kind of emergency measures then being introduced

1978-1986
Index reports the disappearance or execution of 30,000 Guatemalans under the military

'Ideology wants to convince you that its truth is absolute. A novel shows you that everything is relative' — Milan Kundera 1977

1980
Index publishes *Nunca Más* recording by name the 10,000 'disappeared' of Argentina between 1976 and 1980. It sells over 200,000 copies from November 1984 to May 1985 Crown Prince Fahd of Saudi Arabia decrees that Saudi women may no longer take up scholarships abroad even if accompanied by a male

FROM THE ARCHIVE

1981
Twenty-five per cent of the 4,000 people executed or tortured to death in Iraq between 1968 and 1981 are academics

'The Chinese love their land and love their homes. But because their souls have been diminished, they have lost their dignity' — Ma Jian 1997

1982
Robert Kee, presenter of *Panorama*, resigns over UK government criticism of BBC coverage of the Falklands war; 81 per cent of the public feel the BBC got it about right

The Egyptian minister of information bans 'films of violence and sex', and increases the TV time for religious programmes

Mahmoud Darwish, the Palestinian poet, is refused a visa to enter the US despite being part of a poetry reading to raise money for a UNICEF aid programme for Lebanon

Throughout history all cultures have fed one another, been grafted onto one another and, in the process, our world has been enriched. The disappearance of a culture is the loss of a colour, a different light, a different source' — Yasar Kemal on Turkey's war in Anatolia, 1995

1983
An advertisement sponsored by the black newspaper *Voice* depicting the situation of blacks in Britain is rejected by the Independent Television Companies Association as being 'too politically controversial'

Censors in Sweden, Norway and Finland rule that the movie *ET* is unfit for child audiences because it 'portrays adults as the enemies of children'

1985
Index reports the unbanning of a 400-year-old eye-witness report of the Spanish conquest. Missionary José de Acosta's record of atrocities committed in the Americas (1576) is published uncensored in Spain for the first time

'What one writer can make in the solitude of one room is something no power can easily destroy' — Salman Rushdie 1994

1986
The Premier of Queensland, Australia passes a law forbidding any bartender to serve drinks to anyone displaying 'deviant' tendencies

The opening of four South African beaches to both races over Christmas 1985 results in 13,741 black bathers being warned and 300 charged with public indecency and other by-law contraventions.

In the mid-1980s, as thousands of Sudanese die of hunger, Sudanese journalists who report on famine face imprisonment and torture

Indiana Jones and the Temple of Doom is banned by the Indian Film Certification Board for portraying Indians in a poor light, and *Rambo First Blood Part 2* for its anti-Soviet, anti-Vietnamese content

INDEX 1972-97

'I'm a citizen of that country but the law says that if I play for whites my own mother cannot come and hear me' — **Abdullah Ibrahim on South Africa 1983**

1987

Members of the Peruvian Tupac Amaru Revolutionary Movement occupy two ('86) and then six ('87) radio stations and accuse the president of 'political stupidity' and genocide

Thai officials ban a pop song by the group Carabao for poking fun at democracy and implying that a leader in a democracy should be elected

'As the most powerful state, the USA makes its own laws, using force and conducting economic warfare at will. It also threatens sanctions against countries that do not abide by its conveniently flexible notions of "free trade"'— **Noam Chomsky 1994**

1988

In off the record remarks, US Secretary of State Henry Kissinger advocates a total ban on reporters and TV cameras in the Occupied Territories

Under the 'Library Awareness Programme', the FBI asks librarians to monitor the reading of 'persons from countries hostile to the USA'

1991

Hitoshi Igarashi, the Japanese translator of *The Satanic Verses* is stabbed to death at Tsakibu University after having received threats from Islamic militants

'A quarter of a century ago the United Nations Organisation was born bearing the great hopes of mankind. Alas, in an immoral world it too has grown up immoral' — **Alexander Solzhenitsyn 1970, from his Nobel Prize speech which he was prevented from making.** *Index* **published it in 1972**

1995

The world's media has its eyes on the war in former Yugoslavia but *Index* reports that 24 out of 51 journalists murdered that year — a bad one for journalists — are Algerian

1996

French rappers Kool Shen and Joey Starr are condemned to three months' imprisonment, a six-month ban and a US$10,000 fine for 'verbal abuse of the police' in their lyrics

At the present rate of female foetal abortion in China, there will be 70 million men condemned to celibacy by the year 2000

'If we are too careful, slow, hesitant and reserved, the new order could be built by others, in particular the nationalists and chauvinists' — **Václav Havel predicts the rise of nationalism in eastern Europe, 1994**

Researched by Jessie Banfield

Right: The General — Credit: BBC

Tolerance

UMBERTO ECO

The birth of ethics

I AM of the firm belief that even those who do not have faith in a personal and providential divinity can still experience forms of religious feeling and hence a sense of the sacred, of limits, questioning and expectation; of a communion with something that surpasses us. What you ask is what there is that is binding, compelling and irrevocable in this form of ethics.

I would like to put some distance between myself and the subject. Certain ethical problems have become much clearer to me by reflecting on some semantic problems — don't worry if people say this discourse is difficult; we are perhaps encouraged into easy thinking by the 'revelations' of the mass media, which are, by definition, predictable. Let people learn to 'think difficult' because neither the mystery nor the evidence are easy to deal with.

My problem was whether there were 'semantic universals', or basic concepts common to all humanity that can be expressed in all languages. Not so obvious a problem once you realise that many cultures do not recognise notions that seem obvious to us: for example, that certain properties belong to certain substances (as when we say 'the apple is red') or concepts of identity ($a=a$). I became convinced that there certainly are concepts common to all cultures, and that they all refer to the position of our body in space.

We are animals who stand upright, who find it exhausting to keep our heads bent down and, consequently, we share a notion of up and down, tending to favour the first rather than the second. Equally we have notions of right and left, of staying still or walking, of standing up or lying down, of crawling or jumping, of waking and sleeping. Since we all have our arts and crafts, we all know what it means to beat a resistant material, to penetrate a soft or liquid substance, to pulp, to beat, to grind, to kick, perhaps even to dance. The list goes on and on: it takes in seeing, hearing, eating and drinking, swallowing and excreting. Certainly every human has notions of what it means to perceive, to remember, to desire, to fear, to feel sadness and relief, pleasure and pain, and to emit sounds that express these feelings. Therefore (and here we enter the legal sphere) there are universal ideas about constraints: nobody wants anyone to stop them speaking, seeing, listening, sleeping, swallowing or excreting, or going where they want; we suffer if we are tied up or kept in isolation, struck, wounded or killed, or subjected to physical or psychological torture that diminishes or stifles our capacity to think.

You see that up to this point I have only considered a sort of solitary and animal Adam, who doesn't yet know the meaning of sexual relationships, of the pleasures of conversation, of love for his own children or the pain of losing a loved one. But already for us by this point (if not for this Adam or Eve) this semantics has provided the basis for an ethics: we must, above all, respect the rights of everyone's body, including the right to speak and think. If humanity had always respected these rights, there wouldn't have been the Massacre of the Innocents, Christians thrown to the lions, the St Bartholomew's Day Massacre, heretics on the rack, concentration camps, censorship, children down mines, people raped in Bosnia.

But how is it that our human beast, male or female, mindless and savage in the way I have described, once its instinctive repertoire of universal concepts has been elaborated, can come to understand not only that it wants to do certain things and not have other things done to it, but also that it should not do to others what it would not have them do to it? Because — fortunately — Eden rapidly acquires a population. The ethical dimension begins when the other comes on the scene. Every law, whether moral or statutory, regulates interpersonal relationships, including those with that other who imposes it.

Even you, Cardinal, attribute to the virtuous non-Christian the conviction that the other is within us. We are not dealing with a vague sentimental disposition here, but with a fundamental condition. As even the most secular of the human sciences teaches us, it is the other and his gaze that defines and shapes us. Just as we cannot live without eating or sleeping we cannot understand who we are without the regard and the response of the other. Even those who kill, rape, rob, oppress, do so in exceptional moments; the rest of the time they beg their peers for approval, love, respect and praise. They even demand that those they humiliate acknowledge fear and submission. Lacking this recognition, the newborn baby abandoned in the forest will not become human (unless, like Tarzan, it desperately seeks the other in the face of an ape) and we can die or go mad if we live in a community in which everyone has agreed never to look at us and which systematically behaves as if we did not exist.

How then can there be or have been cultures that approve massacre, cannibalism, the physical humiliation of others? Simply because they restrict the concept of 'other humans' to the tribal community (or ethnic group) and consider the 'barbarians' non-human; not even the Crusaders felt the infidel was a neighbour to be excessively loved. The fact is, the recognition of the role of others, and the need to respect in them the needs we consider essential for ourselves, has developed slowly over thousands of years. The Christian commandment of love was enunciated with great effort, and only accepted when the time was ripe.

But, you ask me, can this idea of the importance of the other furnish an absolute base, an immutable foundation for ethical behaviour? It would be enough for me to reply that even the foundations that you define as absolute do not prevent believers from sinning in the knowledge that they sin, and the story would end there; the temptation to evil is present even in those who have a solid and revealed notion of Good. Let me relate two anecdotes that have given me much food for thought.

One is about a writer who, after his own fashion, called himself a Catholic. I won't give his name because we spoke privately and I am not an informer. It was during the time of John XXIII and my old friend, celebrating the Pope's virtues enthusiastically, said (with obvious paradoxical intent): 'Pope John must be an atheist. Only someone who doesn't believe in God can love his neighbour so much!' Like all paradoxes this contains a germ of truth. Setting aside the atheist (someone whose psychology escapes me, because, like Kant, I can't see how it is possible not to believe in God, arguing that you can't prove He exists, and then firmly claim that He doesn't exist and that you can prove it), it seems evident to me that a person who has never experienced transcendence, or who has had it and lost it, can still give sense to his own life and death, can find comfort in the love of others and in the attempt to guarantee everyone else a life worth living even after his own death. Certainly there are those who do not believe and yet are not obsessed with giving meaning to their own death; there are also those who say they believe and yet would be prepared to tear the heart from a living child to preserve their own life. The power of a particular ethical system is to be judged by the behaviour of saints, not by those fools *cuis deus venter est*.

This leads me to the second anecdote. When I was still a young Catholic of 16 I was involved in a debate with an older acquaintance who was well known as a 'communist' in the sense in which we used the term in the frightful 'fifties. As I warmed to the subject I asked him the decisive question: 'How could he, a non-believer, give any sense to that senseless thing, his own death?' This was his reply: 'Before I die I will ask for a civil funeral. In that way, though I won't be here any more I shall leave an example for others.' I believe that you would also admire this profound faith in the continuity of life, the absolute sense of commitment that inspired this response. This is the idea that has moved

There are universal ideas on constraints: nobody wants anyone to stop them speaking, seeing, listening...we suffer if we are tied up or kept in isolation, struck, wounded or killed, or subjected to physical or psychological torture that diminishes or stifles our capacity to think

many non-believers to die under torture rather than betray their friends, to contract plague themselves to cure those suffering from plague. It may also, sometimes, be the one thing that makes philosophers philosophise and writers write: they leave a message in a bottle because in that way what they believe in or what they find beautiful can be communicated to those who come after and who may, in turn, believe and discover beauty in those same things.

Is this feeling really so powerful that it can justify an ethical code as defined and inflexible, as firmly grounded, as that of those who believe in revealed morality, in the survival of the soul and in rewards and punishments? I have tried to base the principles of a secular ethics on natural phenomena (and as such, from your perspective, the result of a divine project) such as our physical being and the idea that we know instinctively that we have a soul (or something which performs that function) only by virtue of the presence of others. Hence it appears that

UMBERTO ECO

what I had defined as a secular ethics is at bottom a natural ethics, recognised by believers too. Brought in the fullness of time to proper maturity and self-awareness, does not this natural instinct provide a foundation with sufficient guarantees? Certainly we may think it insufficient in itself to spur people to do good; particularly since as far as a non-believer is concerned, no-one need know about secret wrongdoing. A non-believer doesn't believe there is anyone watching him from on high and consequently — precisely for that reason — knows that no-one is there to forgive him either. If he knows he has done wrong his isolation is boundless and his death desperate. For this very reason, such a person would be more likely than a believer to try to wash himself clean in the public confessional, asking pardon of others. He knows in every fibre of his being that there is no God to forgive and knows, therefore, that he must forgive others first. Otherwise how can we explain the fact that it is not only believers who feel remorse?

I do not want to draw a hard and fast line between those who believe in a transcendent God and those who do not believe in any supra-individual principle. Remember, Spinoza's great book was called *Ethics* and opened with a definition of God as cause of Itself. This Spinozian divinity, as we well know, is neither transcendent nor personal; and yet even from the idea of a great and unique cosmic Substance into which we shall one day be reabsorbed, there can emerge a vision of tolerance and benevolence precisely because we all have an interest in the equilibrium and harmony of this unique Substance. We share this interest because we think this Substance must, in some way, be enriched or deformed by what we have done over the millennia. What I would hazard (not as a metaphysical hypothesis, but as a timid concession to the hope that never abandons us) is that even from this point of view you can postulate once more the problem of some kind of life after death. Today, the electronic universe suggests to us that there can exist sequences of messages that transfer themselves from one physical support to another without losing their unique characteristics and survive as pure immaterial algorithms at the very instant in which, leaving one support, they are not yet inscribed on the other. Who knows if death, rather than an implosion, might not be an explosion, a re-formation somewhere in the vortices of the universe,

Right: Adam and Eve from the **Manafi' Al-Hayawan** *(The Usefulness of Animals, Iran 13th century)*
Credit: Pierpont Morgan Library, New York

THE BIRTH OF ETHICS

of the software (which others call the soul) which we fashion in the course of our lives, and which is made up of memories and personal remorse (and therefore incurable suffering), or of a sense of peace at duty fulfilled — and love.

But you say that without the example and the word of Christ every secular ethic would lack a fundamental justification with the strength of irresistible conviction. Why take away from the secular person the right to use the example of the forgiving Christ? Try, Cardinal Carlo Maria Martini, for the benefit of the discussion and the inquiry to which you are committed, to accept for a moment the hypothesis that there is no God: that man's appearance on earth is the result of an unfortunate mistake, that not only is he consigned to his mortal condition, he is also condemned to be aware of this, and is thus the most imperfect of creatures (allow me the Leopardian tone of my hypothesis). To find the courage with which to await death, this man, of necessity, will become a religious animal and aspire to construct narratives capable of furnishing him with an explanation and a model, an exemplary image. Among the many he is able to conjure — some splendid, some terrifying, some pathetically consolatory — he achieves, in the fullness of time, the religious, moral, and poetic power to conceive of the model of Christ, of universal love, of the forgiveness of enemies, of a life offered in human sacrifice for the salvation of others. If I were a traveller from a far-off galaxy and I found myself facing a species that had been able to offer such a model, I would fall down in admiration of such God-creating energy; yet discovering it to be responsible for so many atrocities, I would deem it pathetic and despicable and would see its redemption only in the fact that it had succeeded in wanting and believing its story to be the Truth.

We may drop that hypothesis and leave it to others: but let us admit that if Christ was only the subject of a great story, the fact that this story was imagined and desired by immature fledglings who knew only that they knew nothing, would make it every bit as miraculous (miraculously mysterious) as the fact that the son of a true God was truly incarnate. This natural and earthly mystery would continue to move and soften the hearts of non-believers.

Because of this I maintain that, in its fundamental aspects, a natural ethic — respected for the profound religious spirit that inspires it — can find points of contact with an ethic founded on faith in a transcendent being; the latter, in turn, cannot but recognise that the natural principles are engraved on our hearts as part of some great scheme for salvation. If there remain, as there certainly do, areas where there is no overlap, this is no different from what we encounter in disputes between different religions. And in conflicts of faith, Charity and Wisdom must prevail. ❏

Umberto Eco, *linguist, semiologist and professor at Bologna University, is author of* The Name of the Rose *and* Foucault's Pendulum. *His most recent novel is* The Island of the Day Before *(Martin Secker & Warburg, 1995)*

© *All rights reserved. Excerpted from* In cosa crede chi non crede? An exchange of letters between Cardinal Carlo Maria Martini and Umberto Eco *(Liberal, 1996)*

Translated by Rosalind Delmar

JUSTICE
An independent legal human rights organisation

Asylum
fair and effective procedures

Criminal Justice
fair trial rights; intelligence led policing

Europe
anti-discrimination laws; data protection and privacy

Support justice Join JUSTICE!
59 Carter Lane, London EC4V. Tel 0171 329 5100.
Fax 0171 329 5055. E-mail: justice@gn.apc.org

ARIEL DORFMAN

Language of survival

What separates intolerance from violence? Is there any way of making sure that one does not turn into the other? An encounter I had over 10 years ago may provide a way into these questions, a tentative answer

LANGUAGE OF SURVIVAL

ONE NIGHT in June 1986, I joined hundreds of citizens who had gathered in the Plaza Italia in Santiago de Chile, supposedly in order to say goodbye to Halley's Comet, though in reality we were there to ask the comet to take away General Pinochet, Chile's dictator at the time, to take him magically away and leave him out there in the emptiness of space, not bring him back on the comet's next visit to this planet in 75 years. Tyrants hate being made fun of — and Pinochet was no exception. The army quickly broke up our meeting. A tall, glint-eyed, hawk-nosed lieutenant, his face blackened with grease, made sure his troops forgot no-one with their rifle butts — and when the beating was over, told our group to start running.

So we ran, as best we could, limping and bloodied, up Avenida Providencia — and I straggled a bit behind, because I was not as young as most of the others and my leg hurt me, which meant that I was by myself when a young recruit stopped me in my tracks. He could not have been more than 20, perhaps less. He pointed his submachine gun at me, his finger trembling on the trigger. 'Stay away from me,' he barked, 'Hands up, stay away, five metres away, five metres away. *A cinco metros*,' he said, crazed, in a panic, almost imploring me. Death was no more than a nerve pulse away, a twitch of a nerve away. As I slowly raised my hands, I had the flash of an intuition, I understood that this young man who was about to ruin his life — and definitely mine — by eliminating me from the earth, was not really seeing the person he was about to shoot, not seeing my useless body, my empty hands, my extreme vulnerability. I understood that this young man, incredibly, was terrified of me, and that if he pulled the trigger it would be in the name of that terror. His instructors had convinced him that he was in danger from some alien force and I had, inconceivably, come to represent that force. So, in order to save my life, I did the one thing I have been perfecting all my life: I tried to communicate with him. Gently, almost normally, I asked him to look, I didn't even have a candy bar in my hands. I used the name of a candy bar, *una negrita*, that I had eaten as a child, the *negrita* that he had certainly chewed in his own childhood, as if to remind him of his innocence and mine, our innocence that is so easy to lose. And then I mentioned that I had two sons, one a bit older than him, another a bit younger, that they were waiting for me back home, I asked him where he was from — anything to establish a

Left: Book burning in Chile 1973

relationship, to get closer to him, to come nearer than the five metres he was demanding and that he required in order to kill me.

'Shut up,' he said, and I obeyed.

We stayed there for a few more seconds; and I became acutely aware of how different we were: he was poor and uneducated and I was well-to-do and deft with words, he was of indian ancestry and my folks obviously came from somewhere else, from the Europe that had excluded him; life had not been good to him and now he had a way of turning the tables, and marking someone else permanently with his power.

But that is not what he did. Instead, he blinked and I watched something brutal and sad drain out of his eyes, he breathed deeply as if ridding his lungs of a cloud, he steered his weapon away from me, and motioned me to get the hell out of there.

To have said goodbye to Halley's Comet that night in Santiago may have been a mistake for my body, but it did teach my mind something about the nature of intolerance. I had always presumed that fear is what breeds violence, but I had known it only in theory, and now I had witnessed that theory incarnated in a real human being. I had been the potential victim of that fear, had seen that violence disappear as the fear itself melted in front of my eyes, had survived because I was able to convince the soldier that I was neither dangerous nor different. My words broke the isolating circle he had drawn around himself. I had used words to contact his humanity and stimulate his empathy, I had used our common vocabulary to place his skin in my skin and his eyes inside my eyes, to feel the world from my perspective. What art, what literature does: children who dance together find it difficult to slaughter one another in the streets.

It is ironic that I used language that night to save myself, to create a territory where that soldier could meet me as a human being. Ironic because I have in my life been guilty myself of extreme acts of intolerance and the instrument of that intolerance was language. I am at the moment entirely bilingual and yet, as a child in New York, exiled from my native Argentina, I repudiated the Spanish language I had been born into with resolute fanaticism, detested everything associated with my mother tongue, would not speak it for 10 years. My return to Latin America slowly seduced me back into Spanish — until many years later, inspired by the all-or-nothing nationalistic mentality of the 1960s, I found myself rejecting English with the same absolute conviction with which I had turned my back on Spanish when I was a child. It took me many years to return to English without renouncing Spanish, it took me a good part of my life to accept the richness of being bilingual, the joy of being a hybrid, at home in two cultures and two linguistic systems, it took me almost forever to go beyond the fear that I felt at my own duality. It took me much too long to understand that I could not accept plurality in the world unless I was willing to tolerate it inside my own being.

Perhaps that is why I so strongly proclaim one of the solutions to the dilemmas of intolerance to be the right use of language.

And yet, I am aware, of course, that to share a language with someone who considers you his enemy is no guarantee that he will not try to eliminate you. I have not forgotten the German Jews, the Bosnian Muslims, so many people discriminated against because of their skin, their religion, their sexual preference, their tribal origins, massacred by men who speak their tongue, who long ago uttered the same nursery rhymes, who today lip-sync the same songs on the radio. What makes the other menacing could turn out to be precisely the fact that he or she partakes of our same syllables. Perhaps we kill the other because we fear that we could become him.

My tactic with that young soldier that night in Santiago might have backfired: I could well have pronounced a word that made him feel guilty, impure, incomplete, reminded him of some polluted image that swam inside and that he desperately needed to eradicate. I could have triggered my own death, my words of conciliation and familiarity prodding him into pulling that intolerant and intolerable trigger.

And yet, he didn't.

He saw me, from a different class and a different race, with different skin and a different colour of eyes, as a member of his community, or merely perhaps, a member of his species, he saw me as a human being and spared my life.

He conquered his own fear.

And, for a moment that could have lasted an eternity, that young man was no longer intolerant.

Even so, his lack of intolerance was gained by my own effacing of my identity — I appeased him by trying to rid myself of whatever it was that might make him feel threatened, might make him kill me. So that my action that night may be a good tactic for survival, but is not one I would recommend for a long-term coexistence, where along with establishing our sameness and brotherhood, we have to create something more than a mirror in which the more powerful looks and sees himself, we have to create an acknowledgement and, above all, respect for our differences. We have to go beyond tolerance to recognition and dialogue: peace can only come from the act of recognising one another.

Whether that soldier spared my life because I was the same or because I was different, whether because of language or in spite of language, whether it was because he understood me or because he misunderstood me, whatever the reason, the ultimate truth is that two men met on a war-torn street in Santiago de Chile and one of them did not kill the other, and the man whose life was not taken that night carries that soldier with him.

To try and puzzle out the lessons from our brief meeting the night Halley's Comet did not take General Pinochet from the earth — but did not take me away either and left me alive to wonder if the next time that comet comes to visit, in the year 2062, our world will not finally be a place where stories such as these have become obsolete and unnecessary.

It is the least I can do for that young man. ❏

© *Ariel Dorfman*

Ariel Dorfman *is a Chilean expatriate and human rights activist, as well as novelist, playwright and journalist. Currently research professor of Literature and Latin American Studies at Duke University, his works include* Widows *and* Death and the Maiden

RONAN BENNETT

Divided by the same language

Extreme language and glib explanations obfuscate the roots of the Irish troubles and do nothing to further the search for a peaceful solution

THE WORD 'fascist' has started to appear with increasing frequency in connection with Irish nationalism in general and republicanism in particular. Those deploying it fall roughly into two camps. There are politicians and political commentators like Dr Joe Hendron of the Social Democratic and Labour Party who, fighting Sinn Féin in West Belfast during last May's special 'Forum' elections, denounced his opponents as 'fascists'; or John Bruton, the Irish Taoiseach, who last year accused republicans of using 'Nazi tactics'; or Kevin Myers of the *Irish Times* or Eilis O'Hanlon of the *Irish Independent*, who routinely attack republicans for what they see as their backwards-looking cultural and political chauvinism: typical Myers — 'Apart from the obscurantist right, the most reactionary, conservative, unimaginative group of all in Irish life — made all the more unbearable by its hand-wringing piety — has been the militant republican left.'

This is little more than the familiar knockabout stuff of politics, a rather crude form of negative campaigning, which, like all negative campaigning, seems to satisfy the campaigner more than the campaigned: Joe Hendron saw Sinn Féin sweep to victory in West Belfast by a margin of two to one. But there is also at work a subtler argument, developed by liberal and liberal-left historians, critics, writers and academics, which, though it generally avoids the worst of the politicians' excesses, runs broadly along the same line of thinking. Roy Foster, the historian and

RONAN BENNETT

biographer of Yeats, has argued modern Irish republicanism as the outgrowth of a racist Gaelic separatist impulse, sustained by myths, pieties and simplicities deriving from everything from the Conquest, through to the Plantation, the Penal Laws, the Famine and the Rising — a point of view endorsed by the writer and academic Arthur Aughey, who has argued that a 'pervasive notion of general cultural superiority fulfils a vital psychological and political function in Irish nationalism'. Irish nationalism, according to Aughey, is inherently culturally exclusive and politically intolerant.

Colm Tóibín, the novelist and critic, has sought explanations for the origins of the present 'Troubles' in 'good and bad blood'. The violent struggle for the land, the wrongs perpetrated, the sufferings and the cruelties have poisoned the blood. We are not far from the 'tribal' interpretation here, from the notion of two mutually antagonistic, mutually uncomprehending, self-defining and hermetically sealed peoples locked in an irrational, atavistic slaughter. In a recent essay on Pol Pot, Tom Nairn, citing Tóibín, rejected the centrality of the city to the Troubles, locating their origins in 'a centuries-old struggle over land rights'. 'Whatever else it may have become, today's Sinn Féin is the inheritor of Republicanism's old social ideal: the rural and pious peasant-family utopia which inspired the Irish Constitution, and regulated most of its strategic development from 1922 until Ireland's entry to the European Community in 1975. The resultant generational warfare may penetrate or even take over cities, the urban sites to which extended families of land-dwellers have moved or (sometimes) been expelled. But the violent side of the conflict invariably has its origin in the peasant or small-town world they have left behind.'

Nairn went on to argue that the violence was aggravated by the 'agonising process' of urbanisation, during which 'rural emigrants look backwards as much as forwards, and pass from the remembrance to the often elaborate re-invention of the worlds they have lost. They are helped in this by other strata without direct connection to the land. Some urban classes — above all the intellectuals — have a parallel if different motivation: they are seeking to "mobilise" lost-world psychology in order to build a new world, that of the modern nation-state.' From this, it is but a short step to ethnic nationalism of the Balkan variety (the term 'ethnic

Right: Divis flats in Catholic Belfast — Credit: Judah Passow/Network

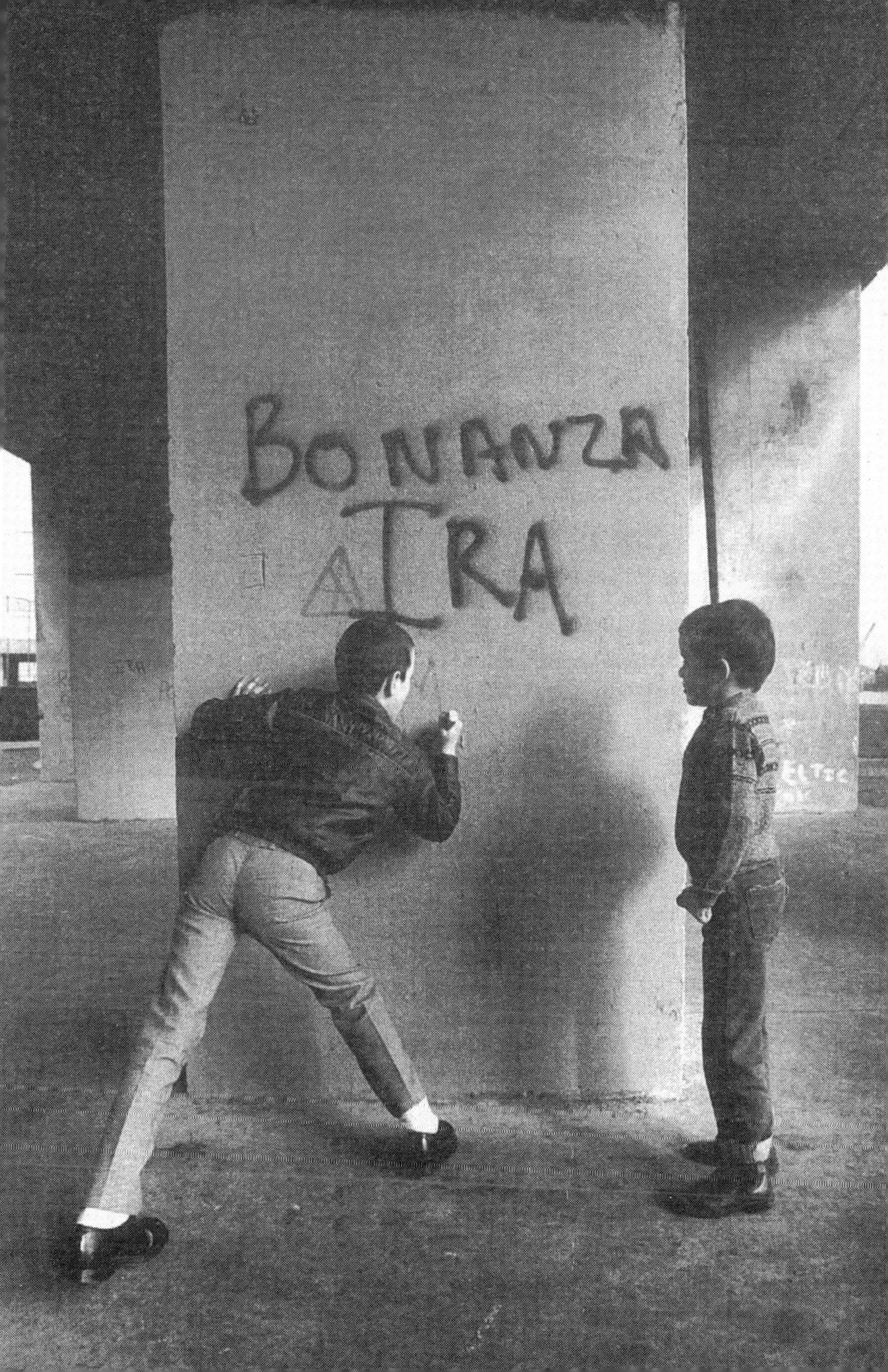
BONANZA
IRA

cleansing' started to appear in writing on Ireland soon after the break-up of the old Yugoslavia), and from there — though historians might argue about the particularity of the term — it is not far to fascism.

But is the use of 'fascist' in relation to what is happening now in Ireland legitimate? Are the Troubles really the product of timeless peasant bloodlust transposed to the city? Are republican leaders like Gerry Adams and Martin McGuinness really seeking to create an ethnically pure state? Are their supporters looking backwards to a warmly imagined Gaelic past? Are IRA volunteers motivated by an implacable hatred of the invader and the planter? These are crucial questions, for if the answer to any of the above is yes, the implications for British politicians thinking about resurrecting the peace process are grave. How do you negotiate with a fascist? How do you compromise with an ethnic cleanser? Why should you? In such circumstances, the question of a settlement becomes one not of political practicality, but of morality and principle, and infinitely more problematic.

There is another interpretation — less abstract, less spectacular, probably less interesting for those who look for over-arching theories of modern manifestations of nationalism. It is that the republican movement, its members and supporters are motivated less by the myths, pieties and simplicities of an imagined Gaelic past than by their more recent history. This is not to say that the Famine or the 1916 Rising have not played their part in helping to shape the political consciousness of the present generation of Irish republicans. But of far greater importance has been the reality experienced since Partition and the creation of the northern state in 1921.

It is interesting that the analysis and media coverage of the early years of the Troubles — from the Civil Rights marches in Coalisland and Derry in 1968, through the Battle of the Bogside in August 1969, to the arrival of British troops and the eventual suspension of Stormont — put the emphasis on recent injustices. That this perspective has changed is due more, I believe, to the revulsion at IRA violence than to a greater understanding of the roots of the conflict. In the early days, the analysis focused on the specific: on the gerrymandering of Derry; on poverty, deprivation and religious discrimination; on the exclusion of Catholics from power; on the sectarian bias of law and order; on the failure of unionism to agree to any kind of meaningful reform. Republicans like Adams and McGuinness, when describing their early political involvement, talk about police violence during peaceful demonstrations or being turned away from jobs because of their religion. Adams says in his autobiography that although he came from a family of republicans, republicanism was rarely discussed in the house when he was young; McGuinness did not even come from a family with a republican past: in interviews he has repeatedly referred to the shooting dead by the British army in Derry of two young men — Beattie and Cusack — as a milestone in his political journey.

There have been many more milestones since, from internment and Bloody Sunday to Drumcree, each of which has impacted directly on republicans. In the republican imagination, Bobby Sands, the IRA prisoner who died on hunger strike in 1981, plays an infinitely greater part than Yeats. His death, and those of the other nine hunger strikers, resonates with this generation of republicans far more than the deaths of the Famine. And though the hunger strike is often held up as yet another example of the republican fixation with blood sacrifice and martyrdom — part of the overall 'all-in-the-blood' package in which ethnic nationalism now comes wrapped — reading the surviving hunger strikers' account of that time makes it clear that it was in fact a last desperate escalation by men who had decided that the only way to break the deadlock of their 'dirty protest' against intolerable prison conditions was to up the stakes as far as they would go.

We are not dealing with bloodlust or martyr complexes in Ireland. We are dealing with specific political problems and the grievances which have emerged from them. The problems are complex and deep rooted, they have led to appalling acts of violence. No-one says resolving them will be easy, but if we persist in interpreting them as a manifestation of ethnic nationalism and a late-twentieth-century form of fascism we not only miss the real point, but make a hard task infinitely harder. ❏

Ronan Bennett *is a novelist and screenwriter*

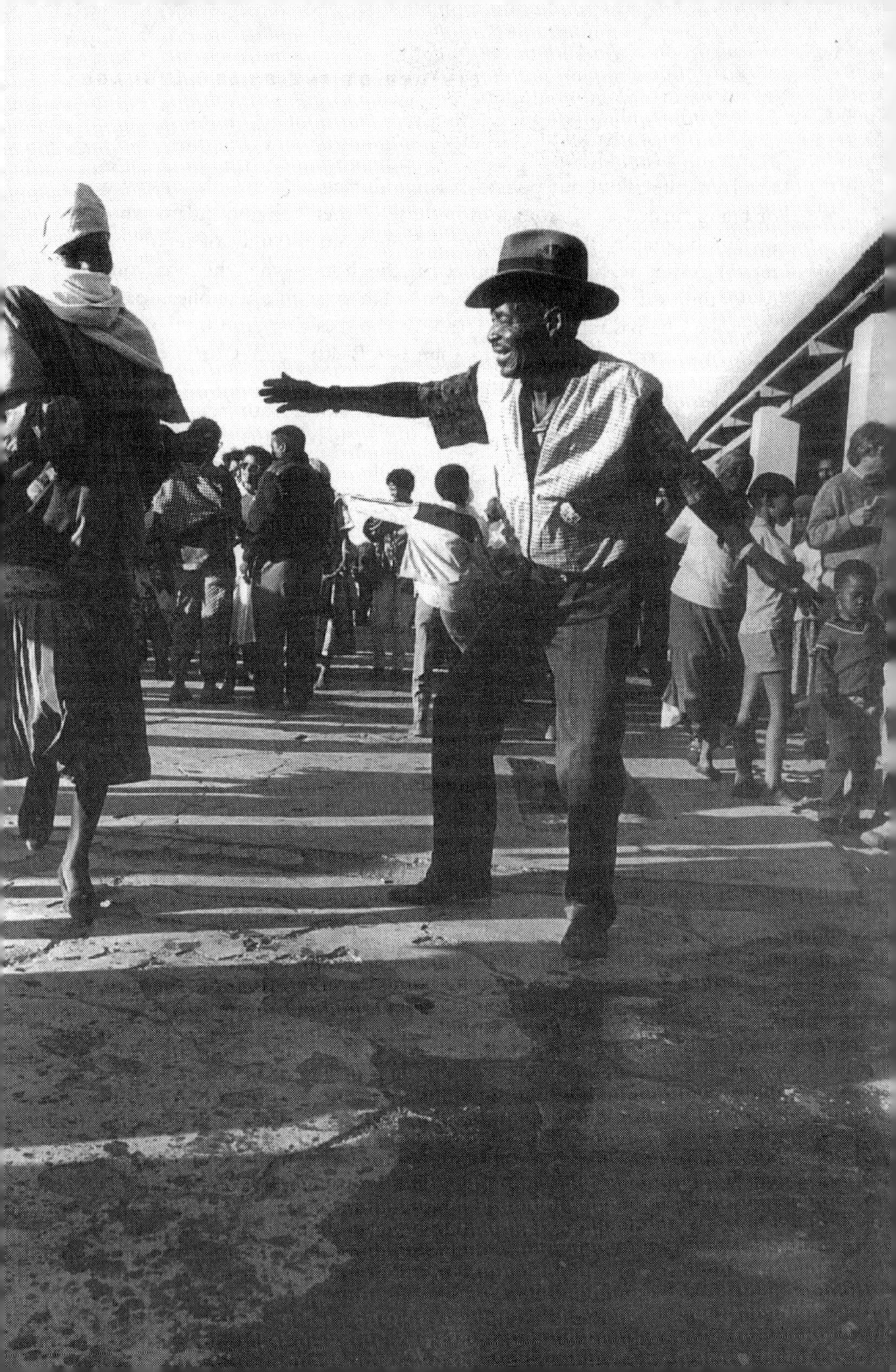

NADINE GORDIMER

Artful words

Because, as the philosopher Swedenborg reminds us, the written word is humankind's exclusive property, there is common recognition that the responsibility of writers for this treasure is great. Yet there are as many disagreements on, as definitions of, the role of literature in society

SOME see the role of literature in society purely aesthetically, as the exploration of the possibilities of the word, of the patterns of language to be endlessly arranged and disarranged.

Some modern writers, as Susan Sontag remarks, make every effort to disestablish themselves: not to be morally useful to the community, not to be social critics but social pariahs and spiritual adventurers who don't want to dirty their hands in contact with the messy business of mundane human problems, which include wars as well as injustice, poverty and homelessness.

Thomas Mann opposes this attitude with the claims of society, which, he says, writers must have 'The courage to recognise and express — that is the quality which makes literature.'

And a cry comes from exiled Polish poet Czeslaw Milosz: 'What is poetry which does not save nations or people? A connivance with official lies!'

South African writers have been faced with that challenge in our poetry, our prose, our plays, in our very recent history. Transforming the world — another definition of the role of literature — by esoteric literary style was hardly a possibility in the world of apartheid, a world of mass removals of our people, the silencing of our people in detention without trial, the banishment of our people to Robben Island, the hijacking of the word, language, to express racist rhetoric in the mouths of our then

Left: Celebrating the return to the land, South Africa 1994 —Credit: Paul Weinberg/Panos Pictures

leaders. If we were to meet the challenge at all, it had to be in the light of what Walter Benjamin defined as Bertolt Brecht's formulation: the aim, the responsibility of the writer was to cause the audience, the reader, to be astonished at the circumstances under which he or she was living and functioning.

From that premise came what is known as our protest literature. And if the aesthetic exploration of the word was taken out of its velvet casket, it could not be disdainfully abandoned. Certainly not by any writer of integrity to the art as well as to his or her social and political convictions. For whatever is written, with whatever purpose, whether to express the struggle for freedom or the passion of a love affair, can only reach towards the power of truth in the measure in which the writer is capable of exploring the splendour of language brought into its service. In Germany writers had to clear their language of Nazi claptrap, the euphemism of 'Final Solution' for 'mass murder'; in South Africa we had to clear our languages of apartheid claptrap, the euphemisms of 'Resettlement' for 'banishment', and 'Permanent Removal' for 'assassination'. We had to clear our heads before we could sit down to write; and some of us had to pay dearly, not alone with the banning of our books, but with personal bans on continuing to write at all, as the price of writings that asserted the truth against connivance with official lies.

There would be no point in dwelling on the past if it were not for the truth of another member of the writing community: Milan Kundera's much-quoted dictum, 'The struggle of man against tyranny is the struggle of memory against forgetting.' I make no apology for reminding myself and you of the kind of situation in which I and my fellow writers in South Africa did our work during the years of apartheid. Perhaps this is the best way we have of ensuring that what happened shall not be allowed to happen again, resurrect under new motives, and that censorship shall not find toleration among us for what *seems* to be the good of other forms of building our new society, until it is too late to realise what we have done.

Our new South African Constitution guarantees freedom of expression. The word is free at last. From the point of view of legislation, literature is freed at last, not only from the grasp of censorship but also from the distortion of literary values which meant that no matter how badly and carelessly some writers used the treasure of the word, wrote his or her language, the work was praised because it was published in opposition to tyranny. This was inevitable: a circumstance of war.

ARTFUL WORDS

There are constraints other than legal affecting us — important small publishing houses in financial straits, semi-literacy, lack of libraries in former segregated black townships and schools — but these may be openly tackled, they belong to the general need and the general determination to create a culture with a dimension for the imagination that was not recognised in our country ever before. Our task now is to put the past aside, while admitting the huge cultural debts which are its legacy, and to look for ways to reimburse, invigorate, in our new South Africa, a long-deprived society.

Those in the outside world who, through *Index*, supported the struggle for freedom in South Africa, know, as part of the cultural family of the world, that if art is at the heart of revolution it is also at the heart of reconstruction. *Index* will continue to be invaluable to us as we guard our hard-won freedom of expression at home, and as we keep alert to whatever threatens that freedom, wherever this happens. For the Word, written or spoken, is our precious common property. ❏

© *Nadine Gordimer 1997*

Nadine Gordimer *won the Nobel Prize for Literature in 1991. Her more recent novels include* My Son's Story *(1990) and* None to Accompany Me *(1994), and the short story collection* Jump *(1991). Her lectures,* Writing and Being *were published in 1995*

In August 1968, Karel van het Reve, our then correspondent in Moscow, smuggled a letter of Pavel Litvinov and Andrei Amalrik, addressed to Stephen Spender, to Amsterdam. Five days later, the Soviet troops invaded Czechoslavakia.
This letter would eventually lead to the publication of Index on Censorship.
Our congratulations on your 25th anniversary, and if we can ever be at your service again...

Het Parool
Wilbautstraat 131, 1091 GL Amsterdam

SALMAN RUSHDIE

Notes on writing and the nation

1.
> THE OUSEL singing in the woods of Cilgwri,
> Tirelessly as a stream over the mossed stones,
> Is not so old as the toad of Cors Fochno
> Who feels the cold skin sagging round his bones.

Few writers are as profoundly engaged with their native land as RS Thomas, a Welsh nationalist, whose poems seek, by noticing, arguing, rhapsodising, mythologising, to write the nation into fierce, lyrical being. Yet this same RS Thomas also writes:

> Hate takes a long time
> To grow in, and mine
> Has increased from birth;
> Not for the brute earth...
> ... I find
> This hate's for my own kind...

Startling to find an admission of something close to self-hatred in the lines of a national bard. Yet this perhaps is the only kind of nationalist...nationist...a writer can be. When the imagination is given sight by passion, it sees darkness as well as light. To feel so ferociously is to feel contempt as well as pride, hatred as well as love. These proud contempts, this hating love, often earn the writer a nation's wrath. The nation requires anthems, flags. The poet offers discord. Rags.

2.
Connections have been made between the historical development of the

twin 'narratives' of the novel and the nation-state. The progress of a story through its pages towards its goal is likened to the self-image of the nation, moving through history towards its manifest destiny. Appealing as such a parallel is, I take it, these days, with a pinch of salt. Eleven years ago, at the famous PEN congress in New York City, the world's writers discussed 'The Imagination of the Writer and the Imagination of the State,' a subject of Maileresque grandeur, dreamed up, of course, by Norman Mailer. Striking how many ways there were to read that little 'and'. For many of us, it meant 'versus'. South African writers — Gordimer, Coetzee — in those days of apartheid set themselves against the official definition of the nation. Rescuing, perhaps, the true nation from those who held it captive. Other writers were more in tune with their nations. John Updike's unforgettable little hymn of praise to the little mailboxes of America, emblems, for him, of the free transmission of ideas.

Danilo Kis's example of a 'joke' by the state: a letter, received by him in Paris, posted in what was then still Yugoslavia. Inside the sealed envelope, stamped on the first page, were the words This letter has not been censored.

3.
The nation either co-opts its greatest writers (Shakespeare, Goethe, Camoens, Tagore), or else seeks to destroy them (Ovid's exile, Soyinka's exile). Both fates are problematic. The hush of reverence is inappropriate for literature; great writing makes a great noise in the mind, the heart. There are those who believe that persecution is good for writers. This is false.

4.
Beware the writer who sets himself or herself up as the voice of a nation. This includes nations of race, gender, sexual orientation, elective affinity. This is the New Behalfism. Beware behalfies! The New Behalfism demands uplift, accentuates the positive, offers stirring moral instruction. It abhors the tragic sense of life. Seeing literature as inescapably political, it replaces literary values by political ones.

It is the murderer of thought. Beware!

5.
Be advised my passport's green. America I'm putting my queer shoulder

to the wheel. To forge in the smithy of my soul the uncreated conscience of my race.

Kadaré's Albania, Ivo Andric's Bosnia, Achebe's Nigeria, García Márquez's Colombia, Jorge Amado's Brazil.

Writers are unable to deny the lure of the nation, its tides in our blood. Writing as mapping: the cartography of the imagination. (Or, as modern critical theory might spell it, Imagi/Nation.) In the best writing, however, a map of a nation will also turn out to be a map of the world.

6.
History has become debatable. In the aftermath of Empire, in the age of super-power, under the 'footprint' of the partisan simplifications beamed down to us from satellites, we can no longer easily agree on what is the case, let alone what it might mean. Literature steps into this ring. Historians, media moguls, politicians do not care for the intruder, but the intruder is a stubborn sort. In this ambiguous atmosphere, upon this trampled earth, in these muddy waters, there is work for him to do.

7.
Nationalism corrupts writers, too. Vide Limonov's poisonous interventions in the war in former Yugoslavia. In a time of ever-more-narrowly defined nationalisms, of walled-in tribalisms, writers will be found uttering the war-cries of their tribes.

Closed systems have always appealed to writers. This is why so much writing deals with prisons, police forces, hospitals, schools. Is the nation a closed system? In this internationalised moment, can any system remain closed?

Nationalism is that 'revolt against history' which seeks to close what cannot any longer be closed. To fence in what should be frontierless. Good writing assumes a frontierless nation. Writers who serve frontiers have become border guards.

8.
If writing turns repeatedly towards nation, it just as repeatedly turns away. The deliberately uprooted intellectual (Naipaul) views the world as only a free intelligence can, going where the action is and offering reports. The intellectual uprooted against his will (a category that includes, these days, a high proportion of the finest Arab writers) rejects, too, the narrow

NOTES ON WRITING AND THE NATION

Kurds celebrate another new year in exile, The Netherlands 1996
Credit: Rob Huibers/Panos Pictures

enclosures that have rejected him. There is great loss, and much yearning, in such rootlessness. But there is also gain. The frontierless nation is not a fantasy.

9.
Much great writing has no need of the public dimension. Its agony comes from within. The public sphere is as nothing to Elizabeth Bishop. Her prison — her freedom — her subject is elsewhere.

> Lullaby.
> Let nations rage,
> Let nations fall.
> The shadow of the crib makes an enormous cage
> upon the wall.

© Salman Rushdie, April 1997

Salman Rushdie *won the Booker Prize in 1981 and the Booker of Booker's Prize in 1993 for the novel* Midnight's Children. *His other works include* The Satanic Verses *(1988),* Haroun and the Sea of Stories *(1990) and* The Moor's Last Sigh *(1995)*

Right: Pro-government militia man, Kabylia, Algeria — Credit: Abbas/Magnum

Intolerance

SELIM ZAOUI

The terror that stalks the mountains

This is the story of one family driven by violence from their home in the mountains and now caught up in the murderous chaos that is tearing Algeria apart and has so far cost a quarter of a million civilian lives

NIGHT falls like the blade of the guillotine on the Mitidja plain, a vast swathe of fertile land between the Atlas Mountains and the Mediterranean that encircles the Algerian capital. Until France, the colonial power, rid it of its plagues, it was malaria-infested marshland. In the process of draining and developing it, the French created the myth of the worker-soldier.

Independent Algeria created a counter-myth of its own: 'The day the Mitidja returns to swamp, the Algerian people will have wiped out all trace of colonialism,' goes the popular saying. Today, the fabled orchards have given way to a concrete jungle, prey to cholera and in fear of even worse plagues — the nameless and faceless terror that mindlessly stalks the land.

Inside her ramshackle hut, hastily thrown together from odds and ends on the site of what was once a French farm before the agricultural revolution shut it down, Houria is preparing her family's evening meal. Her husband Zidane and her eldest son Salah should soon be off on their separate ways to spend the night with friends or family in Birkhadem, an Algiers suburb about an hour by bus.

Here, in this wretched corner of the Mitidja, where the ancestral land

THE TERROR THAT STALKS THE MOUNTAINS

abandoned by its owners produces nothing but slums, 'death roams like a blind camel'. To prevent any unfortunate incidents, every adult male must be sent well out of the way. To be on the safe side, Houria takes care not to know too much of their whereabouts; the civil war is no respecter of infants, the old or the sick. Who knows? Zidane and Salah could well run into a fake roadblock at any time on their nightly trips.

A shot rings out in the darkness. It comes from the shack next door where Houria's great-uncle lives. She puts out the light; Zidane and Salah fling themselves under the big bed with its sprung mattress. Another volley of shots. Silence. And then the voice of aunt Baya rolling out in the night like a clap of thunder: 'Come back! Finish me off! In the name of the beast that nursed you I implore you! Don't leave me struck to the ground, abandoned, helpless, solitary as a ghost.'

The murder squad — some five or six men dressed in camouflage or jeans and with their fingers twitching on the triggers of their kalashnikovs, according to witnesses — have melted back into the night leaving no trace but the blood of their victims spattered on the ground. Uncle Derridja is sprawled on the newly tiled floor like a dismembered automaton, his face blown away by a gun fired at close range straight into his mouth. One of his teeth is embedded in the wall.

His son Nabil, three days off his twentieth birthday, is still breathing, but his chest is soaked in blood. Mohammed, Derridja's brother, wounded in shoulder and stomach, summons the strength to mumble, 'I managed to hold on to his right index finger...I heard his confession: "There is no God but Allah..."'

There's no telephone to call the police; in any case, they wouldn't come, too afraid — and rightly so — of an ambush. A neighbour's car arrives to take Mohammed and Nabil to the military hospital at Aïn-Naadja, 15 kilometres away. The young man dies on the way; his uncle 'returns to God' next morning.

The head of the local municipal guard, a civilian militia some 50,000-strong raised by the Ministry of the Interior, arrives next day under heavy escort just as the bereaved family is returning from the cemetery. The official visitor summons the extended family, 13 households, to drum into them the words that ring from one end of Algeria to the other: 'The state cannot put a soldier alongside every citizen at risk. However, it can encourage you all to join one of the self-defence groups. Each one of you who does will be given a weapon to defend yourselves, your household and your honour.'

It's like talking about rope in the house of a hanged man. That, of course, was exactly what the late uncle Derridja tried to do when he sought the protection of the local mayor, an elected representative of the Front Islamique du Salut (FIS), removed not long ago by force and replaced at a moment's notice by a representative of the military (DEC). Having said his piece, the militia commander leaves with no word of comfort nor gesture of support for the grieving family. Between them, the two brothers have left 17 mouths to feed, a baby to bring up and three daughters to marry off.

There is nothing on television that night or in the nights that follow about this massacre; the press is silent. Nothing out of the ordinary about that. Since June 1994, information relating to security has to pass through a 'communications cell' in the government headquarters in Algiers. The ministerial decree that set it up 'advised' the national media to publish only information that was 'credible and accurate'. To which end, journalists should 'play down and seek to minimise the effects of terrorist attacks'. In short, it was their job to 'highlight the inhuman nature of these assaults', stressing 'throat slitting, attacks on ambulances and the murder of babies and the sick'.

But since it didn't fall within the government guidelines, the assassination of Derridja, Mohammed and Nabil fell into a black hole. The news that day reported only the umpteenth massacre on the same night in the nearby village of Ben-Achour. The death toll there, according to official sources, was 16 dead, all women and infants, butchered with naked steel.

Fortunately, Houria, like many these days, has forgotten how to read. Not a day goes by without the press reporting yet another massacre — within the prescribed categories, of course — somewhere or other in the Mitidja: Tixeraïne, Douaouda, Boufarik, Ben-Chebel and so on. The killings reach up to Blida, a garrison town and headquarters of the army in charge of the region. Since the time of the Ottomans, Blida has been nicknamed *El-Qahba*, the whorehouse, on account of its super-brothel of Fellini-like proportions. This was closed down in the 1970s by President Houari Boumediènne, Algeria's puritan head of state at the time, and the town is now an Islamist stronghold. Before it was banned in 1992, the FIS won the town; today it is under the control of Hamas, a legal Islamist party led by the veteran Muslim Brother, Mahfoud Nahnah.

If one is to believe only the news that gets past the 'communications

THE TERROR THAT STALKS THE MOUNTAINS

A family of Bon Sfer, a village in the Kabylia

cell', the renewed activities of the terrorists that erupted during Ramadan in the first two months of this year and that have continued to escalate since — 100 dead in a massacre one night in mid-April, 45 the next week and so on — are confined to the narrow triangle bounded by Algiers, Medea and Blida. Are we to suppose that the epicentre of the violence is confined to one specific location, or that we are being unusually well informed on these killings? The whole of Algeria knows the truth: death is at work everywhere, reaping its remorseless harvest of shot and steel. There is no shortage of news fulfilling the 'reliable and credible' rubric from which journalists can select their daily quota of killings deemed fit to break the media silence.

But what if this violence is no more than a smokescreen concealing another kind of violence, one that is rotting the country to the bone? Who bothers to look at the country's agriculture, the public health infrastructure, the roads and railways, the water shortages, the return of diphtheria and kala-azar, at the galloping destitution? Kala-azar, also known as the 'Biskra nail' or the 'Sahara pox', leaves the skin deeply pockmarked and is frequently transmitted by dogs. An open letter from southern Algeria, recently addressed to the minister of health, reveals that a pack of around 100 *sloughi* —native breed of dog — have been terrorising the town of Ouargla. After one of these strays had savaged a schoolboy to death and ripped off the arm of a woman it had pursued inside her yard, a self-defence group got together to patrol the area. 'Is there any longer a state that considers itself responsible for protecting its citizens?' asks the writer of the letter. One hundred and eleven cases of kala-azar were recorded last year in the prefecture of Bechar; in the first month of this year alone there were 60.

Human life is not worth a 'rotten onion'; the daily struggle just to survive is grinding the population into the ground. The state treasury has never before dedicated such vast resources from its petro-dollars to 'refashioning a regime that confuses the preservation of Algeria with perpetuating its own hold on state power', complains the man in the street. One third of the active population has no work; bowing to the demand of the IMF, the government has withdrawn subsidies on semolina, oil, sugar and powdered milk.

The generation of independence should, in fact, have been weaned on fresh milk: but then came the agricultural revolution, 'a bloody fiasco', they mutter under their breath. The story is unique in the annals of history:

persuaded by a European adviser, a Marxist, that the only true revolution was that of the proletariat, Algeria's thenpresident, Houari Boumediène, bartered away his oil for an imported industrial infrastructure and the creation of a working class — instead of the reverse.

Industry is scuppered; agriculture is shipwrecked. According to the Paris-based newsletter, *Spécial Maghreb*, Algeria is not only the world's leading importer of powdered milk, it imports almost half the entire quantity of durum wheat traded on world markets. The land that was the granary of the Roman Empire, that invented dry farming 2,000 years ago and that bred the clementine at the beginning of this century, today sells Moroccan oranges because they cost less than the home-grown variety, olive oil 'Made in Italy' and almonds from Tunisia.

The price of bread has skyrocketed since the start of the civil war in 1992 and now costs one to 10 dinars (US 20 cents). Meat costs 54 dinars a kilo, one-tenth of the local minimum wage which, in itself, is scarcely enough to pay the inflated price of imported medicines that dominate the market in the absence of local products: contraceptive pills from Hungary, Indian or French aspirins, testosterone and indigestion remedies from Iran.

Surgical spirit, cotton-wool, sticking-plaster and mercurochome have disappeared from the open market since the beginning of the war in the hope of depriving the Islamist guerrillas of emergency medical supplies. Anaesthetics are considered 'strategic' material; as a result, many country hospitals are forced to operate without. When Houria needed to have a tooth out recently, it cost her a fortune to buy the anaesthetic from a private dentist who had a secret stock for his own patients. 'Those whom Allah loves will never have to go to hospital' is how they see things in Algeria today. A patient frequently has to provide everything for an operation: sheets, cotton-wool, syringes, surgical thread, x-ray film. Everything, of course, is available in the souk on the black market.

ALL this goes over Houria's head. The chaos of her everyday life merely reflects that of the country as a whole. A daughter of the 'war of liberation', Houria was born in a village in Little Kabylia, a trapezium bounded by Bougie Setif, Jemila Jedelli. During the 'pacification of the countryside' by the French general Maurice Challe, designed to rob the Algerian freedom fighters of local support, her hamlet was emptied and the population transported to a resettlement camp in 1959. She remembers the curfews and the barbed wire — also the doctor and the school.

SELIM ZAOUI

At the funeral of a murdered militiaman, Kabylia, Algeria — Credit: Abbas/Magnum

When she was six years old, the arrival of independence uprooted her once more, this time to Algiers, her father having decided not to return to the family lands. She stayed at school until her marriage to a cousin, in accordance with clan custom. Like her, Zidane was also an immigrant from the interior. She worked as a housemaid, he as a building labourer; they had 'four children and three daughters' and a primitive but solid house near Cité Jmanfou — from the French phrase 'Je m'en fou' (I don't give a damn) — one of the most notorious shanty towns perched above the capital.

Had not Colonel Chedli Benjadid, then president, decreed in 1984 that

Algiers should be 'cleaned up' and all shanties bulldozed, she'd be there still. *El Moujahid*, mouthpiece of the ruling Front du Libération National (FLN), spoke at the time of 'slum clearances'.

One bitterly cold morning, summoned by the police, an earth mover poked its great nose into her home. They had to up sticks. Gathering her brood, her television, gas cooker, a pile of mattresses and seething with suppressed rage, Houria once again took to the road, back to her village in Little Kabylia. A motorcycle cop escorted them to ensure that the family didn't backtrack. Back in her ramshackle family hut, at the end of the world though only 15 kilometres from the municipal centre, she had to start from scratch. The riots of October 1988 against government cronyism relieved her sense of powerlessness. The multi-party municipal elections of June 1990, the first of their kind, gave her, at last she thought, a voice in affairs.

She voted FIS, and left the shack in the village without running water or electricity for a solid house only steps away from the town hall. But it was not to be. No sooner had she deposited her belongings than the newly elected FIS mayor, a member of the Beni Y tribe and closely related to his FLN predecessor, in return for a backhander, forced her to give up half the building to an emigrant who had just returned from France. The 11 January 1992 coup d'état sent the so-called 'man of God' to prison.

His successor, the local DEC serving the military junta — also a member of the Beni Y — once again put tribal preferences ahead of public service. For instance, only one business licence was granted to a non-Beni Y during his tenure. On 30 June 1993, an Islamist gang set fire to the town hall; the DEC fled; and no-one came either to replace him or investigate the crime. Overnight, the state faded away. The dispensary shut up shop, followed by the maternity services and finally the chemist. The government boycotted all localities operating under the Islamist banner. Teachers had already been condemned to forced unemployment when the Islamic Army of Salvation (AIS), the armed wing of FIS, burned down their school, college and student canteen. The shuttle bus linking the countryside and the coast was cancelled. The forest of Guerrouche, known as Kabylia's 'lung', became the haunt of cutthroats.

It was at this point that the army decided to dismantle its radar base, built at great expense deep in the mountains, and pull out, leaving the field to the AIS. A delegation of villagers went secretly to the head of the district, the under-prefect, asking him for state protection against the rebels. 'What are you complaining about?' he retorted. 'You voted these guys in, now live with them.'

In the winter of 1994, the village was cut off from the rest of the world for 28 days by snow until the AIS stole a snowplough from a neighbouring municipality to cut a route through to the main road. From summer 1993 to spring 1995, Houria's region lived under the shadow of the *sharia*. Zidane, found with a fag end in his mouth, was beaten up. Houria, on a visit to the tomb of Sidi A, a local holyman and patron of her tribe, seeking his protection, found his gravestone adorned with a massive turd.

This sacrilege was the calling card of the AIS. Indoctrinated with the fierce puritanical Wahabism of Saudi Arabia, these militants have no truck with 'superstition': the worship of 'cults' has been banned. Leaving the shrine, Houria bumped into one of the 'beards' who ordered her to veil her six-year-old daughter, Manal. Fearing that at any moment one of his colleagues would demand her eldest daughter, Lamia, in marriage, Houria spirited her away to stay with her own mother in Algiers.

By the time the army decided to make its reappearance, the Islamists had extended their control throughout at least one-third of the hinterland where almost 84 per cent of the population live. Their 'pacification' of the area bore no relation to that of the colonial army under General Challe: where his troops had invested the mountains 24 hours a day, the National People's Army (ANP) stuck to barracks. The AIS and other armed groups like the Groupe Islamique Armé (GIA) had no difficulty in continuing their forays from the shelter of the forest. Islamists and army watched each other from a distance: the day belonged to the ANP, the night to the Islamist militias.

In this war without front lines, Houria's cousin Khelifa, a lorry driver, was beaten almost to death by the AIS for supposed 'collaboration' with the *'taghout'* — oppressive — regime. Eighteen months ago, another, Hamid, was picked up at a military roadblock. There has been no news of him since. His small daughter approaches every man she sees in a *jellaba* with the question, 'Papa?'

A good pupil of the IMF, the government is denationalising everything in sight. They have even privatised state 'security', that is to say repression. In addition to the professional army, some 125,000-strong, the government also supports an armed police force of 50,000 and a civilian militia of around 60,000 'patriots', those who support the 'democratic and modernising camp'. Given the nature of the conflict and the landscape in which it is waged, this is derisory. If the French could not hold down the country with 2 million troops against 9 million Algerians, what can a poorly equipped and unmotivated army do against three times the population? Most of the troops are, in any case, believers who are not moved by calls for the establishment of a 'more just state'.

'Patriots' get three times the national minimum wage. One of Houria's brothers-in-law, at one time living in Toulon, had no hesitation in 'donning the uniform' as it was called in the days of the *harkis* — Algerian soldiers who fought with the French. Pressed by a recruiting sergeant, Zidane chose to scarper to Algiers in the hope of finding a place to stay and work. At first, Houria waited for him in the village. None of the children could go to school any more; the army doctor examined patients but had no medicines; water dripped from the tap only one hour a day; no buses; no taxis; no newspapers.

With his refusal to serve in the militia hanging over him, Zidane was scared to return. There was no post, but the war, and above all rumours of war, spread unhindered. One morning in the autumn of 1993, an unholy noise sent Houria scuttling beneath her camp bed. A swarm of helicopters were shelling the mountains with napalm. That afternoon she saw 28 plumes of smoke rising from the earth. The fire continued to burn in the forest for two days.

Alone with her seven children, Houria could take it no longer. Everyone was fleeing the municipality; not a soul remained in the village. The army watched the exodus of a whole people without budging. With a knot in her stomach, Houria donned her scarf and left for Algiers with nothing but a bag stuffed with second-hand clothes and a transistor radio sent by her brother in Paris. This time she left the gas cooker, the fridge, the black and white TV — along with a cow, its calf and a splendid vegetable garden — behind. The calf had only just been born and it preyed on Houria's mind that she had not had time to perform the traditional rites of preparing the sacred dish of couscous sprinkled with *aghez* — colostrum. A 'patriot' quickly took over her house, the calf and its mother.

Perched on the roof of a truck bound for Algiers, surrounded by her brood of kids, Houria weeps. From her lofty perch, she watches an endless stream of folk fleeing their land. Here a mattress strapped to a back; there a carpet rolled under an arm. Of all the press, only the francophone

SELIM ZAOUI

Tribune had the courage to feature this exodus on its front page. Throughout 1995, the exodus from Little Kabylia continued to swell to bursting the crowded suburbs of the capital.

Along the Kabylia corniche, the most beautiful road bordering the Mediterranean, a forest fire has driven the entire wildlife of the jebel on to the beach. It is impossible to erase the image of a young wild boar and a Barbary ape, crouched on the sand between the forest in flames and a sea of oil, howling at the carnage.

Death also howls in Algiers. The noise of ambulance sirens, bombs and bazookas reverberate through the city centre. From Reghaïa on the east of the capital to Blida a string of little islands of breeze-block and corrugated iron has sprung up. The legendary Mitidja, the mantle of the urban sprawl, spread between the jumble of refugee shacks and villa bunkers. The city's political elite have, for their part, squatted in the luxury hotels and tourist villages of the Algerian riviera.

Mutual hatred drives the war and annihilates all hope of an end. Houria no longer recognises the city, by day an overcrowded labyrinth of streets and alleys, by night deserted. Where black money and corruption flow as freely as blood. Mercedes and hearses, deposit boxes in the banks and coffins in the streets. Zidane has constructed a shack to house his family in a part of the Mitidja occupied only by people from his own region. It's frying-pan to fire: no running water nor electricity, far from a road, hospital, commissariat, school or shop: 'Just like back down there.'

A breeding ground of 'patriots', with fantastic pay, at the mercy of the insatiable GIA cut-throats. They no longer have confidence in the 'outsider', no matter where he's from — Oran, Setif or anywhere in Algeria.

Zidane does odd jobs for cash in hand, currently he is a labourer for a doctor who is building a villa 'with a garage and swimming-pool'. His children have started school in the next-door municipality. Salah, his eldest son, has got involved with a moorish cafe. Houria has got a ration card from a '*khaïriya*', a local charity, which entitles her to free coffee, semolina, milk and, during Ramadan, even some meat.

Houria no longer has faith in anything. Totally disenchanted by the behaviour of the FIS mayor in her native village, she expects nothing from anyone, neither the authorities nor the Islamists. Zidane believes the state itself is manipulating terrorism which, according to those best placed to

Right: Masked government anti-terrorist gendarme, Kabylia, Algeria — Credit: Abbas/Magnum

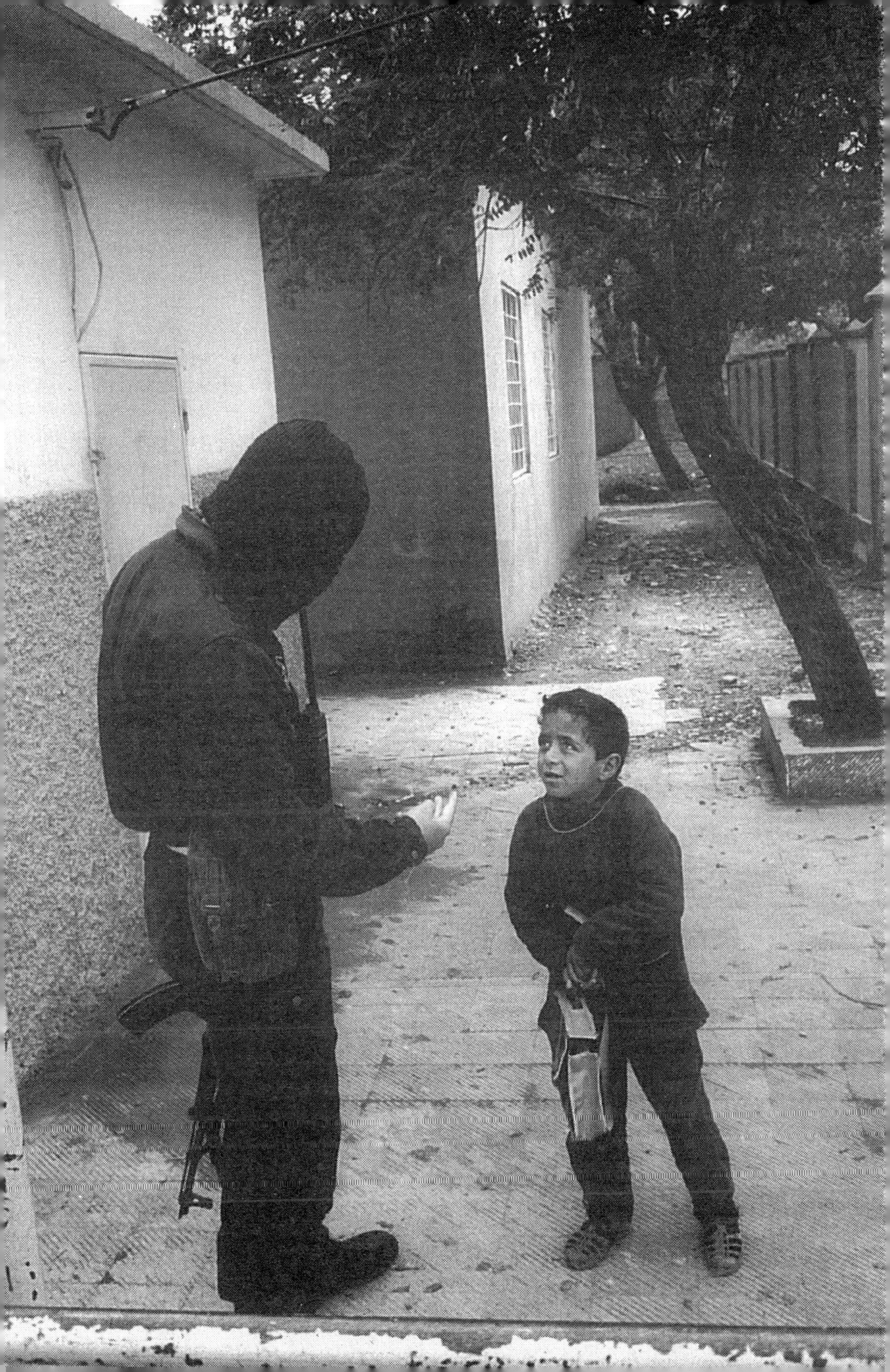

know, strikes only at the ordinary people, the very same who voted for FIS. He has some faith in Hocine Aït Ahmed, leader of the Socialist Front (FFS), and his slogan: 'Neither military dictatorship nor fundamentalist state.' Since his uncle Khelifa was beaten up by the AIS for 'collaborating' with the ruling military, Salah has switched to supporting the army.

HOURIA suddenly finds herself a stranger in her own country. She hasn't a clue what is going on on the political front: General Liamine Zeroual, president and minister of defence, delivers his discourse in classical, literary Arabic; Saïd Saadi, head of the Rassemblement pour la Culture et la Démocratie (RCD), holds forth in a form of 'modernised' Berber. Even less can she comprehend the language of Algerian feminism couched in trendy French that she's watched on a French TV channel in Algiers. Is Houria a democrat? The word rings strangely in her ear. In her ear the word chimes with nothing familiar. Is she an Islamist? Beyond question she is a devout Muslim — but she has never worn the veil, just a head scarf.

She calls herself a 'khobiziste' after *khobz*, the Arabic for bread: in her own eyes she's simply a mother responsible for feeding her family. She's given up her vegetable garden to join her husband and son in Algiers. Yet neither dare spend the night at home. She says: 'I've done my best to stay out of prison, but still I find myself stumbling on the threshold.' ❑

Selim Zaoui *is an Algerian journalist*

Translated from Le Monde *by Judith Vidal-Hall*

OLIVIER ROY

Getting into the game

WE HAVE a tendency in the West to identify secularism and democracy. But in most of the Middle East, as in Algeria for instance, the two things are not synonymous. Secularism is most often identified with conservative societies. In Algeria, as in Turkey, secularism is associated with conservative forces — in both cases the army. The difference is that Turkey is a republic with a political space and a democratic process — even if those involved in this process are not themselves democrats.

We are too fixated on democracy as an ideology, hence the present Algerian paradox: we support anti-democratic groups purely because they are secular and, in our terms, more likely one day to become democratic — though, in fact, there's no question of that. What's at stake is a political system and its institutions: a constitution, elections, a parliament, political parties and so on.

In those countries where there is room for political manoeuvre, as in Turkey, but even in a country like Jordan which is not remotely democratic, the Islamists are part of the game and must be integrated into the political process. I question the position of the 'eradicators' and their view that it will never be possible to integrate the Islamists into the political process. What is more, their doctrine pre-empts any future possibility of democracy itself because it can only operate in a dictatorship. There is no democratic way of 'eradicating'.

It is clear from what is now going on in Algeria that FIS is moving towards a centrist position like that of the Muslim Brotherhood. It has tested the limits of its ideology and is coming out of its kindergarten stage: that is to say, from the enthusiasm that characterised the party during the municipal elections of 1989 and the parliamentary elections of 1991.

One can see these centrist movements learning from experience that they can never establish social justice with their ideology. As a result, they transform themselves into just one political party among others. I call it 'Christian democracy'.

The Catholic church was never democratic but, at a given time, Christian politicians accepted democratic institutions without renouncing their faith. In time, this gave rise to the Christian democratic movement. I believe that Muslim countries are currently going through their own encounter with secularism. What is happening in the Muslim world at present is leading to the creation of a secular platform, even in Iran.

For the time being, Algeria is caught in an impasse because the army has no intention whatsoever of sharing power. There was an historic opportunity at the time of Liamine Zeroual's election. He should have used his legitimacy to reorder the political landscape; in short, to make the system work by sharing power and allowing the emergence of a civil society. What we had instead was privatisation for the benefit of the political elite in the course of which an autonomous entrepreneurial class failed to materialise.

Politically, what Zeroual is doing at the moment aims at locking the doors on the present political set-up. The opportunity was lost and, sooner or later, we'll have to go back to first base. But the actors have changed. FIS has, in particular, drawn the right conclusions from the activities of the GIA and matured politically in consequence. FIS is in the process of accepting the idea of political pluralism.

In so far as there is no way of negotiating with the GIA, any solution must be by admitting FIS into the political process. President Zeroual is toying with Hamas but he must provide them with a credible opposition. He wants to carry Hamas with him but not give them a share in power. Paradoxically, the regime seems prepared to allow Hamas the freedom to Islamise society: its sole preoccupation is holding on to power. ❑

Olivier Roy *is head of research at the CNRS, Paris*

Translated from an interview in Le Monde *by Judith Vidal-Hall*

Right: Credit: Getty Images

Global reach

NOAM CHOMSKY

Democracy lite

Last year's electoral campaign in the USA was of 'historic dullness', analysts agree. Despite a propaganda blitz which included almost 1,400 hours of TV campaign ads, the two leading presidential candiates failed to engage with the issues. In the end the main issue for the voters was which candidate they disliked the least

THE PATTERN was set as the primaries opened in January 1996, with record-breaking expenses and publicity, but few voters. Also missing were the issues that had dominated the front pages. The most dramatic case was the budget: the government had been paralysed through late 1995 by debate over whether to balance it in seven years or a bit longer. The issue instantly disappeared when politicians had to face the voters, who 'abandoned their balanced-budget obsession', as the *Wall St Journal* put it — that is, their strong opposition to balancing the budget under any realistic assumptions. The rest of the agenda of the 'conservatives' who had won a 'landslide victory' in 1994 (with 20 per cent of the electorate) also vanished. Newt Gingrich's closest associates struggled to deny any connection to their leader, who was unpopular at the time of the 'conservative landslide' that he led, and became the most unpopular figure in US politics as the public learned about the 'Contract with America' that they had signed — without their knowledge.

There is often a gap between public preferences and public policy. In recent years, it has become a chasm, as policy has followed the business agenda even more closely than in the past. At the time of the 'landslide victory' of 1994, 60 per cent of the public wanted social spending *increased*. Overwhelming majorities think that the government is 'run for the benefit of the few and the special interests, not the people'; that the economic system is 'inherently unfair'; that 'business has gained too much power'; that 'the federal government must protect the most vulnerable in society, especially the poor and the elderly, by guaranteeing minimum living standards and providing social benefits,' including support for the disabled, unemployment insurance, medical and child care. By 20 to one, the public feel that corporations should 'sacrifice some profit' for the benefit of 'workers and communities'. The resilience of generally social democratic attitudes is particularly striking in the light of the huge propaganda assault to persuade people that they hold sharply different beliefs.

Changes in the global economy in the past 25 years have placed powerful weapons in the hands of the masters, who are naturally using them to dismantle the hated social contract and functioning democracy. Real wages and job security continue to stagnate or decline for the majority, while profits soar along with compensation for top executives. Inequality has reached record heights. The propaganda image is that we have to cut costs and reduce government intrusion into our lives. The reality is that costs are transferred from the rich to the poor, and unaccountable private tyrannies 'intrude' even more massively than before. But the public is not supposed to see their actions as 'intrusion'. General Electric, Citicorps and Merrill Lynch are ordinary folks just like us. Our common enemy is government — because it has an immense defect: in principle, it can fall under public influence.

In reality, the parts of government that serve wealth and privilege are immune from attack. To mention only one example, the 'conservatives' who 'hate government' are in the lead in demanding growth of the Pentagon system, which has long been the main device by which the public funds advanced industry. The public is opposed, but that is irrelevant. Gingrich is a typical example of 'really existing free market doctrine', preaching the stern lessons of market discipline to hungry children while holding the championship in bringing federal subsidies to his rich constituents. The Reaganites were masters in the same art, which has a venerable history, and is the underpinning of just about every dynamic sector of the economy.

Current 'reforms' are intended to carry the process further. Each agenda item — health, welfare, taxation, deregulation, devolution — is justified in terms of the need to reduce costs. A closer look shows that they transfer costs, from the rich to the general public, and surely not in response to the public will.

The public must therefore be demoralised and confused. In a standard work, the professor of the science of government at Harvard explained that 'The architects of power must create a force that can be felt but not seen. Power remains strong when it remains in the dark; exposed to the sunlight it begins to evaporate.' The public is not to see where power lies, how it shapes policy, and for what ends. Rather, people are to hate and fear one another. Our enemies are welfare mothers driving Cadillacs, corrupt unions denying workers their freedom, immigrants stealing our jobs, terrorists at our throat, and the rest of the familiar imagery. The more democratic parts of the government are also 'our enemy', while those that socialise costs and risks while subsidising the wealthy remain 'in the dark'.

None of this is surprising in a business-run society, in which perhaps US$1 trillion a year is spent on marketing — that is, manipulation and deceit — and the huge public relations industry is dedicated to waging 'the everlasting battle for the minds of men' and 'indoctrinating citizens with the capitalist story', as its leaders declare (to one another).

The tendencies are clear and understandable, in the US and throughout much of the world. They will persist as long as 'power remains strong and in the dark'. But that is no law of nature. Popular struggles have won many victories, and can start from a higher plane today than in the past. There are no mysterious 'laws' or 'uncontrollable market forces' that we must silently obey, only decisions within human institutions that are subject to will and choice, as they have always been. ❑

Noam Chomsky *is a professor in the Department of Linguistics and Philosophy at the Massachusetts Institute of Technology in Cambridge, Mass. A prolific writer, he has published widely on linguistics, philosophy, intellectual history, contemporary issues, international affairs and human rights. Latest works include* Language and Thought *(1994),* Powers and Prospects *(1996) and* Class Warfare *(1996)*

© *Reprinted from* La Jornada

CHRISTOPHER HIRD

The capable state

As globalisation extends its influence, those who at one time sought the end of the state now demand its restoration: not no government but good government is what is urgently required

THROUGHOUT the 1980s and much of the 1990s, the dominant political consensus in many countries and virtually all international institutions has been anti-state. Privatisation, attacks on welfare systems and the marketisation of culture has dominated the policies of the world's biggest countries and has been forced upon many of the world's poorest countries. There has been the paradox, of course, that attacks on state provision and ownership in the economic and social sphere have often been accompanied by more centralisation and a reduction in personal freedoms. But now there are signs that the hegemony of this ideology is weakening. The concept of the 'capable' state is emerging; not no government, but good government.

For those concerned about human rights, freedom of expression and participation in the political process, the capable state offers an intriguing opportunity. Part of the idea recognises that in the increasingly global and integrated world, the citizens' 'voice' needs to be encouraged and extended; there needs to be greater transparency of government and business action; more information and more mechanisms for participation and for holding governments to account. Furthermore, these are not optional extras, but an integral part of making the state more capable. One of the ironies of this emerging consensus is that some of those promoting it were once in the forefront of attacks on the state.

Every year the World Bank produces its *World Development Report* — a substantial book on a development topic. There is a joke in the Bank that they are still searching for the one person in the world who has read a WDR cover to cover. Certainly, the writing style of the WDRs bears all

CHRISTOPHER HIRD

the signs of a publication which has had to negotiate its way through a complex political minefield and accommodate a number of mutually incompatible opinions. But it is worth the effort of trying to decode its somewhat congested prose. Last year, for example, it wrote approvingly of one economic system:

> The achievements were considerable. They included increased output, industrialization, the provision of basic education, health care, housing, jobs to entire populations, and a seeming imperviousness to the Great Depression of the 1930s. Incomes were relatively equally distributed, and an extensive, if inefficient, welfare state ensured everyone has access to basic goods and services.

The system being described here was Communism and the 1996 WDR provided a comprehensive and far from reassuring review of the transition from Communism to capitalism. The subject of this year's WDR is the state and its changing role in the globalised world. The report promises to be equally challenging of some widely received wisdoms. Its underlying argument will be that the state has the potential to be an enormous power for good; that what the world needs in economics, welfare and citizenship is a 'capable state' — agile in its responses to the new forces of globalisation and equipped with the institutions which enable it to respond to its citizens needs.

The World Bank is a large and intricate bureaucracy which produces scores of books, research papers and other publications every year. One book — however much a flagship publication — does not represent a policy statement of the Bank. However, it is an indication of a shift in thinking among the world's political and economic elite — after almost two decades of an anti-state consensus, the tide is turning. From around the world come examples of how the state — national, regional and local — can intervene to improve the life and livelihoods of its citizens.

It is possible to trace the roots of this rethinking back several years. In 1992 in the USA the book *Reinventing Government* was published. Written by two management consultants — David Osborne and Ted Gaebler — and with the strap-line 'How the Entrepreneurial Spirit is Transforming the Public Sector' the book soon became a best-seller. It is probably one of those books which many own, few have read but all know the message — the state should be steering, not rowing. Endorsed by Republicans and

THE CAPABLE STATE

Democrats, including Bill Clinton, it is clearly a book from which you can take away what you want. But its underlying theme is not less government, but better government.

There are many forces which have led to this reassessment of the state but the most important has been the break-up of the Soviet Union and the end of the command economy. Once the argument for markets had been won, discussion about the role of the state was no longer confused with the language of the Cold War and the ideological capitalism versus Communism argument. But also, the consequences of the transition in some of the countries of the former Soviet Union made it abundantly clear what could happen if the state collapsed. In many parts of the former Soviet Union the old, the poor and the unemployed are living in poverty. For example in 1992 it was estimated that over two fifths of Russia's children were living below the subsistence level.

The most interesting and potentially optimistic aspects of the new debate about the capable state is what it means for citizens' participation in politics, freedom of expression and the creation of a professional, non-corrupt civil service to serve citizens' needs. And some of the most instructive examples of efforts to create a capable state come not from the western capitalist economies but from Latin America, Africa and Asia.

The Ceara region in northern Brazil is a large, poor, thinly populated region of around seven million people. A recently published study by Judith Tendler of the Department of Urban Studies and Planning at Massachusetts Institute of Technology provides a compelling account of how the regional government became the institution through which there has been a substantial improvement in the living standards of most of its population and increased participation in the political process. For those in the West who sneer at the concept of a civil service with a sense of mission, there are some unpalatable lessons.

In 1987 Ceara was in crisis. There was a serious drought, the government was heavily in debt and in the hands of a corrupt elite who awarded many of the state's contracts to their friends. A newly elected president, Tasso Jereissati, embarked upon a four-pronged reform package: health improvement, job creation, public works and agricultural improvement. He used the government's power as a purchaser of supplies to promote employment — a third of the state's procurement was switched from large companies to the small, 'informal' sector. This was an effective way of reducing the corrupt awarding of contracts and thus saving money and also a way of promoting economic development — the small businesses used this base to start selling to others both in and outside the region. (Recently, some large companies have taken to the courts to challenge this policy — an indication of the opposition which faces imaginative state action.) Other effects of the Jereissati policies were the employment of a million farmers in the wake of the drought and a dramatic increase in vaccination coverage against polio and measles among children — from 25 to 90 per cent.

At the heart of the Jereissati approach was the creation of an accountable and committed civil service. Power and responsibility was devolved from the central regional government to local civil servants, who were given personal discretion in much decision making. But at the same time — to keep them honest — the government promoted the formation of consumer groups to monitor the civil servant's behaviour. In addition to this, the government rewarded civil servants who successfully satisfied their clients, and publicised these successes. Together, this intricate web of reforms created a sense of calling in the civil service, a respect for them among the population and a greater involvement of the citizens in the political process. Such an approach to government contrasts sharply with much of what has been going on in countries such as the UK over the last 20 years.

In general, the approach of the state in the industrialised world has been for it to withdraw from many areas in which it has been involved in the past including industry, pensions, transport, education. But in many cases it has then failed to put in place the appropriate institutions to ensure that the market system serves the community. In Britain, attempts at regulation — in particular of telecommunictions, pensions and water — have had some conspicuous failures. In the case of pensions literally billions of pounds of savers' money has been lost; in the water industry, the regulatory structure has not been able to prevent hundreds of millions being handed to shareholders, whilst parts of the country suffer water shortages and important investment does not take place.

Much of this has happened because in Britain at least, the great sweep of privatisation and marketisation was driven by an anti-state ideology and a crude belief in 'free' markets. Often these markets were 'free' only to the extent that they were free from any effective regulation, free from real competition and the few large companies in them were free to exploit their dominant position. The capable state takes a different view. Whilst it recognises that markets may be the best mechanism for consumers to

Kashindwa village, Brazil

express their preferences and that privately-owned business may be the best judges of what to invest in, markets need both to be regulated and their failures corrected.

Interestingly, this shift in thinking chimes well with public attitudes. Recent surveys in Europe have shown a consistent support for the state. In 1990 over 70 per cent of those questioned in a survey in seven European countries believed in the following roles for the state: providing health care, caring for the elderly, helping the unemployed, prompting industry and reducing income differentials. And in terms of government spending, welfare policies were rated more important than law and order and defence.

As if to highlight the range of public thinking about the state, similar surveys in the USA produce different results — four fifths of respondents mistrust government and there has been a decline in support for welfare spending over the last 15 years. This difference in attitude highlights an important — but oft neglected — feature of the state's role: it's a matter of choice for a society what role it wants to give to the state. Countries such as Holland, for example, have succeeded in creating a social consensus which supports relatively high taxation and a comprehensive welfare programme; and this has been accompanied by economic prosperity comparable with other west European countries. Evidence from elsewhere in the world shows that effective social spending by the state consistently improves the population's standard of living. So countries like Sri Lanka have lower infant mortality than many much richer countries; and life expectancy is much higher in for example, Vietnam than it is in many countries with higher per capita income.

Over the last 20 years there has been a worldwide decline in the number of autocratic regimes. In 1974 one in four countries of the world (39) used open elections to choose their leaders; today it is 117 — two in three. Obviously the changes in eastern Europe and the former Soviet Union account for some of this, but in Latin America and Africa there has also been an increase in democratically-elected governments. These changes have been an integral part of the reform of the state in these continents — developments not much reported upon in the mass media. An example is Uganda.

When the government of Yoweri Museveni took over in 1986, the Ugandan state was as decayed and as corrupt as could be imagined. It was riddled with corruption and had been looted by its previous rulers.

THE CAPABLE STATE

Confidence in its institutions — such as the police — was so low that few Ugandan citizens would think of reporting a crime. The economy was one of the poorest in the world and the civil service one of the most corrupt.

The reform programme upon which Museveni embarked identified this corruption as a key obstacle to economic and political progress. A recent paper which reviews the Ugandan experience includes a perceptive review of the history, causes and effects of corruption in countries around the world. Often introduced to countries by outside influences — such as the Spanish in the Philippines or the British Army in Singapore, corruption is not confined to poor countries and 'takes place where there is a meeting of opportunity and inclination'.

In the Ugandan situation, corruption became endemic as poorly paid civil servants found it was the only way of protecting their living standards against inflation. Many have second or third jobs, government supplies were sold privately and 'fees' were charged for the issuing of standard licenses. And hardly anyone was punished. The Museveni reforms had three planks. First, there was the appointment of an Inspector General of Government to investigate corruption and human rights abuses and to publish its findings. Second, a reform of the public service, aimed at producing a smaller, better paid and more effective civil service. Third, the decentralisation of decision making — taking power and responsibility away from the central government and giving it to private sector and local and voluntary groups.

The reform of the civil service included a massive consultation exercise over a period of two years. It has led to a more than halving in the size of the service — almost a third of those who 'lost' their jobs were already dead, past retirement age or completely fictitious. But for those remaining, targets of a 'minimum living wage' have been set and individual civil servants given more management autonomy. The aim is to create a virtuous circle of an honest, well-supervised, well-regarded, decently-paid civil service.

Clearly, a part of this programme is the work of the Inspector General of Government. A number of high profile cases of corruption have been unearthed and some senior figures have been disciplined but given the size of the problem, this is only scratching the surface. Elsewhere in the world — notably Singapore — the battle against corruption and for an honest, accountable and effective civil service has often taken a generation. One important part of the effort in Uganda relies on the role of the press.

Although much of the Ugandan press remains under government control, it has reported on cases of corruption and the abuse of public office and also highlighted the failings of government reform. Workshops on investigative journalism have been organised in an attempt to improve the effectiveness of the media. The intriguing aspect of this has been the fact that these workshops were partly paid for by the World Bank's Economic Development Institute.

The policies being pursued in Uganda highlight a number of features of the capable state — consultation, participation, decentralisation, a free and capable media. But they also show how the concept of the capable state is not divisible. This is not a shopping list from which government's can pick and choose ideas. Without the check of transparency and citizens' voice, governments are not likely to remain honest and accountable; without adequate pay and some public regard, public servants are not likely to serve the public well. And a diverse and free media is an essential part of the cement which holds this all together.

Many western governments could learn from this and one final observation on the media and the state is provoked. In free markets, the media industry — as in others — will tend towards concentration and homogeneity. This concentration will tend to prevent new entrants appearing, reduce the range of papers and programmes and in short, restrict the market in ideas and debate. Television in particular is capable of being, in economic terms, a 'public good' — one person's consumption does not reduce the supply to others and no-one can be prevented from consuming it. In others words, the case for the capable state intervening to maintain freedom and diversity in this market is overpowering — the more so because media pluralism is likely to enhance the state's capability. ❑

Christopher Hird *is a television documentary producer.* The Terror and the Truth, *a series about the way in which countries deal with the legacy of human rights abuses, will be transmitted on BBC2 in June 1997*

Right: Telecommunications 1937 — Credit: Getty Images

Mediascape

DAN SCHILLER

O what a tangled web we weave

The application of digital technology is allowing television to converge with the Internet at an extraordinary rate — and the fight for advertising revenues on the new frontier is fiercer than ever. What are the implications for free access and expression?

TELEVISION and the Internet are pressing against one another, in a trend that raises wide and important issues. Why is this convergence — or collision — occurring? What does it mean to project contemporary television practices on to cyberspace? Might the process of convergence become generalised as a model for the Web's further evolution? How far can it go?

The recent evidence for this convergence is abundant. PC and TV manufacturers are each seeking enlarged markets. TVs that can stand in as Internet terminals, and PCs that can accept television signals are, in turn, obvious market extensions of current consumer electronics manufacturing. Similarly, US computer software companies and broadcast television networks, programme-makers, and stations have started to jockey for competitive advantage as their industries merge. Nowhere did this internecine disagreement come through more forcefully than in the process of developing technical standards for digital TV, which are widely expected to be a vitally important consumer electronics industry product. The computer companies recently scored an unexpected victory in the standards-making contest, setting the stage for what Mark Lander, writing in the *New York Times*, called 'a titanic battle for America's living-rooms' between established TV makers and personal computer manufacturers, 'both of which want to build the digital device that will display these images.' In truth, this epic corporate contest will be even broader, in part because a stable Internet infrastructure has yet to materialise.

Strategic alliances have already begun to proliferate. Last summer, General Electric's TV network, NBC, joined with Intel, the leading semiconductor manufacturer, to launch Intercast, a system which will allow computers equipped with Pentium processors to receive video and audio signals. Microsoft and DirecTV (itself a subsidiary of GM's Hughes Corporation, with minority participation by AT&T) have inaugurated DirecPC, utilising a satellite delivery system to provide television services over a PC for a monthly subscription fee akin to that charged by cable TV operators. Philips Magnavox and Sony are each marketing 'Web TV' set-top boxes, while Time-Warner, like other giant cable system operators, is contracting with suppliers for similar equipment, to work with emerging systems that will beam TV-like Internet channels to suitably equipped television sets.

The tendency with network services is towards transforming the Web into a passive 'push' medium, rather than a 'pull' medium. The Interpublic Group, a major advertising holding company, has gone into partnership with Ifusion Com to create an Internet broadcasting system named Arrive. As with analogous services offered by Pointcast, Backweb Technologies and Intermind, Arrive will deliver customised information, including advertising, directly to users' screens whenever their computers are idle. The result, writes Stuart Elliot in the *New York Times*, is to relieve users of 'the need to search through the overwhelming amounts of data available' — because preselected sources of information are brought to users automatically. In that context, the ability to control the viewer's start-up screen acquires a new and decisive importance.

Both Netscape and Microsoft plan to transform users' desktop screens into what the *Wall Street Journal* calls 'platforms for receiving Internet broadcasts'. Microsoft, for example, is using its Windows operating system software to create 'Active Desktop', a TV-like receiver that is already allied with a leading Internet broadcaster. One of the 'premier' or default channels on Microsoft's Active Desktop will be supplied by PointCast, whose online network already reaches an estimated 1.7 million subscribers with broadcast feeds of news and advertising. Pointcast is currently in negotiations to be acquired by Rupert Murdoch's News Corporation. The *Wall Street Journal* tellingly refers to Microsoft's overall initiative as 'an important experiment in audience-building', and one with special appeal 'to new consumers that haven't been moved yet to go online'.

From another direction, there is America Online's recent appointment of Bob Pittman, the wunderkind who 15 years ago launched MTV, to manage its consumer online service. AOL's subscriber base of 7 million might not look like much when compared with the tens of millions of net surfers, but it's a formidable number when compared to the ratings garnered by any of the existing cable network channels. Efforts are far advanced to link the two media, and to identify ways of migrating audiences from one to the other. Oprah Winfrey, for example — whose talkshow reaches a daily audience of some 15 million viewers on television — is successfully carrying a portion of her audience to her AOL programme service.

Feverish discussion is underway of how best to track what net surfers are looking at — especially with regard to commercial messages. Nielsen, the television ratings service, is actively developing audience measurement techniques for the Web, where it already faces competition. DoubleClick, for example, comprises a network service for subscribing Web sites and advertisers; by monitoring usage it builds user profiles, on the basis of which it instantaneously uploads customised ads. Since March 1996, DoubleClick has identified the preferences of some 10 million Web surfers, with a reported 100,000 more profiles flowing in each day. A new trade association, the Internet Advertising Bureau, helps ensure that the sponsors who are, in the words of Joan Voight, 'trying to turn the once-eclectic Web into the ultimate 24-hour marketing machine', do not lack for an institutional voice.

'[A]dvertisers,' writes Voight, a reporter for *AdWeek*, 'want to work hand-in-hand with publishers to coproduce the material that packs Web pages.' ParentTime, a Website jointly produced by Procter & Gamble and Time-Warner, provides parents with interactive advice and promotes Time-Warner magazines such as *Parenting* and *Sports Illustrated for Kids*. P&G has, in addition, nine brand-specific Web sites, with dozens of others waiting in the wings; but ParentTime is a collaborative effort by the world's leading advertiser and a megamedia corporate ally to experiment with interactive programme forms specifically targeted at consumer advertisers' most-needed audience: women.

The effort of advertisers to increase women's use of the net has been widespread and concerted. Ed Meyer, then CEO of Grey Advertising, was asked in March 1995 by *Advertising Age* what 'key issues' had to be explored with regard to new media. He responded: 'One of the biggest issues is how we get women to use new media applications and embrace these new technologies. With 70 per cent of traditional advertising directed to women, it's vital to the success of new-media opportunities to appeal to and be used by women.' Women's use of the Internet has duly increased, at least in the US; women accounted for less than 10 per cent of Internet users a few years ago but, according to one tally, totalled nearly one-third by summer 1996. It's significant, in this context, that one of Microsoft's six introductory TV-like channels is a magazine for women called UnderWire.

Already the horizon of online network television is shrinking toward experiences that give Web users incentive to interact under the sign of

●●●●●●●●●●●●●●●●●●●●●●●●●●●●●●●●●

When advertisers come to foot an appreciable proportion of overall media costs, they come to dominate that medium's workaday self-consciousness, which in turn places new pressures and limits upon that medium's relationship with its audience

●●●●●●●●●●●●●●●●●●●●●●●●●●●●●●●●●

one or another brand, even beyond the new channels themselves. Sponsored chatrooms, for example, encourage users to exchange personal messages that contextualise their use of particular commodities — detergent say, or malt liquor — within the span of everyday social interaction. Thus is an emergent cultural practice consecrated to consumption, the most hallowed ground we have. Interactive genres of different kinds, from drama to news to games, seem certain as well to evolve further, under the watchful eye of sponsors who can lard them in all sorts of creative ways with product mentions and demonstrations.

On one side, then, 'push' services threaten to reduce use of the net to a more passive television-type experience. On the other side, however, there are ongoing reformulations of Web experience that put a premium on forms of active engagement — but only insofar as the latter can be rechannelled within the straitened terms of attention and priority demanded by sponsorship.

There is little doubt that TVs and PCs are converging, and that a series of unfolding applications are beginning to recast the Web. What then are

DAN SCHILLER

the implications of these developments?

It is not 'television' that is converging with cyberspace, of course, but a historically specific set of practices that we can more properly gloss as 'commercial networked television'. Commercial networked television is hardly new. It's crucial to stress that, long before the Internet, commercial networked television had already acquired the defining institutional identity that now bulks large in its ongoing convergence with the Web. Each of the two adjectives hints at a crucial feature. First has been the centralisation of television content, or programming. This centralisation should be distinguished from the considerable geographical concentration in programming and related industries that it encouraged. Centralisation of programming via networking meant that large producers and distributors, rather than local or non-profit broadcasters, were enabled to gain market power sufficient to dominate the larger television industry. In addition, thousands of US musicians and untold other performers found themselves unemployed, during earlier decades, because networks and stations successfully pushed to utilise recordings in preference to more expensive and unreliable live performances.

Microsoft is putting US$400 million annually into developing Web content, with no expectation of turning a profit for at least three more years. That's around an order of magnitude above the annual investment that was required by Rupert Murdoch's Fox Broadcasting network [or, for that matter, by Gannett's newspaper, *USA Today*], before each began to pay off. And corporations as a whole are estimated to have spent a couple of billion dollars in developing Web pages. This scale of expenditure makes it all but certain that one or another megamedia company will eventually figure out how to innovate profitable cyberspace genres. But the question of how far such companies will be able to dominate the market for Web-based experiences is a larger and more complex one.

The key goal of Webcasters, on current evidence, is to concentrate and stabilise relations between programme services and audiences. Under active exploration in realising this goal, and therewith claiming additional market power, are 'push' services, exclusive licensing agreements, a star system, blockbuster programming investments, and operating system software. But it must never be forgotten that this multifaceted attempt to stabilise the relation between programming and audience is itself largely a function of the second abiding aspect of a commercial networked model — its embedded reliance on advertiser sponsorship. The *Wall Street Journal* was perfectly correct to reduce this sprawling hubbub of business activity to the headline: 'How Net Is Becoming More Like Television To Draw Advertisers.' The explosive growth of Internet broadcasting is tantamount to an admission that advertisers have succeeded in bending the Web to their particular social purposes.

TV is the world's most effective selling tool. Simplifying only somewhat, it was because of its ability to accommodate live-action demonstration, over and above identification and endorsement of products and product applications, that TV succeeded radio as the foremost advertising medium. Advertisers are not yet confident that the Web portends an equally decisive new stage in the ongoing evolution of the sales effort — but they are certain that they cannot afford to overlook that possibility.

So much at least we may take from the celebrated address, already two-and-a-half years ago, by Ed Artzt, then CEO of Procter & Gamble. Before the American Association of Advertising Agencies, Artzt hectored his audience to rouse itself from its slumbers, and to 'seize technology in its teeth' to ensure access for commercial sponsors to new media. Consider how far the debate has travelled — and metamorphosed — in the brief interval since.

Today it is no longer a question of whether advertising and marketing will move on the net. Now, rather, the issue has become how to make the pioneering forms of commercial representation — banner ads and corporate home pages — succeed more efficiently, or give up pride of place to 'new and improved' forms of advertising. Hunter Madsen, vice-president for commercial strategy at Hotwired, makes a strong case for unremitting experimentation, toward less-standardised banners or 'brand modules', and direct interpenetration of commercial and editorial matter ['content cobranding']. The generic forms of advertiser sponsorship and programming on the Web, surely, are nowhere near stabilisation.

But neither is their precise form the chief issue. Advertisers have proclaimed the necessity of colonising cyberspace, and of making it dependent on their ability to provide funding. Does anyone still truly think that they will realise the folly of this ambition, and abandon the net? If advertisers ever recognised that the 'culture' of the net was unreceptive, that time is long gone. They will try, and try again, until.... The reason is structural, having to do with the most basic features of the economy.

The chief historical basis for advertising (whether or not the latter succeeds efficiently in any given instance) is the pan-corporate need to harness consumption to production. Branding, marketing, and consumer product advertising have been historically indispensable adjuncts of an economy that has reached a certain general level of productivity, of social surplus — ie, the amount of goods and services it can produce outstrips the concurrent socioeconomic ability to absorb this surplus. Advertisers have plunged into cyberspace, accordingly, not because of some peripheral or momentary whim to test new waters. They act, rather, as the representatives of a generative social force. The propulsive and multifaceted sales effort that they spearhead has, in turn, enfolded over a continuing succession of media down through the last hundred years.

Let's distinguish two levels of analysis. The first is, what does advertiser sponsorship do to the media that become dependent on it? The second is, to what extent will the net come to be advertiser supported?

There is plenty of evidence that advertiser sponsorship profoundly affects individual media practices, content, and relationships with audiences. It is not mainly a matter of poor ethics or lapsed standards, but of a systematic overall orientation. Advertisers want media to deliver audiences to them, in predictable quantities and at standard and comparably efficient costs. These audiences, moreover, need to be of ascertained composition and 'quality', in the sense that advertisers desire to purchase access to a guaranteed number of women ages 18-49, or men aged 25-54. (Of course, audience sales are often much more nuanced and targeted than this.) In this context, the roll-out of 'push' services on the Internet instances a new effort to recreate an old necessity: access to stable — measurable and delineable — audiences for advertisements.

When advertisers foot an appreciable proportion of overall media costs, they come to dominate that medium's workaday self-consciousness, which in turn places new pressures and limits upon that medium's relationship with its audience. It is not only a matter of 'censorship' to suit the idiosyncrasies of particular sponsors (though neither should censorship of this kind be gainsaid). It's also, and more substantively, a question of emphasis on particular programme forms, and the priorities that they express: particular creative practices rather than others. The practices that saturate our culture, and that are now being transferred wholesale to the net, are market-driven in intent and in effect. That doesn't mean they cannot sometimes result in true artistry, but rather that art itself is generally placed in harness to a narrow and exclusionary social purpose: selling.

How far can this convergence go? Of this we can hardly be confident. The trail is already littered with the effects of poor strategic judgements and corporate missteps. Consider only the recently announced decision by Pacific Telesis, Bell Atlantic and Nynex that their venture into television production, TeleTV, will disband. Or the trade journal *Variety*'s recent pronouncement: that 'convergence' itself is ceasing to be this season's buzzword in Hollywood. Surely there will be additional failures. Nobody can be certain that any particular venture will succeed, let alone that it will transform the net.

But that doesn't mean the whole thing is an open question. Most significant, it seems to me, is that the outcome itself is being left essentially to 'market forces,' that is, to the very corporate behemoths whose actions I have briefly assayed. If present trends are not interrupted, the extent to which a variant of commercial network television comes to prevail on the Web will be very largely determined by profit-seeking companies themselves. Other social interests, prospecting for alternative visions of cyberspace, including churches, public-interest organisations and community groups, educational institutions, museums, libraries, and labour unions, will either be marginalised, or else incorporated — and exploited — by sponsors seeking access to their members, and perhaps a patina of legitimacy.

The debate over the propriety of advertiser-supported radio broadcasting (the so-called 'American system') unfolded through years of public discussion, and drew outbursts of anti-commercial concern from highly placed politicians, church leaders, business people, educators, and philanthropic organisations. In contrast, the 'debate' over commercialism in cyberspace has been a non-starter. The established media have been nearly silent; aside from the question of 'spamming' — basically a diversion — scant substantive attention has been accorded to the grave questions raised by the growing commercial presence on the net. And this, again, is ultimately because an economy that is based on the subordination of consumption to production cannot afford to overlook any new medium that might be harnessed to its relentless sales effort let alone a medium enjoying the demographics evinced by cyberspace.

But nothing guarantees that this particular necessity shall prompt a foreordained future. In actuality, many people and organisations, a diversity of motive and ambition continue to be present, as the commercial imperative unfolds across another new medium. Some are unalloyed boosters; some alienated cynics, seemingly above the dismal venality and small-mindedness of it all. Still others may take pleasure in successfully smuggling private messages — cybergraffiti — into sponsored spaces, or in covertly intruding in other ways. But what of those more active dissenters, who seek to carry forward on the net the long-standing oppositional traditions of independent film and video artistry, and of free thought and association more generally? We may place our hopes with them — with our hearts, at least, if not yet with our heads. ❑

Dan Schiller *is professor of communication at the University of California, San Diego*

©*Reprinted courtesy of ACM from* netWorker *magazine (Vol 1.1., March 1997)*

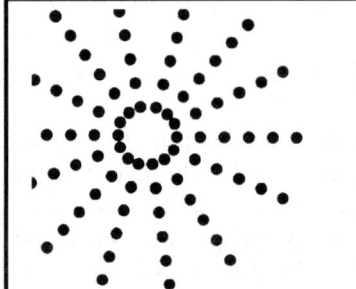

THE REUTER FOUNDATION PROGRAMME

"As a journalist, I have long admired Index's work. As director of the Reuter Foundation Programme I am even more convinced that what Index is doing in accumulating detailed information about threats to press freedom, and putting those threats in context, is absolutely vital."

Godfrey Hodgson (Director)

GABRIEL GARCIA MARQUEZ

The best job in the world

SOME 50 years ago, there were no schools of journalism. One learned the trade in the newsroom, in the print shops, in the local cafe and in Friday-night hangouts. The entire newspaper was a factory where journalists were made and the news was printed without quibbles. We journalists always hung together, we had a life in common and were so passionate about our work that we didn't talk about anything else. The work promoted strong friendships among the group, which left little room for a personal life. There were no scheduled editorial meetings, but every afternoon at 5pm, the entire newspaper met for an unofficial coffee break somewhere in the newsroom, and took a breather from the daily tensions. It was an open discussion where we reviewed the hot themes of the day in each section of the newspaper and gave the final touches to the next day's edition.

The newspaper was then divided into three large departments: news, features and editorial. The most prestigious and sensitive was the editorial department; a reporter was at the bottom of the heap, somewhere between an intern and a gopher. Time and the profession itself has proved that the nerve centre of journalism functions the other way. At the age of 19 I began a career as an editorial writer and slowly climbed the career ladder through hard work to the top position of cub reporter.

Then came schools of journalism and the arrival of technology. The graduates from the former arrived with little knowledge of grammar and syntax, difficulty in understanding concepts of any complexity and a dangerous misunderstanding of the profession in which the importance of a 'scoop' at any price overrode all ethical considerations.

The profession, it seems, did not evolve as quickly as its instruments of work. Journalists were lost in a labyrinth of technology madly rushing the

GABRIEL GARCIA MARQUEZ

On the trail of the 1994 Mexican presidential elections — Credit: Jon Mitchell/Panos Pictures

profession into the future without any control. In other words: the newspaper business has involved itself in furious competition for material modernisation, leaving behind the training of its foot soldiers, the reporters, and abandoning the old mechanisms of participation that strengthened the professional spirit. Newsrooms have become aseptic laboratories for solitary travellers, where it seems easier to communicate with extraterrestrial phenomena than with readers' hearts. The dehumanisation is galloping.

Before the teletype and the telex were invented, a man with a vocation for martyrdom would monitor the radio, capturing from the air the news of the world from what seemed little more than extraterrestrial whistles. A well-informed writer would piece the fragments together, adding background and other relevant details as if reconstructing the skeleton of a dinosaur from a single vertebra. Only editorialising was forbidden, because that was the sacred right of the newspaper's publisher, whose editorials, everyone assumed, were written by him, even if they weren't, and were always written in impenetrable and labyrinthine prose, which, so history relates, were then unravelled by the publisher's personal typesetter often hired for that express purpose.

Today fact and opinion have become entangled: there is comment in news reporting; the editorial is enriched with facts. The end product is none the better for it and never before has the profession been more dangerous. Unwitting or deliberate mistakes, malign manipulations and poisonous distortions can turn a news item into a dangerous weapon. Quotes from 'informed sources' or 'government officials' who ask to remain anonymous, or by observers who know everything and whom nobody knows, cover up all manner of violations that go unpunished. But the guilty party holds on to his right not to reveal his source, without asking himself whether he is a gullible tool of the source, manipulated into passing on the information in the form chosen by his source. I believe bad journalists cherish their source as their own life — especially if it is an official source — endow it with a mythical quality, protect it, nurture it and ultimately develop a dangerous complicity with it that leads them to reject the need for a second source.

At the risk of becoming anecdotal, I believe that another guilty party in this drama is the tape recorder. Before it was invented, the job was done well with only three elements of work: the notebook, foolproof ethics and a pair of ears with which we reporters listened to what the sources were telling us. The professional and ethical manual for the tape recorder has not been invented yet. Somebody needs to teach young reporters that the recorder is not a substitute for the memory, but a simple evolved version of the serviceable, old-fashioned notebook.

The tape recorder listens, repeats — like a digital parrot — but it does not think; it is loyal, but it does not have a heart; and, in the end, the literal version it will have captured will never be as trustworthy as that kept by the journalist who pays attention to the real words of the interlocutor and, at the same time, evaluates and qualifies them from his knowledge and experience.

The tape recorder is entirely to blame for the undue importance now attached to the interview. Given the nature of radio and television, it is only to be expected that it became their mainstay. Now even the print media seems to share the erroneous idea that the voice of truth is not that of the journalist but of the interviewee. Maybe the solution is to return to the lowly little notebook so the journalist can edit intelligently as he listens, and relegate the tape recorder to its real role as invaluable witness. It is some comfort to believe that ethical transgressions and other problems that degrade and embarrass today's journalism are not always the result of immorality, but also stem from the lack of professional skill.

Perhaps the misfortune of schools of journalism is that while they do teach some useful tricks of the trade, they teach little about the profession itself. Any training in schools of journalism must be based on three fundamental principles: first and foremost, there must be aptitude and talent; then the knowledge that 'investigative' journalism is not something special, but that all journalism must, by definition, be investigative; and, third, the awareness that ethics are not merely an occasional condition of the trade, but an integral part, as essentially a part of each other as the buzz and the horsefly.

The final objective of any journalism school should, nevertheless, be to return to basic training on the job and to restore journalism to its original public service function; to reinvent those passionate daily 5pm informal coffee-break seminars of the old newspaper office. ❑

Gabriel Garcia Marquez is the 1982 winner of the Nobel Prize for literature

JAY ROSEN

In quest of journalism

Michael Foley writes:

DURING the US presidential election last November, the Fox Network decided against an election-night special and showed *Beethoven*, a shaggy dog film, instead. Fox is owned by Rupert Murdoch and, whatever one's view of the media magnate, he has rarely failed in judging the public mood.

Here was proof, if proof were needed, that the public had become cynical about public affairs; and that despite huge questions facing the American people, there was no real debate.

Jay Rosen is professor of journalism at New York University and director of the NYU's Project on Public Life and the Press. He is also the guru, the philosopher king, of a movement within the US media, called public, or civic, journalism.

Rosen and the project he heads lives along one of those endless corridors that make up NYU, in Greenwich Village. His offices are crammed with papers, articles and books about the crisis in US journalism — its failure to engage with the political system and the unhealthy state of the US newspaper industry.

Public journalism is a response to all those concerns: a determination to re-connect journalism to the communities it serves; to concentrate on issues rather than on the workings of the political process — the 'horse race' element. Above all, it questions long-held assumptions about journalism and asks if they any longer hold true.

While public journalism as a movement dates back to the presidential election of 1988, it is also a response to other complex political and commercial problems, such as the declining sales of US newspapers.

Rosen speaks with passion and not just to visiting journalists. He campaigns for public journalism and is quietly evangelical. He travels the US with his message and has published extensively.

One of the numerous funding bodies now supporting public journalism projects is the Pew Centre for Civic Journalism. Its executive director, Edward Fouhy, wrote that civic journalists broaden their agenda from the usual overwhelming focus on political and government news and aggressively ferret out issues of interest to citizens who are not members of the elite. 'That means covering an agenda that is set more by citizens, by the people, and less by those who would manipulate them. That means thinking about the news not only from the standpoint of conventional journalistic practice but taking it a step further and thinking about a subject from the standpoint of the public and public interest.'

Of the top newspapers, only the *Boston Globe* has so far taken up the challenge of public journalism. Editors of the *New York Times*, the *Washington Post* and the leading news weeklies, have interpreted public journalism very differently from editors outside the major US cities who are involved in public journalism projects. Articles in the *Times*, the *Washington Post* and the *New Yorker* have warned journalists to be on their guard, accusing enthusiasts for public journalism of abandoning professional judgements and turning over the news agenda to readers for essentially commercial reasons. It has also been suggested that such journalists are becoming community activists and dumping the time-honoured journalistic codes of objectivity and neutrality.

According to Rosen, the elite press in Washington and New York are suspicious of ideas that come from the margins: surely journalists who are any good are already working in Washington and New York.

It is all but impossible to find a common thread linking the various strands in public journalism. At one level, it says simply that journalists should be in touch with the communities they serve. But public journalism is also about democracy and the role of journalism in supporting and strengthening that.

★★★

Jay Rosen:

PUBLIC journalism is simply an experiment in which a number of people are engaging in the hope of discovering how serious journalism can recover its public. That, they claim, is the only way we'll have a serious press. It was a response to a complicated political, commercial and civic crisis that raised questions about the future of journalism as a public art.

Public journalism arose as a response to a whole list of troubles that certain journalists found themselves in after the 1988 campaign. They had just been through what was widely regarded as the worst campaign in modern memory, symbolised by Michael Dukakis climbing aboard a tank to illustrate his tough policy on defence. More than the usual self criticism followed this débâcle and a number of journalists said, 'We are implicated, we have become part of this media system and it's not serving our politics very well. Despite huge issues like the end of the Cold War, it's turning off the American people, public debate is going no where. We have become part of the establishment, we are the permanent professional political class; maybe we should reconsider our relationship to this spectacle and while we are at it start thinking about some other things that ought to concern us. The commercial pressures facing most news rooms these day are very difficult and there are technological changes taking place that may do us in.' A lot of us had noticed that the journalism we were doing in our local communities was not working very well — and not only at election time.

Journalists came to these questions because they were concerned with the survival of their craft. Editors and journalists were already writing about public disaffection with the press, in particular its coverage of politics and public affairs. Simultaneously, the people who employed them, the publishers and owners of media companies, were worried about the erosion of readership. One man in particular, James Batten, former chairman and CEO of Knight-Ridder, our second largest newspaper company, who had been a journalist, understood both sides of the problem. He knew that this was the bread and butter of serious newspapers and that there were good commercial reasons as well as professional ones for the civic crisis to draw the attention of the press.

The companies that own these properties own something that is commercially valuable but also has a public identity, a public duty; some sort of commitment to public values which in America, we would argue, comes along with the First Amendment. The First Amendment is a very important part of the argument. The only criticism I am making of media companies is when they try to pretend that they have no such special position, that they just own a property, like a retail store. That is not what our political tradition and our regulatory tradition says.

There is a distinction between media and journalism. I am interested in the survival of journalism, whether the media wants to support it or not. I do not have to worry too much about the media: I'm confident it will prosper in what is after all a media age. But this public art that we call journalism, this democratic practise, has its own future and I am interested in where it is going to be found. I still believe that some newspaper companies are willing to find it in a stronger connection to community, public life, but it is by no means certain that enough companies are going to believe in this to try and make it work; not at all clear that the commitment of resources from these companies is going to be there. What we need to do is develop the ideal so that whoever wants to support it has something vital and alive to support.

What is really at stake in the public journalism debate is what position the profession is going to take to the possibilities of this idea. My belief is that a form of public journalism will be put into play by others if the US press decides it is not the right thing for it. Some form of public interest media is coming, along with a lot of other media, that is very different. But there is no doubt that the relationship between readers and writers is changing because of, among other things, the Web. That also means a change in the relationship of journalists to citizens and we are trying to think through the implications of that change in two ways: by thinking, writing philosophising about it; and by experimenting in real communities with real newspapers and changing what they do.

It may be that public journalism migrates somehow out of the media into a different world, a more civic world of universities, of foundations, of citizens groups; these people can make media themselves and, if they do, they should have a philosophy of how journalists can practise in some sort of productive relationship to their communities available to them, so that journalists and citizens together make something called the news.

These experiments [in public journalism] run from the solidly professional to the absurd. There is a lot of hype about some of them because the people running them don't appreciate the importance of the

Right: Citizen Kane *1941* — Credit: BBC

IN QUEST OF JOURNALISM

civic tone in everything they do, so they hype it like a commercial product, which is a bad idea.

One of the peculiarities, one of the charming curiosities, of the idea is that it has both a radical and a banal dimension to it. At one level we are saying journalists should be in touch with their communities: that's the banal bit. When I talk with journos who are 60 years old, they get enraged because they know that this is what it used to be like when journalism was part of the life of the city in a way that today's mobile-phone-talking journalists are not. That's the simple part.

The radical part says: journalism is not a self-justifying art; it is not done for the sake of 'doing journalism'. It is supposed to be about democracy and that requires journalists to think about what they are doing to aid the functioning of democracy. Thinking that way is very unusual simply because of the pull of routines, doing the story every day. We are saying: stop, stop the presses; ask yourself what the presses are going to accomplish when you turn them on again. What type of relationship do we have with the community we 'serve'?

Suddenly the actual relationship you are in confronts you. At the very least, there are sources there, but you don't have people who come from there. You don't have conversations that would enable you to take the temperature of what is happening, or a system of monitoring that quickly enables you to grasp the situation. Those are all dimensions of your relationship to the community that suddenly seems not to be working in some way. In a way that does not allow you to produce the truth. When you ask a lot of journalists in public journalism how they came to the idea, they start with stories of some experience of radical disconnection from the community or part of the community.

This is one aspect of the story: the people who are pushing the idea. Then another factor entered the picture: what other journalists wrote and said about it. Particularly the elite press, by which I mean, the *New York Times*, the *Washington Post*, the news weeklies, the capital press. In their hands public journalism became something very different from what it meant to those who were practising it. Part of the charge was that journalists involved in public journalism were abandoning professional judgement by turning over the news agenda to readers for essentially commercial reasons.

Public journalists, the elite press stated, were also activists solving community problems themselves. Another way they put it was that these journalists should junk objectivity and neutrality and become activists for their own idea. Public journalism was also portrayed as a commercial plot essentially out of *Wall Street,* a gimmick dreamed up by some MBAs.

But the idea was already out there when the elite press put this construction on it: the first step in a take over by alien forces who would trash the values of the press. They see them as do gooders, well intentioned, but stupid.

• •

Journalism is not a self-justifying art. It is supposed to be about democracy and that requires journalists to think about what they are doing

• •

Why are they doing it? The elite press believe that if you were any good you would already be working in New York and Washington. You move upward towards the major cities. But this is an idea that comes from a different direction. This is not an idea communicated downward from a professional hierarchy, like a Pulitzer prize, but an idea coming up from below.

The author and journalist James Fallows (editor of *US News and World Report*), says he looked at the Pentagon after Vietnam. There was an institution that had experienced a big failure, but the leadership was not interested in building from first principles. It was the same for the automobile industry after the Japanese invasion. There were others willing to look again at how to succeed, go back to first assumptions and rebuild the edifice. They started to make their voices known. In the Pentagon and Detroit, the reformers were dismissed, ridiculed, until it was realised they were on to something. Fallows' view is that public journalism is in the same position and is getting the same reaction. His attitude is simple: this is an experiment, they are smart but working with limitations, so why not separate the good from the bad and develop it. That would seem to be a common sense approach for the elite press but instead they have rejected it.

Public journalism is part of a larger crisis for professionals in America, the relationship between journalists and the body politic. That's where it's located and public journalism is just an experiment with the terms of that relationship to see if a better one can be found. When it is, the label 'public journalism' will disappear and we shall just call it journalism once more.

Journalism only exists within a culture, within a community. Sometimes it is the community of the nation, but for most journalists it is more local. Your craft has meaning because the civic culture of that place has meaning. It's not the other way around. If that community cannot find in your journalism something useful, something it recognise as its own, some story it can share, then you have failed as a journalist, even if you have lived up to your own professional codes. Civic story telling and civic problem solving will be two aspects of the same thing. This is what a community will ask from its journalists. This is what public journalism is saying now and media companies will come to discover that service of this kind is valuable and that people will pay for it. ❑

*Jay Rosen is professor of journalism at New York University where **Michael Foley**, media editor of the* Irish Times, *interviewed him*

INTER PRESS SERVICE

congratulates

Index on Censorship

on 25 years of moral support

http://www.ips.org.uk

Right: Birth of a Nation, *1915* — *Credit: BFI Stills and Pictures*

The image

DAVID CRONENBERG & J G BALLARD

Set for collision

Even before it opened at the 1996 London Film Festival, David Cronenberg's latest film *Crash*, based on the novel by JG Ballard, was subjected to vitriolic abuse in the right-wing tabloids and to outraged moralising by politicians, none of whom had seen it. Preempting a British Board of Film Classification ruling, Westminster City Council banned its screening throughout London's West End cinemas. Only on 18 March did the often over-cautious director of the board, James Ferman, defy general censure and give it a clean bill of health and an 18 certificate, saying that while 'unusual and disturbing', the film was neither illegal nor harmful. Author and film-maker discuss the renewed furore surrounding *Crash* 25 years after its first publication

David Cronenberg: It'd be interesting to see what you feel the differences are between the book and the movie. In your now infamous preface to the French edition, you said, among other things that you felt the book was in some way a cautionary tale.

JG Ballard: When I was writing the book I certainly didn't think of it as a cautionary tale. I was exploring the apparent links I sensed in the very early 1970s between violence and sexuality and, in particular, between the car and sexuality. Looking back, it seems to me that the book is a cautionary tale where the writer or the film-maker plays devil's advocate and adopts what seems to be an insane or perverse logic in order to make a larger point. Swift did it in *A Modest Proposal*, and film-makers like Kubrick did it in *Dr Strangelove*.

DC: People [also] like to talk about the book being the first techno-porn novel.

JGB: I think it was 1973: I said I like to think of *Crash* as the first pornographic novel based on technology. Of course pornography then had very different connotations: it really meant just explicit sexuality which was a new card in fiction and the movies. There was very little explicit sex in the novel then. The *Last Exit from Brooklyn* trial and the *Lady Chatterley's Lover* trial were only just over; people don't realise that the sort of explicit sexual description you get in novels today, or in films, didn't exist then. Now the word pornography's become all things to all people. It's one of those happily undefined words like fascism that anyone can use for whatever purposes. Generally things you disapprove of, especially paedophile sex and S&M and sex that abuses — pornography that abuses women and so on — I wasn't thinking of that sort of thing.

The book appears to give the impression — and to some extent the film does too — that car crashes are sexually fulfilling. I've never said that; I've been in a car crash and it did nothing for my libido. What I was saying was that the idea of the car crash is sexually exciting or intriguing. By sex I mean all those aggressive sexual energies that impel some young men to chase women drivers who dare to overtake them. The notion that the idea of a car crash is sexually exciting is much more disturbing in a way because it asks much greater questions about who we are. If thinking about car crashes excites us, there's something very strange going on in the human psyche — and that appears to be confirmed by the entertainment culture in which we live which is just saturated and has been for the last 30 or 40 years.

DC: Someone said to me, 'The car crashes in your movie are not very realistic.' I said 'Really, what do you mean?' He said 'Well, there's no slow motion; you're not seeing it from five different angles.' I said 'Have you ever been in a car crash?' He said 'No.' Obviously his understanding of the reality of a car crash was totally formed by Hollywood.

JGB: There is no doubt that cinema is the dominant form in which the twentieth-century imagination shapes itself. It's even more powerful than television which on one level has a greater sort of daily influence. TV surrounds us like all those packets of cornflakes in the kitchen and the Mixmaster and the washing machine and the packet of Daz and so on, but film is where the twentieth-century imagination really expresses itself. The book, the novel, tragically, is moving towards irrelevance. People are not outraged by novels anymore, they were once but not now, film is the dominant medium. But you can't quite dispense with us yet.

DC: The interesting thing for me is that the cinema has always been fed by literature, hugely, right from its inception, and writing is still a crucial part of film-making whether it's a novel or not.

Some time ago I interviewed Salman Rushdie and one of the things I asked him was, 'Do you think the cinema is an inferior art form to the novel?' And he looked at me as though he didn't know what I was talking about because he too had been raised in cinema.

Bergman always felt that he was not a real artist, because for him real artists wrote novels. That's why he rewrote his four screenplays so that they would be more literary, they weren't really like screenplays at all. I suppose there is that lingering, Victorian residue.

JGB: From the age of seven or eight I was a film-goer, with my parents in India, with nanny, it was a form of a babysitting. What TV is as a babysitter today, film was in the 1930s. When my parents couldn't stand this hyperactive child charging around anymore they would tell the Chinese nanny or the White-Russian nanny, 'God! Take him to the cinema!' I loved sitting in these huge empty giant cinemas in Shanghai watching films. I adored films and I've always tried to make my novels like film because I think film has got the grammar and the language in the way the twentieth-century imagination sees itself. I would like to think my fiction, which some people find very difficult, is, in fact, very close to cinema.

DC: But there are things you can do in fiction and in writing that you simply cannot do in cinema and vice versa. I don't think one supplants the other; ideally they enhance, reflect each other. To read the book *Crash* and see the movie *Crash* together would be a much richer, much more dynamic experience than to experience either one alone. I don't think it would be great for fiction to become cinema, to become an inferior version of cinema, or vice versa. I have great respect for the art of fiction, huge in fact.

But I do believe the two are quite different in many ways. To make the movie I had to do really what Jim did which is to be the character, I had to live that life and that is why in the movie there is no superimposed false moral stand taken by the film-maker. The moral stance as understood by

Hollywood is almost a narrative device, or a part of characterisation. You have to give the character moral indignation, you have to be, as a filmmaker, morally outraged. But how many times have we seen films from Hollywood in particular, where we know no-one involved in the film gave a damn about that aspect of it, it was just there as a plot device to motivate the character to jump on the bus or to take his gun, finally, out of the drawer: a mechanical device. I felt when I read the book that it would be much stronger and much more revealing absolutely to accept that that was not the project, and in the course of time you begin to see what meaning the movie might have.

The first thing that struck me when I started to read the book was that the main character was called James Ballard, this is very unusual, especially when it's that book.

JGB: Why invent a character who's working his way through this sort of extraordinary landscape when I can simply use my own name and give this novel what I think is a degree of honesty that would be absent otherwise? I mean by the same token in a way *you* should have called the character David DC. Of course, you don't have first-person narration in films. Unless you'd used a voiceover which I would have rather liked.

DC: It never works.

JGB: It worked in classic films of the 1940s and 1950s — *Double Indemnity* and *Sunset Boulevard* — didn't it? Without voiceovers they would be very alienating movies. Shakespeare used the voiceover: it's called the soliloquy, if you look at *Hamlet* or *Macbeth*, most of the characters are extremely unpleasant. If you look at *Double Indemnity* or *Sunset Boulevard* or *Badlands*, the characters are all extremely unpleasant, yet the voiceover bridges the gap between audience and characters. I think you're right that using a voiceover in your film of *Crash* would have spoilt the film because in a way it would have said we need to bridge a gap.

Where your film is so original is that it introduces this extremely threatening subject matter but doesn't distance it in any way. [David Lynch's] *Blue Velvet* — brilliant film, a masterpiece in its own way — is far more violent than *Crash* and there's perverse sex in it which is at least as perverse as anything in *Crash*. *Reservoir Dogs* is another extremely violent and crude and brutal film, much more likely to incite young men to dangerous behaviour than anything in *Crash*. But in both those films there's a distance: you watch them and you think this is all happening to these perverted nightclub singers and gangsters.

In *Crash* there's no distance, the characters are you in the audience, there's no way you can escape. When I wrote *Crash* 23 years ago people interviewed me at the time and said, 'What is this book?' And I said I wanted to write a book where the reader had nowhere to hide. The filmgoer watching David's film has nowhere to hide. The people on screen are the people in the audience. That's what's so frightening — and a voiceover would [have] used a bit of distance; it would have said, 'I don't want you to feel worried, you people in the audience, this is a strange film, but this is how it happened.'

DC: After I screened the first cut of the film for one of the American distributors, he said, 'I don't know how people are going to access this film. I'm gonna make a suggestion now and I know you're gonna hate it.' I said 'Voiceover, right?' He said 'Right, voiceover.' What he really wanted was the voiceover to be a voice of comfort and to explain the film to everybody.

JGB: The absence of a moral frame around the film is what's so original about it. If you think of the huge output of violent films from Hollywood, all the *Die Hard* films and so on, there's always a saving moral frame: the hero is working for the CIA or whatever it may be, he — Bruce Willis — is not allowed to play a baddie, he's always on the side of the powers that preside over our world and hold it together. It's much more difficult in a public medium like the cinema to eliminate the moral. [But] you've dispensed with the moral frame; you present the events of the film without any apparent easy get-out for the audience, or for the characters within the film. I don't think I've ever seen a film in which there is no moral frame in quite the same way, in which there is no attempt whatsoever to moralise away the events being portrayed. That's *Crash*'s originality: you present these extraordinary events as a sort of metaphor for a larger fusion of all sorts of challenging ideas but without any attempt to justify within conventional moral calculus what is going on. That's not something one wants to say too loud, but that's its great achievement.

DC: One critic did say that the most frightening thing for him about the movie was this lack of a moral stance, but in a sense that is the subject of

SET FOR COLLISION

David Cronenberg on location with Crash — *Credit: Columbia Tristar*

the film, and to impose one would be to subvert what the movie was all about, it would also suggest that I had the answer and I don't, so the movie also raises questions that I don't have answers for, so I wanted to let the characters say, 'What Vaughan is doing, maybe it would be good.' I truly don't believe that if we tacked a little moralising ending on to the end of the film — where they were all arrested and confessed that they had done bad and were misguided — the press hysteria would be different.

JGB: The press need a get-out, one's got to stand by whatever one believes in. *Crash*, both book and film, would have been meaningless if some sort of explicit moral justification was tacked around all this material. The moral framework, if there is to be one, is provided by the audience; the novel and the film are each an extreme hypothesis. As I see it, these tendencies are inscribed in the world in which we live, this strange fusion of sexuality and violence and sensation and this affectless realm that is the late twentieth century. Where do the lines on this graph seem to lead? *Crash*, film and book, represents the end point, an extreme extrapolation, beyond the graph paper, of where these lines are leading. It's not a prophecy, it's just an extrapolation if you like, no moral point is being made but perhaps the truth is being reached. In the case of your film, the narrative drive and the accumulation of images drive one towards credibility. The film does arrive at a point of credibility. Whether one likes this point of arrival, whether one wants to get off this particular train and face up to what stands around the platform, is a different matter, but it's nothing to do with moral frameworks.

DC: A lot of the moral outrage is from people who have not seen the film so how can they be outraged; how dare they say those things if they have not seen the film? They're being outraged because other people are outraged and it all goes back of course to Alexander Walker [*Evening Standard* film critic] who was probably the only one in Britain who had seen the film, to his initial 'Beyond The Bounds Of Perversity', 'Beyond The Bounds Of Depravity'. Even with that I had problems because if you're beyond the bounds of depravity then you're not within the country of depravity, you're somewhere else.

JGB: The first publisher's reader who came across *Crash* in 1972, the year before it was published, was the wife of a famous TV psychiatrist — I think she had some sort of psychiatric training herself — [and she] said in her reader's report, 'The author of this book is beyond psychiatric help.' My reaction was: 'Total artistic success.' I feel the same about the reactions to your film.

The screening of *Crash* at the London Film Festival coincides with this panic that the present Conservative regime feels in the face of almost certain electoral defeat in May. They're climbing aboard every conceivable bandwagon as they've done in their flustered state for the last couple of years: child is savaged to death tragically by a pit bull and the legislation is immediately cobbled together and enacted in a great flurry of moral righteousness to ban all aggressive dogs — rightly maybe. Tragedy of Dunblane where 16 small children are shot dead by this middle-aged paedophile — a ghastly crime and a terrible thing to happen to the children and their parents — and people are quoted linking *Crash* in some way to Dunblane and the murder.

The political parties are really in a degenerate state. You see this in the United States: no-one cares who's elected president because it doesn't really matter. We're moving into the irrelevancy of politics and those who occupy the 650 seats or whatever in the House of Commons are desperate to seize the moral high ground; they're climbing on every conceivable hobby-horse. *Crash* suddenly got on to their radar screen and they've locked on to it. It's a shame because it has nothing to do with the film.

DC: For me, this movie is a kind of existentialist romance. The characters have found that the old forms of love and sex and relationship and many other things no longer work; they're going through the motions but it's not working. And because of an epiphany one of the characters undergoes in a car crash — the nice little lines of traffic which give the illusion of order and control are immediately destroyed in the chaos of any kind of car crash — suddenly you're crossing all the lines, the cars are spinning, you don't know what direction you're facing. His body is torn apart, his life is also torn apart and he's got to put all of those things back together again. He finds they won't go back together again because they'd been coming apart anyway and so he has to reinvent sexuality, eroticism, love, many other things, and they arrive at a very strange place. But in a way it's a bizarrely happy ending.

And that's a legitimate metaphor for what does happen in each individual's life, we end up in a very strange place. On one level, that's my interpretation of the movie; it might not be my interpretation of the book. And yet the movie is also the book: it's a strange, multi-layered interconnection between the two.

JGB: This is a love story. *Crash*, bizarrely you may think, is actually a love story between the two principal characters. You brought out that element which is implicit in the novel. The film is very much a love story — this is one of the few ways left to the late twentieth century to meet itself with deep love and affection — between husband and wife; the story of their rediscovery of their love for each other.

Crash is not a conventional film, there are no conventions *Crash* is relying upon — the horror film, the film noir or whatever. *Crash* creates its own rules from scratch. That's what's unsettling about it because you can't take refuge, you can't escape the thing, it's coming at you like a runaway truck.

DC: That's why the press stuff is so destructive; it's not a violent movie. It's conceptually violent but not physically on the screen. *Braveheart* is a thousand times more violent and yet people think it's this great historical romp for children who walk in in the middle of it. It's not: *Braveheart* is quite excruciatingly horrifying. If I put everybody in *Crash* in a kilt would that be better, give you that distance? ❏

JG Ballard is a prolific novelist, including Crash *and* Empire of the Sun. His most recent works are Rushing to Paradise *(1995) and* Cocaine Nights *(1996)* *David Cronenberg's* extensive and controversial repertoire includes the films Dead Ringers *and* The Fly. Crash *won the Grand Jury prize at the 1996 Cannes Film Festival for its 'originality, daring and audacity'*

© *An edited version of the* Guardian *lecture at the London Film Festival, November 1996*

• Despite the official BBFC decision, the *Daily Mail* took it upon itself to alert every local authority in the UK to the danger of showing this film. In an unprecedented move, 40 councils have asked for a screening of the film before releasing it locally (Ed).

EDWARD LUCIE-SMITH

Beyond fundamentalism

Unlike the word, graphic art in the Arab world retains its power to resist the worst of fundamentalism

I HAVE recently served as a jury member for two major art biennali in the Arab world — Cairo in December 1996 and Sharjah in April 1997. Both events are well established. This was the sixth Cairo Biennale (though the first with an international jury), and the third such event in Sharjah. Taken together, they had much to say about the condition of art in the various Arab nations, and also about contemporary Arabic attitudes to visual representation. If the fiercest kind of Islamic fundamentalism was not present, this was for several reasons.

The first is simple: the nations where fundamentalism currently flourishes most strongly are on the whole not Arabic — Iran and Afghanistan were represented at neither Biennale. There was, however, art from countries where the culture is innately conservative, such as Saudi Arabia, or where fundamentalism is on the rise, such as Algeria (represented in Sharjah only). One interesting thing was that the contributions from these nations were not in fact markedly different from those coming from places where the atmosphere is more relaxed.

In order to understand the situation more fully, it is necessary to know something about the complexity of sources and origins. In addition, it is useful to know something about the position of contemporary Arabic art within its own social context. Indeed, it is essential to look at the latter first, before proceeding to historical questions.

The Arabic artists of today complain as all artists do. In particular, they lament the lack of patronage in their home countries. By this they mean the absence of powerful, well-funded museums of modern art on the western model, the lack of a tradition of private collecting, and the absence of professionally run commercial galleries. It is because of all this that many have expatriated themselves to make careers in the West, though political turmoil is also a factor.

In many Arab countries, however, there is now quite an important apparatus of state patronage, though it operates in an unfamiliar way. As used to be the case in Latin America, promising young artists are often given generous grants to study abroad. A fellow-juror in and from Sharjah told me that he had studied for five years in London at government expense. Patronage of this kind is all the more necessary as there are some countries where art schools do not exist. Where they do, it is in the more 'evolved' societies, such as Egypt. The most important element in the burgeoning official system, however, is a network of competitive exhibitions. The major international biennials are only the top layer. In addition there are many other smaller competitions.

An artist makes his (more rarely her) way through being singled out in these. In a sense the financial value and even the actual hierarchy of the prizes given does not matter. What counts is to be noticed. An artist who attracts attention in this way is encouraged with official commissions of various sorts, and can look forward to being nominated to take part in other events. More than this, an artist who has a success in an international exhibition is seen as someone who confers lustre on his whole nation.

The actual measure used in deciding who should be the prize-winners is a variable. In mixed juries, it is the Arab members who are generally the most anxious for the contemporary element to be recognised. They see modern Arabic art as something which must try to compete on a world stage, not merely a regional one. Non-Arabic jurors, on the other hand, are regularly attracted by elements they perceive as 'arabising', which are to them pleasingly exotic. There are thus two quite different sets of criteria for what seems artistically authentic.

The situation is further complicated by the historical considerations already mentioned. Modern Arabic art begins, not as a direct continuation of traditional forms, modified to meet changing conditions, but as an imitation of western products. A number of modern Arabic artists of the earliest generation were imitators of the European Orientalist painters of the late nineteenth-century. They interpreted their own societies not only using borrowed materials, such as oil paint on canvas, but using borrowed visual conventions. Paintings and watercolours of this type continue to appeal to what is now conservative Arab taste, and one can find a good number of technically skilful artists who make works of this sort. In the Gulf sheikhdoms in particular there is a ready market for depictions of fine Arab horses and hawks, for paintings of *dhows* and camels, and for depictions of traditional local architecture. The one change from the European nineteenth century model is an avoidance, by no means complete however, of the human figure as a prominent element in the composition.

Modernism entered the Arab world largely through the work of the French Fauves, most of all through that of Matisse, whose Moroccan

Both the most modern and most ancient elements in Arabic culture tend to predispose artists to resist the advance of fundamentalism in the contemporary visual arts

paintings had an enormous impact in French-dominated North Africa. Similar influences from French art were felt in Cairo, Damascus and Beirut. Gradually, however, all the leading modernist styles became familiar. As in Latin America, while the styles themselves were easily transported, the sense of their relationship to one another, and of their historical sequence was lost. The results can be found in any Arab-world art Biennale today — there are examples of Expressionism, Cubism, Surrealism, Abstract Expressionism, modified to suit Arab taste. The one significant movement that Arab artists seem to have missed out on is the Neo-Classical revival which flourished between World War I and World War II. In fact, the balanced rationality of classicism is in general not present: the element which all these stylistic experiments, figurative and abstract, have in common is their reliance on subjectivity.

More recently, three things seem to have affected Arab art. The first is the widening diaspora of young Arab artists. At first it was accepted that the place for a young artist to polish his skills was in Paris. Later, especially for artists from the Gulf States, London became an alternative. More recently still, Arab artists have gone to school in Berlin, in Madrid and in various cities in Italy. Each of these imposes its own particular point of

EDWARD LUCIE-SMITH

view — the artist concerned returns to the Arab world with a French, German, Spanish or Italian accent, as the case may be. The second is the development of new forms, which are neither painting nor sculpture. There is growing enthusiasm for environmental art in the Arab world, just as there is in Latin America. Environmental work is much less dependent on the western technical tradition — its procedures are improvised. Making environments and installations, artists, whatever culture they come from, start on more or less equal terms. In addition, the environment and the installation are public rather than private forms. They often have an openly didactic purpose. This suits the political and cultural climate in the Arab world of today. In Cairo, for example, a number of the prize-winning works were installations. One was a comment by an Egyptian on the housing situation in Egypt, and on the possibility of fusing new and very ancient building forms. Another was a comment by a Palestinian on the Palestinian experience of exile.

The third is a tentative search for imagery which is specifically Arabic, but which is at the same time non-figurative. The compromise between the two impulses — the search for what is immediately recognisable as Arab, and for something which skirts around figurative imagery, forbidden by any strict interpretation of the Quran, is to try to marry modernist abstraction to the rich heritage of Islamic calligraphy. This impulse manifests itself in both conservative and radical Arabic societies. The Sharjah Biennale, for example, featured work of this type from Qatar, a relatively conservative Gulf state, but also from Algeria and from Libya. In none of these instances, however, was the national display confined to work of this one type. The Libyan artists, all very young, included one artist who based his work on calligraphic forms, another (trained in Britain) who was a child of Miró and Klee, and a third who offered a watered-down version of French Post-Impressionist figuration.

What conclusions can be drawn from the present state of contemporary Arabic art, particularly in relationship to the rise of fundamentalism throughout the Islamic world? The answer to this question is much less straightforward than one might suppose at first. For example, it is quite obvious that the tendency towards a new kind of abstraction, based on the forms of traditional calligraphy is only one, and probably not the strongest, artistic manifestation among many. There is no sign that it will

Right: Qatari artist Yousef Ahmad at the Sharjah Biennale, 1997

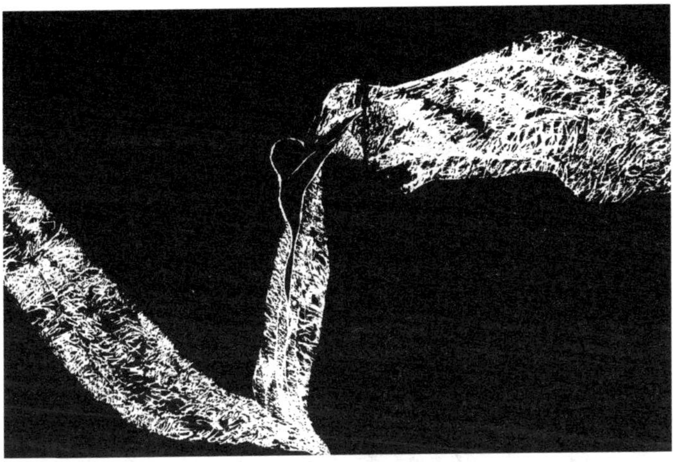
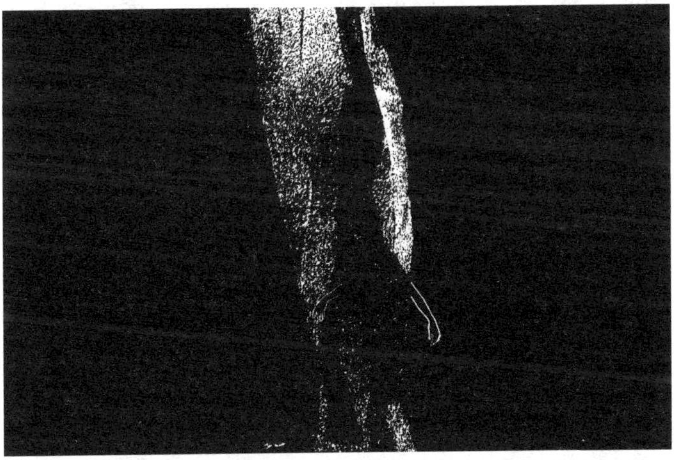
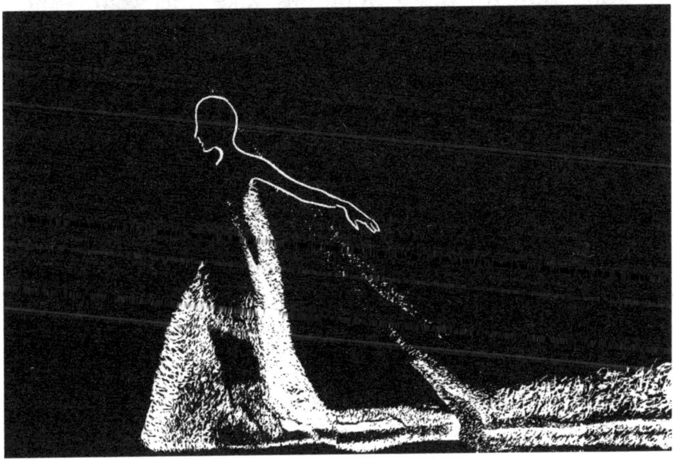

ever be in a position to take over altogether. In Sharjah, in some ways a very conservative environment — teetotal, and with censorship of images considered too openly sexual in magazines and books — the second Sharjah Biennale, of 1995, put far more emphasis on work of this sort than its successor in 1997. Fundamentalism, if it triumphs, will not simply bring with it a new, unified modern Arabic art of this sort. Indeed, it is far more likely that it will try to suppress modernist art altogether, as a corrupt product of the infidel West. Those who involve themselves with the production of contemporary art in the Arab world must all, whatever specific form their activity takes, be regarded as westernisers.

On the one hand, training in art involves activities to which fundamentalists particularly object. One of these, traditional in the western sense, rather than radical, is the practice of drawing from the life. Art schools in Pakistan have been physically attacked by fundamentalist groups for allowing this, and it is no longer possible in Algeria. On the other hand, the political and social statements made by modernist artworks are in general much less specific than those made by embattled contemporary writers. To draw another parallel from the recent history of Latin America — it was much easier for avant-garde conceptual and installation artists to continue their activities unmolested in Argentina, during the worst days of the military junta, than it was for writers of any liberal tendency to express themselves freely. A similar situation prevailed in Chile under Pinochet. But modernist activity of this type, even if allowed to continue, would do so without any official support.

Major contemporary art exhibitions, like the Cairo and Sharjah Biennales, would almost certainly be suppressed, not only because they would be seen as secular and westernising, but because they encourage the sexes to mingle as visitors as well as contributors. The Sharjah Biennale already reserves certain visiting hours for women only.

There are, finally, two other factors which deserve to be considered seriously. There is, in Islamic fundamentalism, an element of the country set against the town. In Turkey, fundamentalism's recent political successes have been linked to an influx of peasant populations from Anatolia into the major cities, particularly Istanbul. Contemporary art in the Arab world is, above everything else, an urban phenomenon. Its history is intimately linked to increasing urban sophistication, and the interchanges which this creates. It is also something which, in a number of the most important Arabic nations has been a vehicle for a discourse about a kind of cultural continuity which reaches beyond things purely Islamic. Contemporary Egyptian artists continually insist on their situation as heirs of the pharaohs, of Roman Egypt and of the Copts. These things, they say, are at least as important to them as their heritage as Arabs. Artists from Syria and Lebanon make the same point. For them, what they produce is the living offshoot of the world's oldest civilisations. Modernism merely supplies a grammar through which they can express their consciousness of this fact.

In the end it is these two things which may provide the strongest bulwark against the advance of fundamentalism in the contemporary visual arts of the Arab world. It may indeed be imposed for a while as a form of political dogma, but both the most modern and the most ancient elements in Arabic culture tend to predispose the artists themselves to resist. ❑

Edward Lucie-Smith is a UK writer and critic. His most recent book is ArToday *(Phaidon 1996).* Movements in Art Since 1945: Issues and Concepts *was reissued in 1995 by Thames and Hudson*

Congratulations for 25 years of Vanguard Journalism!

UTNE READER
The Best of the Alternative Press

INDEX INDEX

Witness in difficult times

THERE is, perhaps, no harsher suffering than that which is solitary and silent. The death squads of Chile, El Salvador and Argentina knew this, and so did the psychiatric torturers in the Soviet Union. The principle is still borne out all around the world, in the 'ghost houses' of Sudan, the Chinese laogai, and now in the Zairean jungle, and many other places. It is a truth that has informed *Index*'s work since the beginning.

Nowhere has this been more evident than in the alphabetic record of abuses and violations that has appeared in every issue of the magazine. To look back at that archive is to be given a sort of ground-level view of world history over the past quarter of a century. All the major political struggles are there and all the names that are now so well known — Andrei Sakharov, Nelson Mandela, Václav Havel, Wei Jingsheng, Aung San Suu Kyi — have appeared at one time or another.

And alongside them are the many hundreds of unknowns, the journalists, writers, dissidents and activists who didn't win prizes or international acclaim. Their courage and their trials are no less for that. Perhaps publishing a straightforward inventory of such cases as these goes against the precepts of mainstream journalism, but it can sometimes attain a peculiar poignancy that no amount of analysis or rhetoric can match.

A magazine of record is more than a simple list of individual cases, however. Reproducing official documents is equally important, partly for the record and partly for what they reveal about the workings of the bureaucratic mind. The linguistic exactness employed in drafting regulations is always striking. The Irish Health Act of 1980, for instance, made it an offence 'to distribute, offer or keep for distribution, any book or periodical publication (whether appearing on the register of prohibited publications or not) which advocates or which might reasonably be supposed to advocate the procurement of abortion or miscarriage or any method, treatment or appliance to be used for the purpose of such procurement.' The telling phrase is 'reasonably be supposed', a verbal doffing of the cap to that stock character so beloved of regulators and legislators: the man in the street, the right-thinking person, the *homme moyen sensuel*, the man on the Clapham Omnibus, Mr Average. He goes by many names. The vast potential for tyranny that is inherent in any bureaucracy, as Hannah Arendt showed, arises from the fact that it tends uncompromisingly towards the average.

A third strand that runs through the *Index* archive is made up of the appeals, open letters and personal testimonies that provide a counterpoint to the factual reporting. It was an open letter, after all, that led to the birth of *Index*. They show what the individual imagination, through a process of intellectual alchemy, can forge from the base material of oppression. In part this is a vital defence mechanism against the arbitrariness of despotism. Rodolfo Walsh's open letter to the Argentinian junta *(see p 110)*, written the day before he fell victim to the very forces he so eloquently anatomises, is both a way for him to make sense of the senseless situation in which he found himself, and a warning to the rest of us that vigilance must be maintained. That warning echoed dismayingly this January, when the body of the photojournalist José Luis Cabezas was discovered in a burned-out car not far from Buenos Aires, in circumstances that strongly suggested police involvement.

There is something about this task of bearing witness, chronicling, testifying, that makes it a crucial human enterprise. Why is it so important for us to tell our stories? For the story-teller, to articulate a traumatic experience gives a measure of control in the face of fear and official denials of the truth of that experience. It is thus an act of individual defiance, a refusal to knuckle under. But it goes further than that, to the heart of why we value freedom of expression so highly. A right to speak can mean nothing without a right to be heard. The important thing about freedom of speech is not just that it gives individuals the right to say what they want, but that it enables them to be visible, to be real, to their fellows. To have a right to free speech is to count for something as a moral being. If we are deprived of it, it becomes far easier to hurt us in other ways as well.

Among the pages that follow is a small selection of some of the documents, open letters and testimonies that have appeared in *Index* over the past 25 years. They are a warning that the bullies are always with us, and a reminder, in Walsh's words, of the continuing need to bear witness in difficult times. ❑

Adam Newey

INDEX INDEX

• •

ALBANIA
Hear our cry

The following letter from writers, journalists, scientists and artists was received shortly after the May 1996 elections, in which President Berisha tightened his grip on power, several months before the outbreak of lawlessness earlier this year

It is already clear to public opinion in Albania and around the world that the electoral farce of 26 May 1996 is the first step towards the restoration of dictatorship. The few freedoms we still enjoy — won through the struggle of the Albanian people after half a century of totalitarianism — will not be here tomorrow. Tomorrow will be too late. The old fear of the state is back and spreading. The most elementary human right, the right to free speech, is under threat. And tomorrow it may be as remote as it was during the period of obscurity we have all struggled to overcome. The free world must not remain indifferent to the restoration of dictatorship in the heart of Europe, as it did with former Yugoslavia, and which led to tragedy for millions of people.

The consequences of these events in Albania will be even harsher if the situation does not change. A dictatorial Albania could become a hotbed of tension for the entire region. A dictatorship without sufficient financial means easily gives rise to arms and drug-trafficking, as well as to other forms of illegal trade, all of which have already started here. Albania could become an open wound with destructive effects on the entire region. With unlimited power, devoid of any democratic control, President Berisha could easily break the hypocritical promises he has made regarding international and regional policy. The free world must not close its eyes in the face of such overwhelming dangers. Likewise, the free world should not seek to justify Berisha's authoritarianism because it presents an alternative to the return of Communism in Albania. The last bastion of Communism in Albania is the personal power of the president himself.

A free Albania facing towards Europe can only be achieved through the democratic integration of all existing political forces in the country. What a post-Communist society badly needs is peace, understanding and dialogue between all political forces, not political apartheid. It needs mutual tolerance and respect, not revenge and discrimination. This pan-Albanian aspiration must not fall prey to the violence and lies of authoritarian state power. If this happens, it will be our common misfortune and a shameful burden on the conscience of everyone who can help Albania's young democracy free itself from the claws of the past.

Brikena Abej, Jorgo Balo, Fatos Baxhaku, Andi Bejtja, Ben Blushi, Delina Fico, Mirela Furxhi, Daut Gumeni, Najada Hamza, Artan Imami, Ardian Klosi, Arben Kumbaro, Fatos Lubonja, Vjollca Mici, Virgjil Mui, Vladimir Myrtezai, Fron Nazi, Gjergj Pei, Edi Rama, Luan Rama, Petrit Ruka, Bashkim Shehu, Armand Shkullaku, Andrea Stefani, Lorenc Vangjeli, Pullemb Xhufi, Ilirian Zhupa **From Index 4/1996**

• •

ALBANIA - ALGERIA

A censorship chronicle incorporating information from the American Association for the Advancement of Science Human Rights Action Network (AAASHRAN), Amnesty International (AI), Article 19 (A19), the BBC Monitoring Service Summary of World Broadcasts (SWB), the Committee to Protect Journalists (CPJ), the Canadian Committee to Protect Journalists (CCPJ), the Inter American Press Association (IAPA), the International Federation of Journalists (IFJ/FIP), Human Rights Watch (HRW), the Media Institute of Southern Africa (MISA), the Network for the Defence of Independent Media in Africa (NDIMA), International PEN (PEN), Open Media Research Institute (OMRI), Reporters Sans Frontières (RSF), the World Association of Community Broadcasters (AMARC), the World Organisation Against Torture (OMCT)

ALBANIA

Following President Berisha's declaration of a state of emergency the Tirana premises of the independent daily *Koha Jone* were set alight by police on 3 March. Fidel's Cafe, a well-known meeting place for journalists and intellectuals, was ransacked. **Alfred Peza** and **Zamir Dule**, both *Koha Jone* journalists, were detained the same day. Foreign news was blocked with 25 western companies and channels affected, including Reuters Television, the BBC, CNN, German networks ARD and ZDF, Italian RAI and French TF1, the Voice of America and satellite Euro News. Associated Press television, photo and news reporters were evacuated from Vlore on 3 March. (A19, CPJ, RSF, Reuters, *Guardian*, *Times*, *Independent*)

A death list was allegedly circulated on 10 March containing names of journalists from *Rilindja Demokratike*, *Albania* and *Tribune*. There were also threats against foreign journalists. On 25 March **Nikolle Lesi**, publisher of *Koha Jone*, was attacked at the Rogner Hotel in Tirana by a secret policeman. The Rogner is an established meeting place for journalists and opposition politicians. Also on 25 March **Wilma Goudappel**, a Dutch freelance journalist for British Independent Television News, was shot and injured by a sniper in Sarande. Goudappel had been covering the situation in Albania and was hit while talking on the telephone. By 28 March no Albanian-language newspapers were publishing because of censorship and practical difficulties. **Lazar Stani** and **Edi Paloka**, editors of the Democratic Party paper *Rilindja Demokratike*, fled to Austria at the end of March, having learned their names were on death lists. Most papers had resumed publication by 11 April, when Parliament lifted censorship restrictions imposed at the height of the unrest. However, the Albanian Reporters' League issued a statement on 19 April protesting against distribution problems faced by some independent papers in parts of the south, including Vlore, Sarande and Gjirokaster. The statement accused 'armed bands and criminals' of waging a systematic campaign to prevent the paper *Albania* from reaching the area, including attacks on distribution vans and their drivers. (A19, CPJ, SWB)

On 8 April the house of **Shpetim Nazarko**, owner of the independent *Dita Informacion*, was attacked by five unknown gunmen. *Dita*'s offices are located in Nazarko's house which was also fired at on 3 March. *Dita* decided to stop publishing after the 8 April attack. (RSF)

ALGERIA

Abdelkader Hadj Benaamane (*Index* 3/1995), the Tamanrasset correspondent of the official news agency APS, was freed on parole on 19 March. He was arrested in 1995 in connection with an internal APS communication concerning the detention of FIS leader Ali Benhadj, and sentenced to three years' imprisonment for endangering national security. (RSF)

Aziz Bouabdallah of the daily *al-Alam al-Siyassi*, who writes under the pseudonym Aziz Idriss, was abducted from his home on 11 April, by two men dressed as police. He is reported to be held in the Chateauneuf barracks in Algiers, but authorities have given no explanation for his detention. (PEN, RSF)

INDEX INDEX

ARGENTINA
Open letter to the junta

A year after the military took power in Argentina, the well-known journalist **Rodolfo Walsh** *wrote an open letter to the junta, denouncing the torture and disappearances that became a hallmark of the 'dirty war'. The day after Walsh wrote this letter he, too, disappeared*

Press censorship, the persecution of intellectuals, a recent police raid on my house, the murder of dear friends, and the loss of a daughter who died fighting the dictatorship, are some of the circumstances which oblige me to adopt this form of clandestine expression, after having worked openly as a writer and a journalist during almost 30 years. The first anniversary of the present military junta has been the occasion for many official documents and speeches evaluating the government's activities during the past year. However, what you call successes were, in fact, failures; the failures that you have recognised were crimes; and you leave out all mention of the calamities...

Having filled the existing prisons, you created virtual concentration camps in all the principal military bases, where no judge, lawyer, journalist or international observer may enter. The military secrecy of the proceedings, which you claim to be essential to your investigations, means that most arrests are in fact kidnappings, which allow torture without limit and executions without trial.

More than 7,000 habeas corpus petitions have been denied during the past year. In thousands of other cases of disappearance, no habeas corpus petition has been presented, either because it seemed useless or because no lawyer could be found to take the case. The reluctance of lawyers is not surprising because 50 or 60 of them have themselves been kidnapped for intervening in political cases.

In this way you allow torture to continue indefinitely. The arrested person does not exist. There is no possibility of the prisoner being brought before a judge within 10 days as the law requires, a law which was previously respected even during the darkest days of former dictatorships.

Saad Lounes, editor-in-chief of the privately owned daily *El Ouma*, was arrested on 11 April and his Sodipresse printing works were sealed. After a gap of 15 months caused partly by a dispute with the state-owned SIA printing house, *El Ouma* began publishing again in March after founding its own printing works. (RSF)

ARGENTINA

In the first week of April an anonymous witness alleged that a high-ranking police officer had planned the killing of photographer **José Luis Cabezas** (*Index* 2/1997) and had asked the murderers to film Cabezas pleading for mercy before he was shot. On the night of the murder, 25 January, the local police reportedly declared a 'liberated zone', refusing to answer calls and thereby giving free rein to criminals.

There is no limit on the time, neither is there any restriction on the methods used. These are a throwback to the middle ages, when torturers amputated the limbs of their victims or eviscerated them. Now it is done with surgical and chemical instruments which mediaeval executioners did not have at their disposal. The rack, thumbscrew, flaying, and saws of the Inquisition reappear in prisoners' testimony, along with the electric prod, the 'submarine' and the air-compressor of contemporary torture...

Between 1,500 and 3,000 people have been killed in secret since you prohibited any information concerning the discovery of corpses, which have in some cases been impossible to hide because of the numbers of victims involved or because the deaths affect other countries.

At least 25 corpses floated on to Uruguayan beaches between March and October 1976. These were only a few of those tortured to death in the Navy's engineering school, before being dumped from ships into the Plata estuary. They included one 15-year-old boy, Floreal Avellaneda, who was found with his hands and feet tied, 'injuries in the anal region, and visible fractures', according to the autopsy report.

A skin diver found a virtual mortuary on the bottom of the San Roque lake near Córdoba. He reported his macabre discovery to the police, but his testimony was not accepted. He wrote to the newspapers, but nothing was ever published...

In the light of such incidents we begin to understand the full significance of the definition of the war being waged by the armed forces, according to one senior officer: 'The struggle we are engaged in does not recognise any natural or moral limits; it is beyond any discussion of what is good or evil.'

These events, which have already shaken the conscience of the civilised world, are not the greatest sufferings undergone by the Argentine people, nor the worst violations of human rights for which you are responsible. In the economic policies of the government, one finds not only the explanation for its repressive crimes, but also a greater atrocity which punishes millions of human beings with carefully planned misery...

These are the thoughts which I wished to share with the members of the junta on this first anniversary of your disreputable government, without hope of being listened to, in the certainty of persecution, but faithful to the commitment I made a long time ago to bear witness in difficult times.

From **Index** *5/1977*

However, the motive for the killing is still unclear. (*Guardian*, Madres de Plaza de Mayo)

ARMENIA

The editor-in-chief of the independent paper *Yerevanian Orer*, **Mikael Hayrapetian**, was attacked on 7 March by two unknown individuals who entered his office and demanded that he erase the next issue from his computer. When Hayrapetian refused, he was badly beaten around the head. Two days later he was admitted to hospital suffering from cuts, heavy cerebral shock and eyesight problems. (RSF, SWB)

AUSTRALIA

Officials at Parliament House have again banned the display of photographs depicting human rights abuses by Indonesian forces in East

INDEX INDEX

Timor from an exhibition in the foyer of the House (*Index* 1/1997). Approval was given for the exhibition late last year. However the President of the Senate and the speaker of the House of Representatives ordered the photographs, including some of the 1991 Dili Massacre, to be removed as the exhibition was being set up on 23 March. (*Jakarta Post*)

In early April the education minister upheld the removal of Gillian Mears' *Fineflour* and Caryl Churchill's play *Top Girls* from the New South Wales Higher School Certificate (HSC) reading list. A review panel barred the Churchill play on the grounds that it is 'dated', shows 'contempt for religion' and contains 'gratuitous violence'. (Reuters)

On 7 April the Cabinet rejected a proposal by the minister for communications, Richard Alston, that adult channels be barred from pay television. R-rated material will continue to be available as long as the channels are available only by subscription, have a personal identification number and are broadcast at selected times of day. The Cabinet also decided to replace the X-rating for videos with a 'non-violent erotica' (NVE) classification. (Reuters)

The Tasmanian government confirmed on 14 April that it would abide by a declaration in the High Court that the federal law on sexual privacy overrides Tasmania's anti-homosexuality laws. Tasmania is the only state where gay sex is illegal. The legislation led to the first Australian case before the UN Human Rights Committee, which in 1994 found the laws discriminatory. (Reuters)

AUSTRIA

Almost all of the country's Internet service providers (ISPs) shut down their networks for two hours on 25 March in protest at a police raid on the Vienna-based service provider **VIPnet**. The raid, in which equipment was confiscated, was prompted by a legal complaint filed with German authorities in March 1996. The complaint was then passed on to the Austrian police. (Reuters)

AZERBAIJAN

Jumhuriyet, the weekly newspaper started by the opposition Azerbaijan Popular Front (APF), was not published in February, possibly by decree of a high-ranking official in the president's office. The executives of the state-controlled Azerbaijan Printing House gave no reason for refusing to print the 13, 20, and 27 issues even though a contract had been signed to print until December 1997. (RSF)

Recent publication: *Time to Abolish the Death Penalty* (AI, March 1997, 19pp)

BAHRAIN

In early March several defence lawyers acting for 81 Bahraini citizens accused of involvement in an alleged Iranian-backed plot to overthrow the government were summoned by the minister of justice and warned that dissemination of any information about the trials would not be tolerated. The lawyers had recently given interviews about the trials to foreign media. The defendants are also charged with membership of an organisation whose aim is to overthrow by force the 'political, social or economic system of the state'. (AI, Bahrain Freedom Movement)

On 15 April **Ali Hassan Yousif** (*Index* 2/1997) was released from prison after paying a fine of US$800. Another poet, **Abdul Karim Yousif Mardi**, has been detained since the beginning of March and accused of circulating poetry critical of the government. (Bahrain Freedom Movement)

BELARUS

On 13 March **Ihar Rynkevich**, executive director of the Belarusian Association of Journalists, was detained by police. He was questioned about his participation in an unauthorised picket on 10 March. At least 11 other journalists in Minsk were detained on 13 and 14 March before and during opposition demonstrations. (CPJ)

The executive director of the Soros Foundation in Belarus, **Peter Byrne**, was deported on 17 March. He was accused of monitoring various opposition activities and of breaking the rules on foreign citizens staying in the republic. President Lukashenka has several times criticised the Soros Foundation for 'interfering' in internal affairs. (SWB)

On 18 March a new law was passed banning the transfer of media equipment, including audio-visual and printing materials which 'could threaten the country's political and economic interests'. Although a ban on the use of the satellite transmission centre by foreign companies was lifted on 26 March, journalists must still submit all material for prior censorship and a duty officer must be present during transmissions. Also on 26 March distribution of *Belarusskaya Gazeta* was interrupted at the Lithuanian border. (RSF, CPJ)

On 24 March the government withdrew press accreditation from **Alexander Stupnikov**, the Belarus correspondent of Russia's NTV. Stupnikov was ordered to leave Belarus by 31 March for activities 'incompatible with his status as a journalist' and for violating the press law. This is thought to be linked to his coverage of a demonstration in Minsk on 23 March. NTV was warned that the station would be banned if Stupnikov's voice or name were mentioned. On 3 April the foreign minister, Ivan Antonovych, threatened to expel more foreign journalists and added that Belarusians might be barred from working for foreign news agencies. (CPJ, A19)

About 70 people were detained on 2 April during opposition protests against the union with Russia. Among those detained or beaten were **Valery Shchukin** from *Tovarishch*, **Iryna Khalip**, a correspondent with *Imya*, **Pavel Bykovsky** from *Belaruskiy Rynok*, **Vladimir Khalip**, an independent doumentary film-maker, **Tamara Khamytsevych**, a photographer for *Vecherniy Minsk*, **Vladimir Kostin**, a cameraman for Belarusian Independent TV, and **Sergei Malinovsky**, correspondent for *Svobodniye Novosti*. **Pavel Kornazytsky**, a reporter for the weekly *Zdravy Smysl*, was sentenced to 10 days' imprisonment on 4 April for covering the protests. On 8 April the trial of **Vladimir Davydovskii**, correspondent for the newsletter of the Association of Belarusian Journalists, began. He is charged with 'participating in an unauthorised demonstration'. (CPJ, RSF, SWB)

Mikola Markevitch, editor-in-chief of *Pagonia*, was evicted from the newspaper's offices on 9 April by the municipal authorities in Grodno. The Municipal Council, which owns the property, had ended the lease of the offices on 31 December 1996, but no suitable new premises were found. *Pagonia* was threatened with suspension in September 1996 after two critical articles were published (RSF)

Recent publication: *Human Rights Violations in Belarus* (International Helsinki Federation, April 1997, 12pp)

BENIN

A new law allowing private ownership of radio and television but imposing harsh penalties for libel was adopted unanimously by Parliament on 28 February. Insulting the president, foreign heads of state and foreign ministers is now punishable by five years in prison or a fine of US$17,700. (RSF, AFP, Reuters)

BRAZIL

Video footage showing military police abusing civilians over a period of several nights was broadcast on Globo Television on 3 and 7 April. An amateur photographer filmed the abuses, which involved beatings and apparent summary executions, in São Paulo state in early March. In response to the furore, the government has set up a National Human Rights Secretariat and the president has approved a bill making torture illegal for the first time. Ten officers have been arrested and charged. (HRW, *Financial Times*, Reuters)

Recent publication: *Police Brutality in Urban Brazil* (HRW/Americas, April 1997, 118pp)

BURMA

An 8pm to 4am curfew was imposed, street barricades set up and a ban placed on gatherings of more than five people in Mandalay on 18 March following riots between Buddhist monks and Muslims. Five days later

INDEX INDEX

CAMBODIA

From the S21 interrogator's manual

The interrogator's manual used at the Khmer Rouge's notorious S21 prison was a practitioner's guide to the theory and practice of torture according to Pol Pot. Its 42 pages cover such areas as the hours of work, the preparation of reports and the proper attitude of the interrogator. The following extract is from part III, 'Views and Stances Concerning Methodology of Interrogation'

1. The measures for each of us during our interrogation of prisoners are of two types:
a. Political pressure, ie, we propagandise and pressure them constantly, consistently and continuously at all times.
b. The use of torture is a supplementary measure.
2. Our experience in the past has been that our interrogators for the most part tended to fall on the torture side. They emphasised torture over propaganda. This is the wrong way of doing it. We must teach interrogators how to do it.
3. The enemy will not confess to us easily. When we use political pressure, prisoners confess only very little. Thus, they cannot escape from torture. The only difference is whether there will be a lot of it or a little. Torture is a necessary measure, we must also nevertheless try our best with political pressure, to make them confess fully. Only when we put maximum political pressure on them, when we put them in a corner politically and get them to confess, will torture become productive. Our political efforts also make the prisoners clear in their answers. And, whether or not we use torture later, make them quicker to confess.

It's better than if we were to just think of only beating them and not to think of propaganda at all. The doing of politics demands a stance of utmost perseverance. Don't be hasty. The forms of propaganda that we have made use of in the past are:
a. Reassure them by giving them something, some food for instance. Reassure them that the Party will give them back their posts.
b. Terrify them, confuse them in clever ways. Arrange little ploys to make them give up

---

security was increased around religious sites in Rangoon after street demonstrations and attacks on mosques spread to the capital. At least 90 monks were rounded up after trying to hold a protest near the city centre. Reports from the All Burma Young Monks' Union suggest some

15 monks arrested in Mandalay have already received summary trials and been sentenced to lengthy jail terms. (Reuters)

Recent publication: *Pleading Not Guilty in Insein* (All Burma Students' Democratic Front, February 1997, 82pp)

CAMEROON

Aboulaye Math, president of the Movement for the Defence of Human Rights and Freedoms, was arrested on 27 February, shortly before travelling to the United States to attend a human rights training programme. He was

any hope that they will ever live again or ever be able to survive.
c. Draw them into some ordinary conversation, but formulated so that it is of some use.
d. Bring them over to thinking about their families, their wives, their children and their life. Make it clear to them that their guilt is a minor one. When they confess, or have not yet done so, we must guide them and reassure them that they are not the big leaders. Don't step up the pressure all the time. Say something like 'Don't make us torture you or torture you severely. It's bad for your health, and its makes it harder for us to deal with each other in the future'.
e. If they reveal small matters, encourage them to reveal the big ones. Tell them that if they reveal important matters, the Organisation (Party) will be lenient with them.
f. Tell them that if they slander revolutionaries, such as saying that they are traitors, they fall into the trap of trying to destroy revolutionary forces. Thus their guilt would be just as heavy...

4. The Question of Torturing
a. The purpose of torturing is to get their responses. It's not something we do for fun. We must hurt them so that they respond quickly. Another purpose is to break them and make them lose their will. It's not something that's done out of individual anger, or for self-satisfaction. So we beat them to make them afraid, but absolutely not to kill them. When torturing it is necessary to examine their state of health first, and the whip. Don't be so bloodthirsty that you cause their death quickly. You won't get the needed information.
b. It is necessary to be fully aware that doing politics is most important. Torture is only secondary, subsidiary and supplementary to some political expediency in certain areas. So politics takes the lead at all times. Even when torturing, it is always necessary to do constant propaganda.
c. At the same time, it is necessary to avoid any question of hesitancy or half-heartedness, of not daring to torture, which makes it impossible to get answers to our questions from our enemies. This will slow down and delay our work. In sum, whether doing propaganda work or torturing or bringing up questions to ask them or accusing them of something, it is necessary to hold steadfastly to a stance of not being half-hearted or hesitant. We must be absolute. Only in this way can we work to good effect...

From **Index 1/1986**

charged with fraud and released pending trial on 7 May. (OMCT, A19)

Alain Christian Eyoum Nganguė, a journalist with *Le Messager Popoli* arrested on 22 January (*Index* 2/1997), was granted bail on 27 March. (RSF, AI)

On 20 March **Evariste Menouga**, editor-in-chief of the independent paper *Hebdo*, was charged with 'spreading false news' and 'inciting rebellion within the army', following an article he wrote concerning low morale and desertion in the armed forces. (RSF)

CANADA

In March film censors overturned a ban on the video distribution of the film *Bastard Out of Carolina*. The film, directed by Anjelica Huston, deals with sexual abuse and contains an explicit rape scene, which led it to be banned in Nova Scotia, New Brunswick and Prince Edward Island. (Reuters)

On 2 April Canadian Forces veteran Doug Caie pleaded guilty to altering documents requested by a journalist under the Access to Information Act 1994. The documents related to the Canadian army's involvement in Somalia. Caie pleaded guilty at a standing court martial to negligent performance in a plea bargain that saw two other charges dropped. (Reuters)

CHINA

The February edition of the leftist *Zhongliu* (Mainstream) was removed from sale and condemned by the Propaganda Department for 'sabotaging stability and solidarity' after it printed a highly critical review of a pro-Jiang Zemin book, *A Heart-to-Heart Talk with the General Secretary*. (SWB, *International Herald Tribune*)

Foreign newspapers and periodicals suffered restricted sales in early March, with some banned from government newsstands and others subject to censorship. Articles analysing the impact of Deng's death and reporting on ethnic violence in Xinjiang were all removed from publication. Journalists were barred from visiting Yining, the scene of recent rioting. Papers affected include *The Sunday Times*, *Newsweek*, *Time*, and *The Economist*, and an outright ban was placed on three editions of the German weekly *Der Spiegel*. In addition, recently repealed blocks on foreign news organisations' Internet sites, such as those of **CNN**, the *Washington Post*, and the *Boston Globe*, were reinstated shortly after Deng's death. (*South China Morning Post*)

Exiled poet **Liu Hongbin** was expelled from China on 20 March, accused of 'activities incompatible with his tourist status'. Liu, who fled the country after the 1989 democracy movement was crushed, entered the country on a tourist visa in February and reported constant harassment during his stay. Police in his home town of Qingdao kept him under virtual house arrest, seized his British passport and instructed him not to make contact with political activists. Later, in Shanghai, he was detained for questioning and confined to a hotel before police put him on a flight to Hong Kong. (Reuters)

Dissident and critic **Liu Xiaobo**'s appeal against a three-year term of re-education through labour (*Index* 1/1997) was turned down in late March. (*International Herald Tribune*)

Xinhua news agency reported on 2 April that writers are voluntarily renouncing Soviet-style subsidies for life (known as the 'iron bowl' model) in favour of payment on the basis of the quantity and quality of work produced (the 'mud bowl' model). Writer Ji Wenzhang said that although the trend does not guarantee 'freedom for writers, it is a sign of progress since it introduces competition'. (SWB)

The Propaganda Department, the Ministry of Culture and the Press and Publications Administration issued a joint order in April banning the sale of the novel *Wrath of Heaven* by a pseudonymous author known as Fang Wen. The novel is closely modelled on a high-profile embezzlement scandal among the Beijing city government. (*Independent*)

Xinjiang: On 20 March six people were charged with hooliganism and endangering social order in connection with the February riots in Yining. They could face execution if found guilty of the former charge. Exiled Uighur independence groups claim that two religious students were already facing imminent execution for their involvement in the riots. (Reuters, *Guardian*)

Recent publication: *Law Reform and Human Rights* (AI, March 1997, 29pp)

COLOMBIA

Freddy Elles, a freelance photographer who worked for three major Colombian newspapers, was murdered on 18 March. He was found in Cartagena, handcuffed, stabbed and shot in the head. Eyewitness accounts say that Elles had been accosted by three individuals on the afternoon of 17 March. It is thought that his murder may be related to his coverage of police brutality during demonstrations by municipal workers in 1995 and of illegal construction of residences in the Corales del Rosario National Park. (IAPA, RSF)

On 20 March **Gerardo Bedoya Borrero**, the opinion page editor for the Cali daily *El Pais*, was shot dead as he was leaving an apartment building in the city centre. He was a vociferous campaigner against the drugs trade. Police said they had no clues as to who was responsible but General Harold Bedoya, the country's top general and a cousin of the victim, said he 'had no doubt' that it was 'one more crime of the many committed by narco-terrorism in Colombia'. (IAPA, Reuters, *El Pais*)

CROATIA

The bodies of Radio Vukovar journalists **Sinisa Glavasevic** and **Branimir Polivina** were identified in early March in a mass grave in Ovcara, near Vukovar. The two journalists continued to broadcast from the wine cellars of Vukovar Castle as the Yugoslav army forces advanced, until Glavasevic was wounded and they went to the hospital. They were seized from there in November 1991. (PEN)

The independent station **Radio 101** expressed concern in early April that it has been allocated a technically and geographically inferior new transmitter site. Obliged to change sites by the terms of its new licence, Radio 101 can now only reach half of Zagreb (*Index* 1/1997, 2/1997). (RSF)

CUBA

Guillermo Fariñas Hernandes, child psychologist for Pedro Borras hospital, was detained by security police on 6 March. He was taken to a police station and severely beaten before being carried home five days later. Hernandes began a hunger strike on 3 March in protest at corruption, abuse of power and maladministration at the hospital. (CubaNet)

Olance Nogueras Rofes, a journalist with the Independent Cuban Press Bureau (BPIC) was arrested by state security police in a raid on the home in Havana of another BPIC journalist, Luis Solar Hernández, on 23 April. The police also confiscated books, videotapes and documents. (BPIC)

CYPRUS

On 5 March the Turkish Cypriot newspaper *Yenidüzen* reported that its journalists had received death threats by letter from Azmi Karamahmutoglu, chairman of the 'Idealist Hearths Organisation' in Turkey. (IFJ)

EGYPT

Three Cairo University students — **Mustafa Zedan**, **Ahmad Taha Qandeel**, and **Mohammed Abdel-Haleem** — were among five people arrested between 26 and 27 March after participating in a march protesting against Israeli settlement policies in Jerusalem. They were accused of possessing printed materials that would disturb public peace and harm the public interest. On 30 March students **Tamer Soliman** and **Mohammed El-Ba'ali** were arrested and detained on similar charges. They later alleged that state security investigators had tortured them during interrogation in Giza. Three female students — **Samah Helmi**, **Shereen Megahid** and **Areeg Ibrahim** — have been harassed by security forces for their participation in peaceful demonstations at Cairo University. (Egyptian Organization for Human Rights)

ETHIOPIA

Kefle Mulat, editor-in-chief of *Ethio Times*, was sentenced to six months in prison on 9 February for disseminating false information, in connection with an article in the 3 December 1995 issue on an alleged attempt to assassinate Mengistu Haile Mariam. (CPJ)

On 24 February **Atenafu Alemayhu**, editor-in-chief of the weekly *Tomar*, **Kidist Belachew**, former editor-in-chief of the weekly *A'emrio*, and **Tesihalene Mengiesha**, former editor-in-chief of the weekly *Mebruk*, were charged in connection with reports they had published in late 1995 disclosing links between the Muslim aid organisation, Blessed Relief, and Sudanese religious leaders Hassein Ali Turabi abd Mohammed Sirage. Alemayhu remains in detention in Addis Ababa, unable to pay bail set at US$780. (RSF)

Arega Wolde-Kirkos, acting

INDEX INDEX

● ●

CHINA

Hunger strike declaration

The following is extracted from the declaration issued by four student leaders in Tiananmen Square shortly before the massacre on the night of 3/4 June 1989

We are on hunger strike. We protest, we appeal, we repent. We are not in search of death; we are looking for real life. In the face of irrational and violent pressure from the Li Peng government, the Chinese intellectuals must cure their soft-boned disease of being vocal but of never being active for thousands of years. We must act to protest against martial law, to call for the birth of a new political culture, to make up for our past mistakes of being soft and weak for so long.

We all share responsibility for the Chinese nation being left behind many others.

During this movement the government and the students have both made mistakes. The mistakes of the government are dominated by the old mode of class struggle, of a way of political thinking which places them in opposition to the students and citizens.

The mistakes of the students are mainly the crudity of the students' own organisation. There appeared to be a lot of undemocratic elements in the process of seeking democracy. So we appeal both to the government and to the students; they should calmly question and examine themselves. It is our view that as a whole the mistakes of this movement are mainly with the government. Marches, hunger strikes and actions of that kind are democratic methods. They are entirely legitimate and reasonable and do in no way constitute unrest.

But the government has ignored the basic rights endowed to every citizen by the constitution and has declared this movement to be a form of unrest. This stems from their thinking in terms of dictatorial politics and has led to a series of mistaken decisions and to confrontation. Therefore the real creator of the unrest is the government's error. The seriousness of its mistakes is no less than of those taken during the Cultural Revolution. It was only due to the self-restraint of students and citizens and due to the strong appeals of society, including the wise people in the Party, the government and the army that massive bloodshed was then avoided. The government must admit its mistakes. A correction now would not be too late.

The government should draw the painful lessons from this massive movement to democracy. It should learn to listen to the voice of the people.

We think the true realisation of democratic politics is the democratisation of the procedures, the methods and the operation. So we appeal to the Chinese: Get rid of the tradition of pure ideology making, of sloganeering, of objectifying. These are empty democracy. They must start the process of turning a democracy movement centred on the enlightenment of thought into that of an actual operation.

The major errors by the government in decision-making are shown in the phrase they have used to describe the movement: they have called us 'the very, very few'. Through our

● ●

hunger strike we want to show public opinion in China and abroad that the so-called 'very, very few' are people who are not merely students. Those who actively took part in this nationwide movement to democracy, led by students, are citizens with a sense of political responsibility.

It must be acknowledged that to govern a country democratically is a strange concept for every Chinese citizen. So all citizens of China must learn from the very beginning — and in this way we must include the top leaders of the Party and the state. In the process ,mistakes by the government and by the people are inevitable. The key lies in acknowledging their mistakes when they occur, and in correcting them when they occur, in learning from mistakes so that they can be turned into a positive asset and, in the process of correcting mistakes, to learn to govern our country democratically.

The rules of the hunger strike:
a) Location: under the monument to the People's Heroes in Tiananmen Square.
b) Duration: 72 hours, from 14:00 2 June to 14:00 5 June.
c) Rules: boiled water only, no food, no nutritious drinks (such as glucose, fat or protein).

Liu Xiaobo, Zhou Duo, Hou Dejian, Gao Xin　　　　　　　　　　　**From Index 8/1989**

Sensitive issues

After the Communist Party's Sixth Plenary in October 1996, the Central Propaganda Department promulgated eight wide-ranging press regulations:

1. In order to guarantee unity of thinking and to avoid a negative impact on political stability, all sensitive issues, such as the campaign to protect the Diaoyou Islands or the overseas democracy movement, are not to be covered.
2. All cases which have a significant impact or wide involvement should not be reported, such as the case of the former secretary of the Beijing Municipal Committee, Chen Zitong, or the case of Zhou Beifang of the Capital Iron and Steel Works.
3. There have been over 10,000 cases of demonstrations and protests in the urban and rural areas within this past year. All of these are not to be covered.
4. Articles written by dissidents are not to be published.
5. Propaganda departments of different levels must strengthen censorship over the media and deal with problems promptly.
6. Propaganda departments of different levels must strengthen supervision over publication units; those that violate the regulations must be dealt with severely.
7. When reporting on issues concerning Hong Kong, the media must act in accordance with the policy formulated by the Party Central Committee.
8. When reporting on foreign affairs, the media must not reveal state secrets.

From Index 1/1997

INDEX INDEX

editor of the newspaper *Tobia* detained on 6 January (*Index* 2/1997), was released on bail on 28 February. (RSF)

Two hundred students at Addis Ababa University were arrested without charge at a demonstration on 21 March in support of peasant farmers who claim they have been discriminated against in a land redistribution programme undertaken by the regional state of Amhara. Thirty of the students who refused to sign a statement requesting a pardon for having participated in an illegal demonstration, remain in custody. The farmers also claim to have been detained by police for disrupting meetings at which they expressed their opposition to the confiscation of their land. (Ethiopian Human Rights Council, AI, SWB)

EUROPEAN UNION

The European Ombudsman, Jacob Soderman, was advised in late March not to continue his investigation of the Council of Ministers (the most powerful decision-making body in the EU) on behalf of **Tony Bunyan**, British editor of the civil liberties newsletter *Statewatch*. Bunyan had applied to see EU documents relating to immigration and police affairs dating back three years. Although the Council of Ministers referred Bunyan to the newly created ombudsman if he wished to appeal, they now say that Soderman's post does not carry sufficient 'legal competence' for him to investigate. (*Statewatch*, *Guardian*)

FRANCE

In March Cameroonian journalist **Kakmo Pideu** was struck and verbally abused by police at Charles de Gaulle Airport, held in a cell and then sent back to Cameroon. He was in transit on his way to a journalists' conference in Hong Kong. (Gemini News)

Gérard Jubert, editor-in-chief of the magazine *L'Elephant Rose*, was given a 10-month suspended sentence and fined US$52,000 on 3 March after being convicted of violating the public health code by encouraging the use of marijuana. Owing to the size of the fine, the magazine has ceased publication. (RSF)

Theatre director **Gérard Paquet**, who was dismissed by the National Front mayor of Toulon (*Index* 2/1997), was arrested on 1 April and questioned over alleged financial mismanagement. (*Guardian*)

The files of ex-President Mitterrand's anti-terrorist department, which were opened to the public on 10 April, show that he personally oversaw widespread illegal phone-tapping of journalists, lawyers and politicians. Gilles Ménage, who headed Mitterrand's private office, is currently being investigated in connection with the department's activities (*Index* 6/1996). (Reuters)

The transmitters of two community radio stations, **Agora FM** and **97.7 FM**, were torn down by vandals on 12 April. The relay station of another station, TSF Côte d'Azur, was also damaged in the attack, which appears to be racially motivated. (RSF)

GERMANY

In mid-April, prosecutors in Bavaria charged **Felix Somm**, the managing director of the German subsidiary of Internet service provider **CompuServe** (*Index* 2/1996), in connection with the distribution of illegal pornographic and neo-Nazi material. The case is significant because it is an attempt to make the service provider legally liable for material placed on the network by its subscribers. It will also provide a test of the applicability of German laws to the Internet. CompuServe said it expects the case against Somm to fail. (Reuters, *Guardian*)

A new bill to regulate online media was introduced on 18 April. The Information and Communications Services Bill sets standards for child protection on the Internet and attempts to define which online activities should be subject to licensing and other regulatory requirements. (Reuters)

GREECE

On 6 March two Greek journalists were given 15-month suspended sentences for an article which was considered 'an offence against religion'. The article was a review of an English book claiming that Christ survived the crucifixion and fled to

EUROPEAN UNION - INDIA

Europe with Mary Magdalene. On 18 February another journalist was sentenced to 15 months in prison on the same charge after reporting on the supposedly dissolute life of Christ. The sentence was suspended on appeal. (RSF)

GUATEMALA

Francisca Esteban Pérez, secretary of the Committee for La Blanca Community Land and member of the National Indigenous and Peasant Organisation (CONIC), was killed on 12 April by unidentified assailants. CONIC has denounced the murder as part of a wider campaign of intimidation against the peasant movement, especially in La Blanca. Two days previously, 15 armed men, allegedly sent by the landowner Adrian Ponce Cruz, entered Ruben Hu community, firing shots and threatening to kill the inhabitants if they did not leave. The villagers fled to the mountains. The men then moved on to Ruben Pec where again they threatened the people with death if they did not remove themselves from the land. (Derechos-l)

Police raided the offices of the daily *Al Día* on 18 April in a search for photographs and negatives taken by one of the paper's photographers in the San Raymundo district of Guatemala City on 5 March. (Guatemalan Journalists' Association)

Recent publications: *Corporations and Human Rights* — *Freedom of Association in Guatemala* (HRW/Americas, March 1997, 62pp); *Appeals against Impunity* (AI, April 1997, 28pp)

HONG KONG

Schoolbooks that 'do not accord with history or reality' and 'contradict the spirit of "one country, two systems"' and the Basic Law' should be revised after the Hong Kong handover, foreign minister Qian Qichen suggested on 10 March. Although the Hong Kong government was quick to criticise Qian's comments, certain changes have already been made to textbooks in preparation for the transfer of sovereignty, according to the Hong Kong Educational Publication Association (*Index* 4/1996). (*Financial Times*, *Times*)

Foreign journalists wanting to interview Hong Kong's chief executive designate, Tung Chee-hwa, have been asked to submit any articles on Mr Tung for vetting prior to publication, it was reported on 12 March. (*Independent*)

Tung Chee-hwa cautioned **Democratic Party** members at a meeting on 17 March to 'be careful' when speaking about the territory in the future. The Democrats, whom Tung has in the past accused of damaging Hong Kong's reputation abroad, responded with a summary of their recent overseas statements. (*South China Morning Post*, Reuters)

New proposals to restrict public rallies and political groups with overseas links were announced by Tung Chee-hwa's office on 9 April. Under the proposals, rallies or organisations would be banned if they endangered national security; permission would be needed for any group of 30 or more to hold a public protest; any group wishing to operate in Hong Kong would have to register with the government; and any political organisation that 'solicits or accepts funds from overseas' could be restricted. The last measure would directly affect the Democratic Party, whose leaders recently returned from a fundraising trip to north America. (*International Herald Tribune*)

HUNGARY

The data protection commissioner, Laszlo Majtenyi, said on 18 April that documents relating to the ongoing Hungarian-Slovak dam dispute (currently the subject of a case before the International Court of Justice) are not classified and that therefore the Foreign Ministry acted illegally when it denied public access to the documents for 30 years. (SWB)

INDIA

Saidain Shafi, a Kashmiri journalist with the national television network Doordarshan, was shot dead by two unidentified men in Srinagar on 16 March. In his reports for the weekly news programme *Kashmir File*, Shafi was highly critical of militant separatists in the state, and reported receiving

INDEX ON CENSORSHIP 3 1997   121

INDEX INDEX

IRAN

Before the revolution...

The Shah's secret police organisation, SAVAK, issued the following secret guidelines to the press in 1978

1 Any news about the Shah, Empress, Crown Prince, Prime Minister and the royal family should be obtained from official sources.
2 Any plans announced by the Shah and Empress are not to be caricatured.
3 Responsible and high-ranking citizens, and those who are appointed by the Shah, are not to be attacked or accused.
4 Throughout the country and in every news item the concept of the Resurgence Party monarchy and the 17-point Shah Nation revolution are to be mentioned with great reverence, and these are never to be criticised. Their method of implementation may be criticised, but only mildly.
5 News about the Ministry of Foreign Affairs and appointments is to be obtained from official sources.
6 Only official sources are authorised to make available to the press any news about the army and the armed forces.
7 News about the Imperial Court, security organisations and terrorist activities is to be obtained from official sources. The names and ideas of terrorists are not to be mentioned and admired, and they are not to be publicised as champions.
8 News about wage increases, benefits and promotions of employees is to be obtained from official sources.
9 Any news about the state's economic and financial situation and those of industrial concerns as well as problems pertaining to health, contagious diseases and food products is to be reported with caution, because it may cause public anxiety and loss of confidence. Before publication, the relevant officials should be consulted. In any case, there should not be too much emphasis on these matters .
10 Macro-size misappropriations, embezzlement and briberies are not to be exposed and reported in the press.
11 Writers and poets whose object is to criticise and campaign against the regime, are not to be given space in any column.
12 News about workers' strikes and students' demonstrations is to be treated with caution.
13 Criticism should be constructive and problems are not to be exaggerated. Criticism should not be subjective. Policies and approaches are to be noted. The right to reply is to be respected and such replies are to be published in a specific column.
14 The press is to endeavour not to report, consecutively, on a topic that may incite public opinion. The press is not to create expectations or agitation.
15 The public is not to be encouraged to expect too much, such as cheaper housing, more public services and increased wages... **From Index 2/1978**

...and after

To coincide with the Frankfurt International Book Fair in October 1983, the Iranian Writers Association in exile issued the following statement, demanding that representatives of the Khomeini government not be allowed to take part

The great tragedy which has befallen our country is no longer unknown to anyone. For the past five years, a regime founded on the most barbaric, inhuman and primitive set of values and known as the Islamic Republic is governing our fatherland. In Iran, men and women, young and old, even children and pregnant women have recently been placed before firing squads in great numbers simply because they failed to prove their allegiance to the totalitarian regime of the Islamic Republic.

In Iran today, the brute force buried in the depths of history has risen from its grave and is bent on demolishing the entire achievement of Iranian culture and civilisation. Whole social groups, particularly the intelligentsia, are condemned to annihilation merely because of their ideas. The hands of the hungry, stretched out of sheer desperation seeking a loaf of bread are severed. The emotional bond between man and woman is viewed as an unforgivable sin. Under no circumstances is anyone's life, property, dignity or honour immune: the spectre of the executioner's presence behind every door is the dreadful ghost which can turn into a devastating reality at any moment: the reality of the murderer who can assassinate the son in his father's presence, rape the wife in front of her husband, or stone to death women already burdened by unjust social relations at the behest of the religious courts of law.

The nightmare of ignorance and criminality holding Iran in its bleeding claws is not just a national tragedy; for culture and civilisation, liberty and equality anywhere in the world are legacies of centuries-long struggles, efforts and sacrifices undertaken by successive generations of mankind. They are, by their nature, universal achievements and values, their preservation a world-wide human obligation. Silence in the face of what is happening in Iran today is tantamount to acquiescence in the possibility of its happening anywhere in the world...

The Writers Association of Iran, a democratic gathering of progressive writers, which was founded in 1968 but was never recognised by either the monarchical regime or that of Khomeini, has always been a target for brutal attacks.

The Writers Association of Iran considers the presence of the regime's representatives at the International Book Fair a flagrant denigration of books, an insult to culture and to man. In the name of thousands of writers, artists, scholars, students, teachers and professors brought to torture, execution, incarceration, exile or destitution, in the defence of the libraries devastated and bookstores burned down by the Khomeini regime, the Writers Association of Iran requests the Book Fair authorities to expel the representatives of the Khomeini regime from their midst.

The Writers Association of Iran (in exile) Executive Board, Paris. Gholam Hoseyn Sa'edi, Nemat Mirzazadeh, Homa Nategh **From Index 1/1984**

INDEX INDEX

threats for allegedly biased reporting. Separatists have previously issued warnings to Kashmiri journalists working for state-owned media. (CPJ)

Recent publication: *Jammu and Kashmir — Remembering Jalil Andrabi* (AI, March 1997, 8pp)

INDONESIA

D&R journalist **Lucia N Idayanie** was beaten by security guards on 5 March after she tried to interview the Regent of Bantul, Sri Roso Sudarmo, about the August murder of journalist **Fuad Muhammad Syafruddin** (*Index* 5/1996, 2/1997). (Institute for the Studies on Free Flow of Information)

Former opposition MP **Sri Bintang Pamungkas** and his Indonesian Democratic Union Party (PUDI) colleagues **Julius Usman** and **Saleh Abdullah** were detained on 5 March, after being invited to lunch at a restaurant near the attorney-general's office. Bintang was formally charged with subversion two days later and his fellow activists are thought to be facing similar charges. Their arrest was prompted by a greeting card Bintang sent to government officials for the Muslim festival of Eid al Fitr, detailing the PUDI's agenda. Formed as a challenge to the three-party political system, the PUDI is advocating a boycott of the May parliamentary elections, the rejection of President Suharto's re-election in 1998, and preparation for the post-Suharto period. The party and its leadership have been kept under close surveillance since its formation in May 1996. Bintang, its chairman, already faces a 34-month sentence (currently under appeal) for defaming the president in a speech made in Germany in April 1995. (*Straits Times, Reuters, Jakarta Post,* AI)

The book *New Era, New Leader: Badio Rejects the New Order Regime's Engineering*, written by **Subadio Sastroatomo**, a former leader of the now-defunct Indonesian Socialist Party, was banned on 6 March on the grounds that it could provoke unrest and tarnish the government's image. On 17 March the well-known government critic **Ali Sadikin**, who had asked to reprint the book, was also questioned in connection with it. (Institute for the Studies on Free Flow of Information, *Jakarta Post*, Reuters, SWB)

Students **Slamet Bibit** and **Fuad Chafidin** were sentenced to two years' imprisonment on 10 March for sowing hatred against the government. The two had circulated leaflets detailing irregularities during the 1992 elections, including the banning of United Development Party (PPP) and Indonesian Democratic Party (PDI) symbols from public places and the banning of activists from election rallies. (*Jakarta Post*)

The United Development Party (PPP) have accused the ruling Golkar group of biased and repressive behaviour in the run-up to the general election, it was reported on 10 March. Reported incidents in East Java include the banning of PPP calendars and the replacement of PPP banners with Golkar promotional material, while some of the PPP's provisional candidates have been removed from the list by government officials. Other pre-election measures taken by the government are a ban on calls to boycott the elections and a warning that civil servants and their families must vote for Golkar. (*Jakarta Post, Guardian*, Reuters)

Foreign nationals invited to observe Indonesia's elections for the first time are to monitor but not investigate or pass judgement on proceedings, the Home Ministry announced in mid-March. Only formally invited observers will be granted free access to the polls. Journalists planning to cover the election have been cautioned by the interior minister, Yogei Memet, to 'just write the facts. Otherwise foreigners get different and negative impressions of the election process'. (Reuters, SWB)

A proposed march from Bali to Jakarta has been banned by East Java military command, it was reported on 24 March. The march, organised by a PDI faction calling itself the 'Constitution-Loving PDI Cadres', was branded as a political activity liable to disturb security and order. (*Jakarta Post*)

Recent publication: *The Trial of Thought* (AI, April 1997, 26pp)

IRAN

Faraj Sarkoohi (*Index* 6/1996, 1/1997, 2/1997), the editor-in chief of the monthly literary magazine *Adineh*, is still detained without charge. In February the official IRNA news agency broadcast allegations that Sarkoohi had had an extramarital affair with his assistant, journalist Parvine Ardalan, who also disappeared around 24 January. It is feared she may have been arrested. Adultery is a capital offence punishable by death. (Iranian PEN Centre in Exile)

The body of editor **Ebrahim Zal Zadeh** was found in the Tehran City Coroner's Department mortuary on 29 March with multiple stab wounds to the chest. He had been missing since around 23 February. The body has still not been released to his family for burial and there is no official statement concerning how long it had been there. He was the editor of *Me'yar*, a monthly literary magazine which was reportedly forced to close after publishing an article criticising the government's censorship policies in 1995. He also owned the Ebtekar (Initiative) publishing house and is said to be one of the eight writers who offered to share in the punishment of **Abbas Maroufi**, the editor of *Gardoun* magazine who was sentenced to be flogged in February 1996 (*Index* 3/1996). (Iranian PEN Centre in Exile, RSF, AI)

Mohammed Sadegh Javadi-Hessar, director of the newspaper *Toos*, has been banned from practising journalism for 10 years, it was reported in April. A court in Mashhad found Javadi guilty of spreading 'false information' about Iran's Quranic schools. (*Iran News*)

ISRAEL

A two-month suspended sentence and fine of US$240 imposed on **Moshe Arenfeld** were upheld on appeal in February. He was convicted of religious disturbance for spitting on the ground while a procession of Armenian priests carrying the cross passed him on the way to the Church of the Holy Sepulchre in Jerusalem's Old City in March 1995. In the original trial the judge stated that religious disturbance had occurred despite the fact that no physical act aimed at preventing religious activities had taken place. Arenfeld appealed but the appeal court rejected his claim, saying that freedom of expression has its limits. (*Times*)

KAZAKHSTAN

Two radio stations and two television stations have been banned by Kazakh authorities since 24 February. The Kazakh Audio-visual Committee took the decision to disconnect the transmitters of Russia's **TV6-Moskva**, the private Kazakh **Totem TV**, **Totem Radio** and **Radio Max** on 21 February following a review of the files of media outlets requesting broadcast frequencies. Following a decree in December 1996 that all stations were required to renew their contracts (*Index* 1/1997), a new fee (US$30,000 for radio stations and US$100,000 for television stations) is now required to obtain a definitive frequency. The four popular and established stations had all paid this sum. On 3 April the authorities also halted broadcasts of the Russian radio station **Mayak**. (RSF)

KUWAIT

On 24 February six journalists were released from prison as part of a general amnesty declared by the government. The freed journalists are: **Abed Maazouz Ahmad Mustafa, Ali Ghazi Mahmoud al-Sayyed, Walid Hassan Muhammad Qaraqa, Daoud Suleiman Musa, Hassan Ahmad Hassan al-Khalili** and **Muhammad Mahmoud Ahmad Zahran**. They were convicted by martial law tribunals and state security courts between June 1991 and July 1992 for their work with the Iraqi occupation newspaper *al-Nida*. (CPJ)

KYRGYZSTAN

Res Publica journalist **Rysbek Omurzakov** (*Index* 5/1996, 2/1997) was summoned to the Lenin District prosecutor's officers on 24 March and has been in custody ever since. Omurzakov received a two-year suspended sentence for insulting the president in a political leaflet in 1996. In recent months he has received repeated warnings concerning his articles criticising public figures. (CPJ)

IRELAND

Health and safety

The Health (Family Planning) Act, which came into effect on 1 November 1980, set out several amendments to the censorship laws, particularly with regard to any mention of contraception or abortion

Section 12, Paragraph 1:
Section 16(1) of the Censorship of Publications Act, 1929, is hereby amended by the deletion of 'the unnatural prevention of conception or' and 'such prevention or'... The amended portion of the Censorship of Publications Act, 1929, will now read:
It shall not be lawful for any person, otherwise than under and in accordance with a permit in writing granted to him under this section—
(a) to print or publish or cause or procure to be printed or published, or
(b) to sell or expose, offer, or keep for sale, or
(c) to distribute, offer or keep for distribution, any book or periodical publication (whether appearing on the register of prohibited publications or not) which advocates or which might reasonably be supposed to advocate the procurement of abortion or miscarriage or any method, treatment or appliance to be used for the purpose of such procurement.
Paragraph 2:
The reference contained in section 3 of the Indecent Advertisements Act, 1889, to printed matter which is of an indecent or obscene character, shall be deemed to include advertisements which relate or refer or may be reasonably be supposed to relate or refer to any disease affecting the generative organs of either sex, or to any complaint or infirmity arising from or relating to sexual intercourse, or to the prevention or removal of irregularities in menstruation, or to drugs, medicines, appliances, treatment or methods for procuring abortion or miscarriage...
Paragraph 4:
Section 9(1) of the Act of 1946 is hereby amended by the deletion in paragraph (b) of 'the unnatural prevention of conception or' and 'prevention or'...The amended paragraph in the Act of 1946 will now read: The Censorship Board shall examine the issues recently theretofore published of every periodical publication in respect of which a complaint is made to them in the prescribed manner and if they are of the opinion that the issues—
(a) have usually or frequently been indecent or obscene, or
(b) have advocated the procurement of abortion or miscarriage or the use of any method, treatment or appliance for the purpose of such procurement, or
(c) have devoted an unduly large proportion of space to the publication of matter relating to crime, and that for any of the said reasons the sale and distribution in the State of the said issues and future issues of that periodical publication should be prohibited, they shall by order prohibit the sale and distribution thereof accordingly. *From* **Index 2/1981**

The new independent newspaper *Kriminal* (*Index* 2/1997) was ordered to close by the Pervomasky District Court on 12 March. Despite the support of lawyers, public defenders from the parliamentary commission on information and mass media and local human rights groups, it was banned for violation of Article 23 of the civil code, 'publication of non-verified or false information'. The paper, which has published just two issues, was also charged with printing insulting allegations against the prime minister and deputy prime minister and of offending government officials. (CPJ)

MALAYSIA

It was reported on 26 February that the 14 members of the banned **Al-Arqam** Islamic sect (*Index* 4/1996, 5/1996), held without trial for between six and nine months for their 'deviant' religious teaching, were freed in early February. Only one (Ahmad Salim Omar), however, received an unconditional release. The other 13 have been banished to remote districts and placed under restriction orders requiring police permission to travel. The government has announced it will monitor former members of the sect to ensure that they have 'truly repented'. (AI)

Reacting to the growth of sexually explicit articles in general-interest magazines and a rash of books purporting to offer sexual advice for Muslims, the Home Ministry announced plans in early March to tighten censorship and increase the penalties for pornography. Articles with sexual content could be used for educational purposes but not for publication in entertainment magazines and tabloids, the Ministry said. (*South China Morning Post*)

Recent publication: *The Trial of Opposition Parliamentarian Lim Guan Eng — An Update* (AI, March 1997, 4pp)

MEXICO

Tensions have been rising in the states of Guerrero and Oaxaca as clashes between peasants and judicial police grow more frequent. On 15 February in the community of La Soledad, two members of the opposition **Revolutionary Democratic Party** (PRD) were allegedly tortured and arrested by police who accused them of belonging to the rebel Peoples' Revolutionary Army (EPR). The next day four peasants from the neighbouring village disappeared following a police raid. On 21 March, 80 police and civilians violently expelled 50 local human rights activists demonstrating in San Augustín Loxicha for the release of indians illegally arrested and held in prison. A number of people were seriously hurt and one, **Ignacio Niño García**, was arrested. He has not been heard of since. A week later, two PRD members, **Guadalupe Lope Carrasco** and his wife, were shot dead in their car. (AI, *La Jornada*)

MICRONESIA

On 19 March Congress passed a resolution calling for the deportation of **Sherry O'Sullivan**, the Canadian editor of the country's only independent newspaper, *FSM News*. The resolution accused O'Sullivan of reporting with 'gross, extreme, careless and apparently wilfully malicious inaccuracies, distortions and outright falsehoods'. O'Sullivan's two partners in the paper dismissed her on 26 March, accusing her of failing to understand local cultural concerns. On 15 April, immigration officials gave O'Sullivan 15 days to renew her immigration permit or leave. (Pacific Islands News Association)

MONGOLIA

The Justice Ministry banned the private weekly *Yellow Newspaper* on 27 February and ordered the Free Press printing house (a gift from the Danish government to foster an independent press) to stop printing it. Channel 25 TV described the weekly as specialising in 'vanity fair and sensations'. (SWB)

NEW ZEALAND

The film *Salo — 120 Days of Sodom*, banned in New Zealand for more than 20 years, was seized by Wellington customs in late February and is again being considered by the Office of Film and Literature Classification. The film, directed by Pier Paolo Pasolini, was due to show at Wellington's Paramount Theatre as part of

INDEX INDEX

the International Film Festival running from 27 February to 12 March. Two previous attempts to get the film shown, in 1976 and 1993, both failed. (Reuters)

NIGER

On 15 March **Mamane Radiou Dogo**, **Salissou Rade** and **Abdoulaye Moussa**, journalists and technicians working for Radio Anfani, were detained for four days, following a complaint by the military against the bi-monthly magazine *Anfani*, which is under the same management. The magazine alleged that the military had vandalised Radio Anfani's offices in a raid on 1 March. On 21 March the station's director, Gremah Boucar, and night security guard, Harouna Issoufou, were released from detention after being charged with 'swindling' and organising the raid in order to obtain financial aid from international agencies. (RSF, CPJ)

Souleymane Adji, columnist for *Le Républicain*, *Citoyen*, *L'Alternative* and *La Democrate*, is recovering in hospital after being hit on 10 April by a car driven by four men, one of whom wore military uniform. (CPJ)

NIGERIA

Nobel-prize winning writer **Wole Soyinka** was charged in absentia with treason on 12 March in connection with a spate of recent bomb blasts in the country. Eleven other people, including several exiled members of the opposition group the National Democratic Coalition (NADECO), **Olu Falae**, the former finance minister, and **Frederick Fasehun**, president of the Campaign for Democracy, were also charged. (PEN, Reuters, AFP, Guardian)

On 18 March *Today's News Today* news editor **Tokunboh Olorun Tola** and reporter **Bola Owolola** were detained in connection with an article stating that Lagos state police commissioner Abubakar Tsav had been transferred. The paper's editor, **Owei Lakemfa**, has gone into hiding. (CPJ)

Ladi Olorunyomi, a journalist who has worked for the *Concord* and the *Herald* newspapers, was detained on 20 March. No reason was given for her detention. (CPJ)

Recent publications: *Shell and Nigeria — Findings and Recommendations* (PEN Center USA West, March 1997, 16pp); *Abacha's Media Crackdown* (A19, April 1997, 26pp)

PAKISTAN

A home-made bomb exploded at the offices of the Urdu-language paper *Qaumi Akhbar* on 3 March. The office was empty at the time and no-one was injured, but the blast caused extensive damage to the building. (Pakistan Press Foundation)

PALESTINE (AUTONOMOUS AREAS)

David Mizrahi, an Israeli photographer with Israeli daily *Ha'aretz* and Agence France-Presse, was beaten by Palestinian police officers while covering a demonstration in Hebron on 30 March. The officers also seized the film from his camera. Also in Hebron 10 journalists were pelted with stones by a crowd on 11 April after a Palestinian police officer publicly described them as collaborators with Israel. (RSF, CPJ)

Khaled Amayra, correspondent for Sharja Satellite Television of the United Arab Emirates, was summoned for questioning by Preventive Security Services (PSS) agents who came to his home on 23 March. He was interrogated at PSS headquarters in Dura about a broadcast which alleged that the head of Israeli intelligence, Ami Ayalon, in a meeting with PSS head Jibril Rahjoub, had requested that Palestinian security services arrest Hamas activists in connection with the 21 March suicide bombing in Tel Aviv. (CPJ)

PERU

Miguel Real, a Peruvian correspondent reporting on the Japanese Embassy siege for Worldwide Television News, received threats on 5 and 6 March telling him that 'your days are numbered'. Real also claims that the National Intelligence Service is planning to charge him with collaborating with international terrorist organisations. On 15 March, meanwhile, **Guillermo Anton** of American Tele-

Julian Barnes
Lionel Blue
Joseph Brodsky
A S Byatt
Beatrix Campbell
Noam Chomsky
Alan Clark
Emma Donoghue
Ariel Dorfman
Ronald Dworkin
Umberto Eco
James Fenton
Paul Foot
Zufar Gareev
Timothy Garton Ash
Martha Gellhorn
Nadine Gordimer
Gunter Grass
Vaclav Havel
Christopher Hitchens
June Jordan
Ryszard Kapuscinski
Yasar Kemal
Helena Kennedy
Ivan Klima
Doris Lessing
Mario Vargas Llosa
Naguib Mahfouz
Alberto Manguel
Arthur Miller
Caroline Moorehead
Aryeh Neier
Harold Pinter
Salman Rushdie
Edward Said
Posy Simmonds
John Simpson
Alexander Solzhenitsyn
Wole Soyinka
Stephen Spender
Tatyana Tolstaya
Alex de Waal
Edmund White

subscribe!

United Kingdom & Overseas (excluding USA & Canada)

	UK:	Overseas:
1 year (6 issues)	£38	£43
2 years (12 issues)	£66	£79
3 years (18 issues)	£96	£114

Name

Address

B7A3

£ _____ total. ❏ Cheque (£) ❏ Visa/MC ❏ Am Ex ❏ Bill me

Card No.

Expiry   Signature

❏ I would also like to send **INDEX** to a reader in the developing world—just £25.
❏ I do not wish to receive mail from other companies.

INDEX, 33 Islington High St, London N1 9LH Tel: 0171 278 2313

subscribe!

United States and Canada

	US:
1 year (6 issues)	$50
2 years (12 issues)	$93
3 years (18 issues)	$131

Name

Address

B7B3

$ _____ total. ❏ Cheque ($) ❏ Visa/MC ❏ Am Ex ❏ Bill me

Card No.

Expiry   Signature

❏ I would also like to send **INDEX** to a reader in the developing world—just $35.
❏ I do not wish to receive mail from other companies.

INDEX 33 Islington High St, London N1 9LH
Tel: 0171 278 2313 Fax: 0171 278 1878
Email: indexoncenso@gn.apc.org

BUSINESS REPLY SERVICE
Licence No. LON 6323

INDEX ON CENSORSHIP
33 Islington High Street
London N1 9BR
United Kingdom

NO POSTAGE
NECESSARY
IF MAILED
IN THE
UNITED STATES

BUSINESS REPLY MAIL
FIRST CLASS PERMIT NO.7796 NEW YORK, NY

Postage will be paid by addressee.

INDEX ON CENSORSHIP
708 Third Avenue
8th Floor
New York, NY 10164-3005

vision was detained by national police officers while photocopying an MRTA paper in a grocery store near the Japanese Embassy. And journalists **José Antonio Alvárez** and **Rosa Neyra** received numerous intimidating calls and a letter outlining a plan to kill Alvárez, who has been listed as a member of the MRTA by the anti-terrorist police. Human rights groups are calling for an investigation into the storming of the Embassy in April, in which all 14 of the MRTA hostage-takers were killed. (Instituto Prensa y Sociedad, AI, Derechos-l)

A report about human rights and press freedom abuses was broadcast on the morning shows of two leading Peruvian TV channels on 6 April, bringing to light an ongoing intimidation campaign against journalists who have reported on human rights violations. Channel 2 showed the testimony of **Leonor La Rosa**, a former Military Intelligence Service agent, who was tortured because the military believed she leaked to the press the plans of their operations 'Bermuda' and 'El Pino' aimed at intimidating journalists and members of the opposition. Channel 4 also reported on the case of **Mariella Barreto**, an army agent found beheaded and dismembered on 30 March. Barreto was the wife of an army major in jail for involvement in the anti-terrorist group linked to the 1992 La Cantuta massacre (*Index* 8&9/1993), and she was allegedly killed for having told the press where the La Cantuta bodies were buried. (Reuters, Instituto Prensa y Sociedad)

Edmundo Cruz, who works for the 'investigation unit' of the paper *La República*, received a threatening phone call at his home in Lima on 4 April. The anonymous caller told him: 'The invoice is made out; all that's left to do is pay it.' The threat followed a series of articles this year in which Cruz outlined plans by army intelligence to intimidate journalists and lawyer Heriberto Benítez Rivas. Benítez is the defence lawyer representing Leonor La Rosa (see above). (AI)

PHILIPPINES

On 10 March President Ramos ordered state censors to defer the public screening of the film *Sarah Balabagan Story* on grounds of 'national interest' after the United Arab Emirates expressed concern about its subject matter. The film, which tells the true story of a Filipina maid who escaped execution for murder in the UAE in 1994, is believed to be potentially threatening to Philippine-Emirates relations and to the 80,000 Filipinos (including one on death row) currently living in the Gulf state. Separately, a group of Muslims also petitioned a Manila court to halt the screening of the film, calling it 'a great disgrace and insult to the high morality of Muslim women'. It is the first Filipino film to be censored for reasons other than pornography and at foreign request. (Reuters, *South China Morning Post*)

ROMANIA

Three journalists from the local paper *Opinia* were sentenced to a year in prison in Buzau on 13 March for libel. The three published an article claiming the former prosecutor's mother had let her house to the manager of an illegal pyramid-investment scheme. An appeal is pending. (OMRI)

Recent publication: *Unlawful Use of Firearms by Law Enforcement Officials* (AI, March 1997, 11pp)

RUSSIAN FEDERATION

Russia: **Albert Musin**, a human rights activist and freelance journalist for *Ekspress Khronika, Nezavisimaya Gazeta* and the radio stations Ekho Moskvy and Radio Liberty, was released from custody on Moscow in 6 March. He had been detained on 21 February and is wanted for extradition to Uzbekistan, charged with the 'unlawful collection, publication and use of confidential information without the consent of its owner'. It is not clear if the threat of extradition to Uzbekistan has been lifted. (AI, Reuters, CPJ, RSF)

The State Duma affirmed its decision on 5 March to strip **Russian Public TV** (ORT) correspondents of their accreditation for one month as punishment for 'biased' coverage. (OMRI)

INDEX INDEX

NIGERIA
Ordeal by innocence

The following is taken from the defence statement that **Ken Saro-Wiwa** *was prevented from reading in court in September 1995, shortly before he was sentenced to death on the trumped-up charge of complicity in the murder of his fellow Ogoni activists*

My lord, we all stand before history. I am a man of peace, of ideas. Appalled by the denigrating poverty of my people who live on a richly endowed land, distressed by their political marginalisation and economic strangulation, angered by the devastation of their land, anxious to preserve their right to life and to a decent living, and determined to usher to this country as a whole a fair and just democratic system, I have devoted all my intellectual and material resources — my very life — to a cause in which I have total belief and from which I cannot be blackmailed or intimidated. I have no doubt at all about the ultimate success of my cause, no matter the trials and tribulations which I and those who believe with me may encounter on our journey. Nor imprisonment nor death can stop our ultimate victory.

I repeat that we all stand before history. I and my colleagues are not the only ones on trial. Shell is on trial here, and it is as well that it is represented by counsel said to be holding a watching brief. The company has, indeed, ducked this particular trial, but its day will surely come and the lessons learnt here may prove useful to it, for there is no doubt in my mind that the ecological war the company has waged in the delta will be called to question sooner than later and the crimes of that war be duly punished. The crime of the company's dirty wars against the Ogoni people will also be punished.

On trial also is the Nigerian nation, its present rulers and all those who assist them. I am not one of those who shy away from protesting injustice and oppression, arguing that they are expected of a military regime. The military do not act alone. They are supported by a gaggle of politicians, lawyers, judges, academics and businessmen, all of them hiding under the claim that they are only doing their duty, men and women too afraid to wash their pants of their urine. We all stand on trial, my lord, for by our actions we have denigrated our country and jeopardised the future of our children... I predict that a denouement of the riddle of the Niger delta will soon come. The agenda is being set at this trial. Whether the peaceful ways I have favoured will prevail depends on what the oppressor decides, what signals it sends out to the waiting public.

In my innocence of the false charges I face here, in my utter conviction, I call upon the Ogoni people, the peoples of the Niger delta, and the oppressed ethnic minorities of Nigeria to stand up now and fight fearlessly and peacefully for their rights. History is on their side, God is on their side. For the Holy Quran says in Sura 42, verse 41: 'All those who fight when oppressed incur no guilt, but Allah shall punish the oppressor.'

Come the day.

From **Index** *6/1995*

A statement issued by the Oryol municipal administration on 10 April accused journalists from several local publications of 'distorting information received at meetings and from officials of the mayor's office'. The mayor's office suggested that a system of accreditation might be needed to regulate 'unprincipled' journalists. (*Ekspress Khronika*)

Irina Chernova, correspondent for the daily *Komsomolskaya Pravda* in Volgograd, was badly kicked and beaten by two unidentified assailants on 17 April. Chernova had reported being followed for several days prior to the attack. It is thought that the attack may be related to Chernova's investigation into corruption in a local oil company. (Glasnost Defense Foundation)

Chechnya: **Natalya Vasenina**, editor of the Chechen youth newspaper *Respublika*, was released on 20 February, having being held for five months by Chechen rebels (*Index* 6/1996). In early 1996 the Chechen minister of press and information, Abdula Bugayev, had decreed that Vasenina should be removed from her position as editor-in-chief of *Respublika* for writing about Alla Dudayeva, the widow of Dzhokhar Dudayev. (CPJ, SWB)

On 4 March four Russian journalists were kidnapped by armed men in Grozny. They are **Nikola Zagnoyenko**, an Itar-Tass correspondent, **Yuri Arkhipov** and **Nikolai Mamolashvili**, reporters for the public radio station Radio Rossia, and **Lev Zeltser**, a technician in satellite communications. An anonymous caller telephoned the mayor's office in Satka on 4 April and demanded US$2 million for the journalists' release. (SWB, AI, OMRI)

Recent publications: *Torture in Russia — 'This Man-Made Hell'* (AI, April 1997, 76pp); *Torture, Ill-Treatment and Death in the Army* (AI, April 1997, 16pp); *The Right to Conscientious Objection to Military Service* (AI, April 1997, 17pp); *The Failure to Protect Asylum Seekers* (AI, April 1997, 34pp)

SAUDI ARABIA

On 6 April the Egyptian magazine *al-Ahram al-Arabi* was banned from Saudi Arabia by the authorities over an article about the fundamentalist leader Osama bin Laden who was stripped of Saudi citizenship and is now living in Afghanistan. The article says that 'the fact that bin Laden was deprived of his citizenship has strengthened the credibility of his statement that his fundamentalist movement is not bound by nationalities'. The magazine also reports the presence of more than 12,000 Islamist militants in training camps on the Yemen-Saudi border. (RSF)

SERBIA-MONTENEGRO

Montenegro: The Montenegrin bureau of the Serbian government daily *Dnevik* reported receiving 'nuisance phone calls, threats and blackmail' (including threats to kill the bureau chief) in March, following the paper's criticism of an interview with the Montenegrin prime minister, Milo Djukanovic, which appeared in the paper *Vreme*. (SWB)

Serbia: Independent broadcaster **BK TV** was told on 5 March by the state-owned network Radio-Television Serbia (RTS) that its lease for transmitter sites in five locations would expire in 15 days and that the agreement to use three of those would be terminated. BK TV claims it is the only station to have received a lease termination and that the action violates the terms of the lease. BK TV is owned by entrepreneur Bogoljub Karic, who may launch a party to run in the elections this year. After a BK TV blackout at the end of March, a Belgrade court ordered the telecommunications authority and RTS to air BK on its own transmitters. (CPJ, *Guardian*)

On 10 March the government unveiled a new media law, which would bar private radio and television stations from broadcasting to more than 25 per cent of the population. State-run outlets will continue to broadcast to the whole population. No individual or organisation will be permitted to control more than 20 per cent of the newspapers published in the country. Also, all media receiving financial or material aid from abroad will have to inform the authorities. (RSF)

Mladen Popoyic, director of

the cinema service at RTS, was dismissed on 30 March. Popoyic had criticised RTS's reporting on 5 December 1996 in *Nasa Borba* and on 10 January in the weekly *Nin*. (RSF)

SIERRA LEONE

Defamation charges against **Pat Kawa** (*Index* 2/1997), a *Punch* correspondent in Bo, were dropped when the case was thrown out of court on 3 March. (CPJ)

Footprints magazine editor **Mohammed Karim** and journalist **Njai Kanhbai** were arrested on 3 March on charges of possession of drugs. They were released three days later and are planning to take the police to court for wrongful arrest and detention. On the same day *Footprints* publisher **Harry Evans** was detained in connection with an article in the 28 February edition which alleged that the minister of presidential affairs used his position to avoid import duties of US$23,000 on 50 imported cars. He was released without charge on 12 March. (CPJ)

In late March the government introduced amendments to the press law, requiring all editors to have 10 years' prior experience, five of them in an editorial capacity, and all journalists to have an educational degree in their field and be registered by the police. It is proposed that all newspapers which began circulation after February 1996 — the majority of independents — will have to re-register, affecting up to 30 of the country's 42 papers. (CPJ)

On 7 April editor-in-chief **Ibrahim Seaga Shaw** and journalists **Gibril Koroma** and **Abayomi Charles Roberts** of the independent newspaper *Expo Times* were conditionally released pending trial. They were charged on 22 March with 'obtaining secret official documents or extracts containing military secret information which could be directly or indirectly used by enemies of the state' following an opinion piece published in the 19 March edition, entitled 'Abacha's Wild West Gangsterism'. (CPJ, RSF, *For Di People*)

SINGAPORE

On 10 March **Tang Liang Hong** (*Index* 2/1997) was found guilty of libelling prime minister Goh Chok Tong and 10 other ruling party members. Tang's defence was struck down after he failed to appear in person at the trial. He has refused to return to the country for fear of arrest. (*Guardian, Sydney Morning Herald*)

SOUTH KOREA

Novelist **Kim Ha-Ki** (*Index* 5/1996) was sentenced to three-and-a-half years in prison on 11 February on charges of 'illegally entering North Korea' and 'revealing state secrets'. (PEN)

Controversial labour legislation rushed through Parliament in late December (*Index* 2/1997) has been replaced by a new law, introduced on 10 March. The revisions give immediate recognition to the banned Korean Confederation of Trade Unions, modify anti-strike rules, and delay by two years the implementation of clauses which facilitate the laying off of workers. At the insistence of opposition groups, another unpopular law which restored powers to the domestic intelligence Agency for National Security Planning will also be revised. (Reuters, *Independent*)

SPAIN

In late March the Supreme Court ruled that secret military intelligence documents detailing the operation of covert government actions against the Basque separatist group ETA between 1983 and 1987, when 28 suspected militants died, should now be declassified, despite a decision by the current government to keep them secret for reasons of national security. (*International Herald Tribune*)

SRI LANKA

In March parliamentarian Joseph Parajasinham urged the government to launch an inquiry to determine the fate of 23 youths detained in July 1996 during an army operation in Jaffna peninsula. None of the 23 has been heard of since. Thousands of Tamils have disappeared while in army custody since the army began its counter-offensive against separatist rebels in the east in 1990. (*Sunday Times*)

Recent publication: *Reform at Risk? Continuing Censorship in Sri Lanka* (A19, March 1997, 44pp)

SYRIA

March marked the tenth anniversary of the detention of poet and journalist **Faraj Ahmed Beraqdar** (*Index* 1 &2/1994, 1/1996). He was arrested in March 1987 on suspicion of membership of the Party for Communist Action (PCA), and held without trial for over six years before being sentenced to 15 years' imprisonment in 1993. It is believed that he has been tortured and denied medical care during his imprisonment. (PEN)

Five long-term prisoners — **Jadi Nawfal, Ya'qub Musa, Hassan Ali, Hassain Salama** and **Thabit Murad** — were released from Sednaya Prison in February. They were among 17 people arrested in 1991 and 1992 and charged in connection with a leaflet issued by the banned Committee for the Defence of Democratic Freedoms and Human Rights (CDF). However, five of the 17 — **Nizar Nayyuf, Aktham Nu'aysa, Muhammad Ali Habib, Afif Muzhir** and **Bassam al-Shaykh** — remain in prison. (AI)

TAIWAN

Charges of criminal libel against journalists **Ying Chan** and **Hsieh Chung-liang** (*Index* 1/1997) were dismissed on 22 April. The judge indicated that the use of criminal charges in a defamation case was inappropriate, and that the article that gave rise to the charge, which claimed that the ruling Kuomintang had offered to donate US$15 million to President Clinton's re-election campaign, dealt with a matter of legitimate public interest. A civil suit filed by Liu Tai-ying, the Kuomintang's business manager who was named in the article, was also dismissed. (CPJ)

TANZANIA

Freelance journalist **Adam Mwaibabile** was released on bail on 21 March pending appeal against a one-year sentence for possession of a 'secret government document'. The document in question was a letter from the Ruvuma regional commissioner's office instructing the town council director not to issue a business licence to Mwaibabile (who also operates a vending kiosk) for the year 1995-96. However on 21 April the High Court in Dar es Salaam quashed the sentence after the state attorney admitted that Mwaibabile had been wrongly convicted. (MISA)

The Association of Journalists and Media Workers (AJM) started court proceedings in late March challenging the constitutionality of several laws impinging on press freedom, including the 1976 Official Secrets Act, the 1976 Newspaper Act, the 1976 News Agency Act and the 1993 Broadcasting Act, which it says are 'outdated, undemocratic and going against the freedom to receive information'. (AJM)

TOGO

On 19 February the independent weekly *Forum Hebdo* was suspended for six months by the attorney-general. Its publisher, **Gabriel Agah**, was also sentenced in absentia to one year's imprisonment and fined US$1,900. (CPJ)

Lucien Messan, editor-in-chief of the independent weekly *Le Combat du Peuple*, went into hiding on 4 March. Earlier that day he had been forcibly taken to the office of the interior minister, Colonel Seyi Memene, who threatened him with arrest unless he substantiated allegations made in the previous day's edition that a journalist from the international radio station Africa 1 had received US$17,300 for reporting favourably on the recently established Constitutional Court. (RSF)

The Lomé fire brigade has filed defamation charges against **Augustin Assiobo**, the editor-in-chief of the independent weekly *Tingo-Tingo* (*Index* 2/1997), in connection with an article in November last year. Assiobo has been detained without trial since 5 February. (RSF)

TUNISIA

Hechmi Jegham, a lawyer and president of Amnesty International's Tunisian

INDEX INDEX

SOUTH AFRICA

The written word is buried

The following appeal was issued by Nadine Gordimer, in her capacity as vice-president of International PEN, on 7 July 1986

There is a double crisis of censorship in South Africa. First of all, one that concerns the freedom of the press. The suppression of all sources of independent news gathering, with information restricted and released or withheld at the pleasure of police communiqués, gags the press and blindfolds the population to the true enormity of events. Journalists and photographers not only are unable to do their work — many are harassed and arrested, themselves becoming the subjects of the oppression it is their task to record. Others are being forced into hiding by the threat of arrest.

The smaller papers, which represent real press opposition in South Africa, for example the *New Nation* and the *Weekly Mail*, maintain a precarious, week-to-week existence with a skeleton staff and many columns mutilated by lines blacked out. The most important and prominent among journalists detained is Zwelakhe Sisulu, editor of the Catholic Bishops Conference paper, the *New Nation*. I call upon writers everywhere to condemn Sisulu's detention and do all in their power to obtain his release.

The second crisis of censorship: literary freedom. The Publications Appeal Board, which has been banning books for more than 20 years, is no longer the principal arm of censorship. Countless provisions of the state of emergency and the new powers given to the police under other legislation now succeed, entirely without the cumbersome process of the Publications Appeal Board, in preventing the sale and distribution of books. These decrees strike directly at source: publishers find their printers do not want to accept anything that may put them at risk; booksellers not only refuse to distribute what they think may be a contravention of one of umpteen laws, some go so far as to remove from their shelves books that have been freely on sale for years. *Intimidation* has taken over much of the work of the censors. Indeed, it has gone beyond what formal censorship as such could accomplish. The written word is buried under the fears not of those who write — self-censorship is not something South African writers have submitted to — but under those who distribute. This is because *anyone* who disseminates in any way what may be regarded as subversive may be prosecuted under today's laws.

I call upon writers everywhere to review their efforts to fight apartheid. Repressive laws can no longer, by any standards, be divided between those that affect writers and those that do not. The word will not be free so long as the present regime lasts, backed up by the reluctance of the United States and other western powers to bring real pressure to bear on the South African government.

From **Index** *8/1986*

Section, was detained on two separate occasions at the central police station in Sousse on 8 and 9 March. He was questioned about his contacts with foreign media and human rights and other organisations, and was advised to inform the Tunisian authorities of any future contacts. (AI)

TURKEY

Hatun Temuzalp, Ali Can Kaya, Arzu Görmez, Dilsan Acar and Muammer Kalkan of the socialist bi-weekly *Proleter Halkin Birligi* (Proletarian People's Union) were detained in Istanbul on 7 March. Three other people who work for the same paper — Tekin Yazar, Ali Ekber and Haydar Celik — were detained at their homes. Hasan Acan, a subscriber to the newspaper, was also taken into detention. On 14 March they were taken to court, where Temuzalp, Kaya, Görmez, Kalkan and Yazar were released and the others were formally arrested. The arrests appear to be connected with the anniversary of the killing by police of at least 17 people during a week of unrest in March 1995 in Istanbul. (AI)

On 14 March Aysenur Zarakolu, director of the Belge Publishing House (*Index* 4/1995, 6/1995, 2/1996), and Erturul Kurkcu were sentenced for 'insulting the army' by translating and publishing a Human Rights Watch report. Kurkcu was given a 10-month suspended sentence and Zarakolu was fined. The 1995 report, *Weapons Transfers and Violations of the Laws of War in Turkey*, criticises Ankara's handling of the conflict in the southeast and quotes an unnamed US diplomat as describing Turkish policemen as 'brutal thugs'. (Reuters)

On 24 March Aydin Dogan, owner of *Radikal* newspaper, and Yesim Denizel Beduk, the editor, were charged under the anti-terror laws for 'publishing the statements of a terrorist organisation'. *Radikal* published an interview with Abdullah Öcalan, leader of the Kurdistan Workers' Party (PKK), in December 1996. In the interview Öcalan called for talks with the authorities but threatened attacks on major cities if his call was rejected. (Reuters)

On 25 March it was announced that Mete Göktürk, a senior prosecutor, is to be tried for insulting the judiciary and Justice Ministry in ATV's weekly debate programme *Political Arena*. In the programme, broadcast in November 1996, Göktürk criticised the current policy on sentencing. (Reuters)

Composer and human rights activist Sanar Yurdatapan (*Index* 5/1996, 6/1996) was detained on 16 April as he returned to Turkey from Germany. He was taken to the Anti-Terror Branch of Istanbul police headquarters and formally arrested on 22 April. Yurdatapan is one of the main activists with the Initiative for Freedom of Expression in Turkey. Police say that two false passports, which were intended for two former members of the PKK, were found in his possession. (AI, A19)

Recent publication: *Torture and Mistreatment in Pre-Trial Detention by Anti-Terror Police* (HRW/Helsinki, March 1997, 50pp)

UGANDA

Niciphore Agwanyi, a freelance journalist who has been detained since 20 August 1996, was found guilty of attempted extortion on 14 February and sentenced to a fine of US$92 or one year in prison. Agwanyi claims that the person who accused him of extortion had bribed the police to arrest him after he found out that Agwanyi was going to write an incriminating story about him. (CPJ)

Amos Kajoba, editor-in-chief of the *People*, was detained for five hours on 24 March in connection with an article reporting a security meeting of West Nile leaders. On instruction, Kajoba reported to the police on the following two days and 2, 4 and 8 April. (Uganda Journalists Safety Committee)

UKRAINE

The paper *Ridna Zemlya* was effectively banned by Nikolai Gogol, director of the regional printers, on 8 March because it had 'fatally offended the head of the regional state administration', Stepan Volkovetsky. The paper accused Volkovetsky of

INDEX INDEX

intrigue, hypocrisy and currency speculation. Gogol has previously refused to print the opposition newspaper *Prikarpatskaya Pravda*. (*Ekspress Khronika*)

The body of **Petr Shevchenko**, Lugansk correspondent of *Kievskie Vedmosti*, was found at a deserted petrol station on 13 March. A number of journalists feared he had been murdered, after he expressed fears of persecution by the Ukrainian Security Service (SBU). In early March the SBU criticised Shevchenko's articles for 'distorting reality'. This followed a series of articles co-authored by Shevchenko about disputes between the mayor and the local branch of the SBU. The SBU denies any involvement in Shevchenko's death. (CPJ, *Ekspress Khronika*)

Parliamentary hearings into freedom of expression ended on 10 April with the recommendation that President Kuchma undertake a reform of existing media regulations to bring them into line with constitutional guarantees and international standards. The hearings criticised the executive branch and individual officials for encouraging politically biased programming in state radio and television. (SWB)

UNITED KINGDOM

In February several British Gulf War veterans reported being harassed and intimidated following their efforts to prompt an investigation into Gulf War syndrome. In 1995, lawyer Hilary Meredith was ordered to sign a document promising not to release information about the use of organophosphates during the war. Despite evidence that the Ministry of Defence was aware at least two years ago that unsafe chemicals had been used extensively, Parliament was not informed and as yet veterans have received no compensation. Some 1,500 British (and 20,000 American) veterans have so far reported sickness. (*Independent, Telegraph*)

The government announced on 5 March that it would attempt to stop the Italian hardcore satellite channel **Satisfaction Club** from beaming into Britain. Heritage secretary Virginia Bottomley said: 'I will always put the rights of our children before the bogus rights of pornographers.' (*Guardian*)

On 12 March three members of the extreme right-wing group **Combat 18** were jailed for between 12 and 17 months each on charges of possessing threatening and abusive material with the intention of distributing it to stir up racial unrest. (*Times*)

On 18 March the British Board of Film Classification (BBFC) passed David Cronenberg's film *Crash* uncut, giving it an 18 certificate. The BBFC had been considering the film since November 1996. Despite the decision, local authorities may still prevent the film from being screened. (*Times, Independent, Guardian*)

Eamon Collins, a former Irish Republican Army (IRA) member who wrote a book about the organisation, was run down and badly injured in late March, shortly before his book, *Killing Rage*, was published. Collins has been subjected to death threats and assassination attempts since he gave evidence against IRA members after being arrested by British authorities in 1985. (*Guardian*)

BBC and ITV executives said on 22 April that they would not transmit an election broadcast by the **Prolife Alliance** if it included footage of dead foetuses because it would breach guidelines on taste and decency. A cut version of the broadcast was shown instead. The Alliance has placed the footage on their website (http://www.enterprise.net/prolifealliance/). An election broadcast by the far-right **British National Party** was shown by the BBC and ITV after the removal of a sequence involving a clearly identifiable Asian family. Anti-racist groups had demanded that it be banned. (Reuters, *Daily Telegraph*)

USA

Following a February ruling banning tobacco advertising in Tacoma-Pierce County, Washington, Philip Morris USA decided to replaced its usual advertising with the message: 'Restrict Access, Not Speech'. The Tacoma-Pierce County regulations limit any outdoor tobacco advertising to a black and white 'tombstone' format with only

UNITED KINGDOM · USA

USSR
A chronicle of current events

The following statement was issued in May 1974 by **Andrei Sakharov** *and two colleagues, in response to the controversy generated by the circulation of the underground publication* A Chronicle of Current Events, *which monitored and detailed the persecution of dissidents and intellectuals*

The harsh verdicts — without foundation in our opinion — pronounced in the recent trials of Sergei Pirogov and Victor Nekipelov (each was sentenced to two years' imprisonment) are the occasion for this appeal concerning a question of principle. The starting point of the Pirogov case was the defendant's natural, humanitarian endeavour to deliver the diary of a suicide victim to his relatives. Pirogov had acquired this diary by chance; the man was unknown to him. The indictment considered this act the dissemination of libel because the diary contained remarks on the unwarranted — in the author's opinion — role of the Party in our life. Nekipelov's unofficial poems played some part in his case.

But the major impulse behind the indictment in both cases was contained in the words: 'A chronicle of current events'. And our appeal is directed to this subject in particular.

Both abroad and in our country, *A Chronicle of Current Events* is well known as the anonymous information bulletin which publishes news about the persecution of individuals for their beliefs or for the dissemination of information. In numerous verdicts of Soviet courts and in statements by representatives of the official point of view, the *Chronicle* has been declared libellous. We believe that the information in the *Chronicle* is factually correct, with the possible exception of a few accidental inaccuracies (Pirogov said this during his trial) and further, that this information is vital and essential for society.

We ask authoritative international organisations to express publicly their considered judgement of the *Chronicle*. We call to your attention that all numbers of *A Chronicle of Current Events* have been published abroad. Much specific testimony of witnesses from the Soviet Union who have spoken out openly has been published — the statements of dissidents and foreign correspondents, the testimony of émigrés given under oath, and other direct and indirect testimony. The Soviet authorities punish very severely all actions connected with the circulation or publication of the *Chronicles*. We consider that labelling the *Chronicle* as libellous is based on the mistaken identification of any negative information about Soviet life with libel.

We believe such identification to be an extremely harmful and regrettably persistent survival of the era of ideological terror. Only open and reasoned discussion, which you can initiate, will be able to break the vicious circle of these prejudices. We are convinced that *A Chronicle of Current Events* is a historically necessary product of the ethical and social demands of Soviet society, a manifestation of the healthy spiritual forces in Soviet society.

Andrei Sakharov, Andrei Tverdokhlebov, Vladimir Albrecht   From **Index 3/1974** price and availability information. In other specified areas tobacco advertising is prohibited entirely. (Reuters)

Lawyers for **Mumia Abu-Jamal** filed new evidence in the case with the Pennsylvania Supreme Court on 10 March. A new witness, Pamela Jenkins, will testify that in late 1981 police pressured her to falsely identify Abu-Jamal. (Equal Justice USA)

On 24 March the Supreme Court rejected an appeal against a provision in the Communications Decency Act 1996 which requires that cable channels with mainly sexually explicit content be scrambled by the cable operator to prevent non-subscribers from stumbling on the signal when children might be watching. (Reuters)

In April America Online (AOL), the country's largest Internet service provider, rejected a request by the Anti-Defamation League to remove a site operated by the Ku Klux Klan. The site decries 'the race mixers and mongrelisers' who believe 'the insane notion that two peoples can occupy the same space at the same time.' It also contains links to more virulent Internet sites. AOL's terms of service allow it to remove 'inciteful and provocative' material. (Reuters)

Spanish businessman **Javier Ferreiro** was arrested in Miami on 1 April on charges of violating the trade embargo against Cuba. Ferreiro, who lives in Havana, is accused under a 1963 regulation of illegally exporting US goods worth more than US$400,000 to Cuba via the Dominican Republic. (Reuters)

On 3 April the USA voted against a UN Human Rights Commission resolution urging countries to move towards abolition of capital punishment. The resolution, which is not legally binding, passed with 27 in favour, 11 against and 14 abstentions. The other 10 voting against were China, Algeria, Bangladesh, Bhutan, Egypt, Indonesia, Japan, Malaysia, Pakistan and South Korea. (Reuters)

Hearings began on 4 April in the American Library Association's challenge to a New York state law criminalising computer transmission of 'indecent' material which is 'harmful to minors'. The state law is similar to the controversial online decency provisions of the Communications Decency Act, currently the subject of an ongoing appeal before the Supreme Court (*Index* 1/1997). Meanwhile, FBI director Louis Freeh warned on 8 April that 'increasingly paedophiles and sexual predators are using the Internet and online services to target and recruit victims and to facilitate the distribution of child pornography.' Freeh was testifying at a Senate appropriations subcommittee hearing. (Reuters, *Computing*)

The public consultation over the television ratings system introduced in January (*Index* 2/1997) continues. The initial deadline for comments to be filed with the Federal Communications Commission was 8 April. The system has sharply divided opinion among the public and politicians. (*New York Times*, First Amendment Rights Working Group)

Recent publication: *Death Penalty Developments 1996* (AI, March 1997, 29pp)

VENEZUELA

Félix Faría Arias, a student in Baruta near Caracas, was abducted and beaten by members of the security forces on 8 March. He was seized by two men as he entered his halls of residence and forced into a Land Cruiser. The men beat him continuously as they drove around Caracas and threatened to kill him if he did not tell them about the activities of the opposition party Bandera Roja (Red Flag). The abductors identified themselves as members of the Dirección de los Servicios de Inteligencia y Prevención, a special unit of the security forces. Faría has been detained previously in relation to his political activities and he was an eyewitness to the killing of a student at Caracas University by security forces in April 1991. (AI)

VIETNAM

In the first case of its kind Philip Morris Vietnam Inc, the company representing

Marlboro cigarettes, was fined US$2,700 on 7 March for violating a ban on liquor and tobacco advertising. (*Saigon Times Daily*)

New regulations to establish government control of the Internet and its content were announced on 11 March. According to the current decree, information available on the Internet must conform to press and publication laws with fines and possible criminal prosecution to be imposed on those found accessing prohibited information. Users are to be restricted to the service provided by the state-run telecommunications company, and the use of public telephone lines to access the Internet is banned. (*Asia Intelligence Wire*, Reuters, HRW, *Financial Times*)

YEMEN

On 13 April police officers entered the home of **Fouad Qaid Ali**, a journalist with the independent bi-weekly *al-Ayyam*, and threatened to break his legs if he continued to call for a boycott of the 27 April parliamentary elections. Ali has since gone into hiding. (RSF)

Writer and academic **Muhammad al-Saqqaf** is currently facing charges of 'humiliating the president of the state... the Cabinet, or parliamentary institutions' and publishing 'false information' which 'threatens public order or the public interest' (Articles 197 and 198 of the Penal Law). In August and September 1996 al-Saqqaf wrote two articles for the weekly *al-Wahdawi* in which he criticised the High Elections Committee. (CPJ)

Recent publication: *Ratification Without Implementation — The State of Human Rights* (AI, March 1997, 52pp)

ZAIRE

Jean-Philippe Ceppi, correspondent for the French daily *Libération* and the French-language service of the BBC, was expelled from Lubumbashi on 23 February after reporting on the retreat of the Zairean army in face of the rebel advance. **Karen Lajon**, a correspondent in Lubumbashi for the French weekly *Le Journal du Dimanche*, was expelled on 21 March, after being held for four hours in the capital, Kinshasa. (RSF)

Bola Kikuabi, a senior magistrate and human rights advocate, has been detained in Kinshasa since 26 February for 'threatening state security'. Sources, however, believe he is being detained because he denounced atrocities committed by Zairean troops retreating from Bukavu. (SWB, Radio France Internationale)

The privately owned station **Television Kin Malebo** (TKM) was suspended for three months by the information minister on 3 March, in accordance with a decree dated 14 February which bans radio and television stations from producing, broadcasting or retransmitting programmes of a political nature (*Index* 2/1997). (RSF)

Ghislaine Dupont, special correspondent for Radio France Internationale, was ordered to leave Kisangani on 11 March, accused of carrying out a 'disinformation campaign' on air. **Thomas Sotinel**, western Africa correspondent for the French daily *Le Monde*, was also ordered to leave the town on the same day. (RSF)

Bohulu Bongombe was dismissed from his post as deputy minister of public works on 14 March for making statements on a private television station which the government considered 'incompatible with his status and the governmental solidarity to which he is supposed to adhere'. (SWB)

Growing support in Kinshasa for anti-government ADFL rebel forces of Laurent Kabila led to a ban on demonstrations in March. Meanwhile, Zairean journalists have been banned from publishing information on the civil war which comes from any source other than the Ministry of Defence. (*Guardian*, RSF)

On 31 March, the ADFL rebels started confiscating all means of communication such as mobile phones, faxes and radios from local people in areas under its control, particularly in the eastern town of Goma and the third-largest city, Kisangani. (*La Tempête des Tropiques*)

Two US journalists, including

Jennifer Glasse of the network ABC, were attacked by soldiers during a demonstration held by supporters of Etienne Tshisekedi in front of the Parliament building on 7 April. In a separate incident a Belgian radio correspondent was also hit several times by soldiers. (SWB)

On 21 April the information minister announced new regulations for foreign journalists, including the creation of an 'ethics committee' to evaluate 'misinformed and unbalanced' articles, and compulsory registration with the Zairean Press Union. (RSF)

Recent publication: *Memorandum to the UN Security Council — Appeal for a Commission of Inquiry to Investigate Reports of Atrocities in Eastern Zaire* (AI, March 1997, 11pp)

ZAMBIA

Boyd Phiri, a reporter on the privately owned paper the *Chronicle*, has been charged along with editor Lweedo Hamusankwa (*Index* 2/1997) with 'publishing false news with intent to cause fear and alarm to the public' in connection with an article detailing the theft of arms and ammunition from an army barracks. (MISA)

Martin Wamunyima of the state-owned *Times of Zambia* and Ketson Kandafula of the *Zambia Daily Mail* were attacked and harassed at a press conference held on 11 March by the opposition United National Independence Party (UNIP). (MISA)

The country's major media organisations condemned as 'oppressive' and 'undemocratic' a draft of a Media Council of Zambia (MCZ) Bill, released by the government on 7 April (*Index* 2/1997), which seeks to establish a system of annual licensing for journalists and a statutory media council to regulate the press. The government temporarily shelved the legislation on 15 April, 'to provide for further consultation and debate'. (MISA, SWB)

The *Post*'s special projects editor, Masautso Phiri, gaoled for contempt of court (*Index* 2/1997), was released from prison on 11 April after serving the full term of his sentence. He regards the sentence as 'illegal' and has instructed his lawyers to make an application to the Supreme Court for a ruling on the law of contempt. (MISA)

ZIMBABWE

The organisation Gays and Lesbians of Zimbabwe (GALZ) condemned an ad carried in the 4 March edition of the state-owned *Herald* as hate propaganda and incitement to violence. The ad described homosexuals as rapists and called for them to be flogged. (GALZ, Reuters)

On 17 March the Supreme Court ruled the compulsory carrying of identity cards unconstitutional as it contravenes freedom of movement. The case was brought by lawyer Bryant Walker Elliot after he was arrested travelling from his office to the gym without his identity document. (*Herald*)

***

General publications: *Ethics in Journalism — Case Studies of Practice in West Africa*, ed Kwame Karikari (Panos Institute/Ghana University Press, 1996, 156pp); *Attacks on the Press in 1996* (CPJ, March 1997, 376pp); *Respect My Rights — Refugees Speak Out* (AI, March 1997, 32pp); *Africa — A New Future Without the Death Penalty* (AI, April 1997, 33pp); *Digital Terrestrial TV — Descrambling the Issues* (InterMedia Special Report, April 1997, 35pp)

***

Compiled by: Penny Dale (Africa); Victoria Millar, Sarah Smith (Asia); Ann Chambers, Vera Rich (eastern Europe & CIS); Emily Walmsley (Latin America); Michaela Becker, Philippa Nugent (Middle East); Briony Stocker (north America & Pacific); Jessie Banfield (western Europe)

Right: Credit: J C Tordai/Panos Pictures

Unquiet city

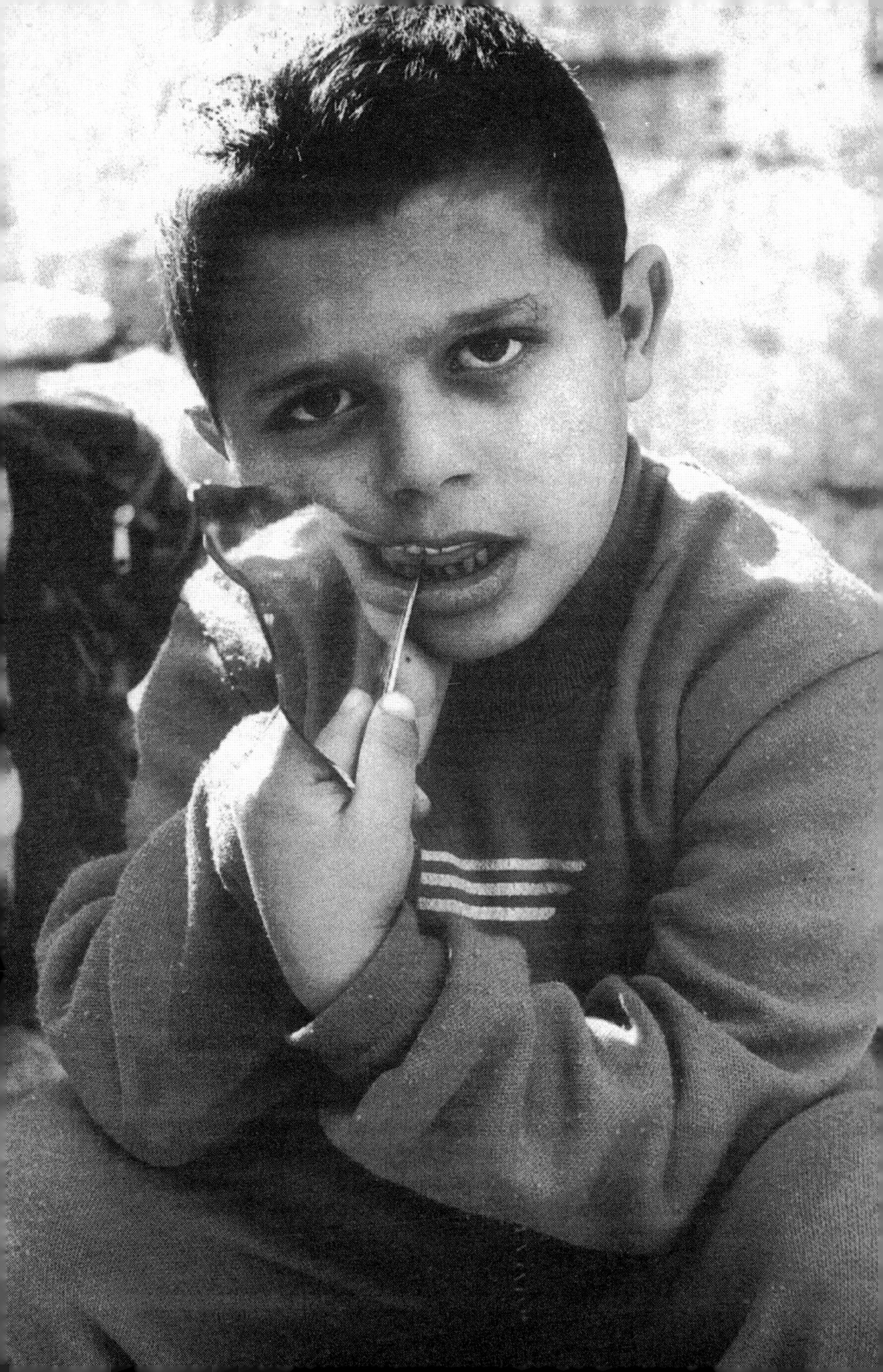

JERUSALEM, THE UNQUIET CITY

In the streets of Jerusalem

Left: Credit: Mark Power/Network
Above: Credit: J C Tordai/Panos Pictures

PHOTO FEATURE

JERUSALEM, THE UNQUIET CITY

Left: Credit: Rapho/Network
Above: Credit: J C Tordai/Panos Pictures

PHOTO FEATURE

Above: Rapho/Network

Right: Zhaotang, Yunnan, south west China — Credit: Rhodri Jones/Panos Pictures

Asian values

RONALD DWORKIN

Forked tongues, faked doctrines

WHEN *Index on Censorship* was born, the principal invasions of free expression were brutal, fundamental and uncomplicated. Dictators and military governments, over much of the world, controlled the press and throttled independent speech. In the last decade, however, that brutal threat has seemed to recede as democracy — at least in a nascent and often in a surprisingly vigorous form — has replaced tyranny in Russia, eastern Europe, South Africa, south America and elsewhere, and some of us therefore turned our attention to less fundamental and more complicated problems for free speech.

In previous *Index* articles I wrote about some of the new dangers that have arisen, not in fascist or Communist or theocratic dictatorships, but in contemporary democracies that are in principle committed to freedom of expression. Some feminist groups in the USA have campaigned to censor sexually explicit literature and film, for example, on the grounds that such materials 'silence' women by making them less likely to contribute to and less effective in political discourse. Several democracies have adopted laws and 'speech codes' censoring racist or other forms of hate speech that we properly despise: German law, for instance, makes it a crime to deny the existence of the Holocaust. These campaigns and laws, I said, are particularly attractive in western democracies because they urge censorship in the interests not of the powerful but of the vulnerable; in the name not of injustice but of equality. They must nevertheless be resisted, I argued, because if we deny freedom of speech to opinions we hate, we weaken the legitimacy of our entire political system, particularly the legitimacy of the very laws we pass to protect victims of stereotype and prejudice.

It is crucial that we continue to resist these attractive but dangerous exceptions to our basic commitment to free speech. But as this anniversary issue of *Index* goes to press, we are dramatically reminded that the old, brutal, uncomplicated forms of censorship are still routine over a great part of the world. After the Tiananmen Square demonstrations of 1989, during which Chinese soldiers killed hundreds of protesters, the British administration in Hong Kong adopted a set of civil rights laws guaranteeing freedom of speech and demonstration. But the Chinese have now made plain that these laws will be repealed when China takes over the government of Hong Kong on 1 July, and that the territory will thereafter be subject to China's general policy of ignoring basic human rights. In a document issued on 9 April, Tung Chee-hwa, the former shipping magnate designated by China to be Hong Kong's first chief executive under its rule, declared that 'Hong Kong is extremely vulnerable to external forces', and that the new government must 'strike a balance between civil liberties and social stability, personal rights and social obligations, individual interests and the common good.'

'Balanced' is code for 'denied': a right to free speech that must be 'balanced' against so exhaustive a list of other supposed values means a right that can be exercised only when those in power judge that the speech in question is innocuous to them. The cynicism of Tung's position becomes even clearer, moreover, when we look more carefully at his list of allegedly competing values. We know why he began his justification with a reference to 'external forces'. It is universally accepted, even in democracies that prize free speech, that freedom cannot be absolute, and the most familiar and plausible reason for qualifying it is a foreign military threat. Government may properly punish the publication of military secrets in time of war. But Hong Kong is not now, nor will it be in the foreseeable future, threatened by military force, from Taiwan or anyplace else. The external force Tung has in mind is the force of political and possibly economic pressure designed to improve China's human rights policies, so he is actually making the bizarre argument, in this part of his remarks, that constraints on free speech are necessary in order to prevent external criticism of China for not respecting free speech.

He also argues that free speech must be balanced against 'personal rights' and 'individual interests'. That is another familiar idea in democracies: it is the justification for libel laws that allow people to sue when they believe that what someone else has said of them is false and damaging. (We worry, in democracies, that such laws may inhibit political speech too much, and in the United States, the power of public officials to sue for libel is very sharply restricted for that reason.) But Tung's reference to individual's rights is as cynical as his reference to external force. He will not permit a free press and free demonstrations and then allow individuals to attempt to prove the falsity of statements about them. He will rather use political criteria to decide what may be published or said and then cite the bare possibility of false and harmful statements about particular individuals as a blanket justification for prohibiting the rest.

So Tung's reference to traditional grounds for limiting freedom of speech — foreign threats and personal rights — is a smokescreen, and his real argument emerges only when we ignore these and concentrate on the other grounds he mentions. It is now common for those Asian politicians who denigrate human rights to appeal to the cultural relativism that has, sadly, also become popular in western universities. They say that 'Asian' values do not attach so high a priority to individual rights as 'western' values do and that it is cultural imperialism for western governments to attempt to pressure them to abandon their own cultural inheritance as the price for economic co-operation. That is the nerve Tung tried to touch with his reference to 'stability', 'social obligations' and 'the common good'. He meant to suggest that Asian values are less selfishly individualistic than western ones, and that they place relatively greater importance on the competing values of collective enterprise and responsibility.

The concept of 'Asian' values is itself a fake: the nations of Asia are culturally diverse, and each of them combines a host of ethical traditions, some sharply different from others. We can, however, test Tung's claim and the more general defence of despotism it represents, by asking which other 'western' values, in addition to the supposed selfish individualism, would also have to be dismissed as culturally relative if his claim were to have any force. The first of these is, of course, democracy itself, meaning self-government by the people as a whole. The idea that the people should govern themselves is hardly an individualistic or selfish one. It supposes that a political community must act as a kind of partnership in which each citizen accepts some responsibility for collective decisions, and that ideal can be realised only when citizens are invited to participate in government as equals which means, at a minimum, that none can be denied a voice in collective deliberation because his or her ideas are deemed offensive or dangerous.

But presumably Tung and his colleagues would dismiss democracy, too, at least so understood, as just another western obsession. China as a whole, they might say, does not have enough experience with self-government to make it sensible to experiment with western-style democracy at this critical historical moment of transition to an internationally competitive economy. If new political parties were allowed, they might resist the government's sensible, indeed necessary, demands for individual sacrifice, and might thereby attract the votes of people unskilled in political judgement. That is a frightening argument. But it also misses a deeper point: that freedom of speech is essential, not just for democracy as we know it, but for a reason even more fundamental, which is that any government is a tyranny if it does not enjoy, in the main and overall, at least the informal consent of the governed.

It may be, as China's leaders claim, that the Chinese people understand the need for firm, efficient government to transform the nation, that they accept that a majority of them might be tempted, from time to time, to unwise decisions, that they do not want the expensive and divisive apparatus of competing political parties and regular free elections. People do, after all, for better or worse, often prefer hard choices to be made for them by others. But these are nevertheless empty and insulting claims so long as they cannot be tested, and they cannot be tested when people who argue to the contrary are jailed or tortured or killed. Freedom of speech is more fundamental even than democracy, because the former must be honoured even to allow the people to judge that the latter is wrong for them.

We must insist on that point, and repeat it whenever 'Asian' values of collective obligation and social responsibility are cited as justification for censorship. Freedom of speech, which is quite unnecessary to most people's individual ambitions for themselves, has nothing to do with selfishness. It is, however, indispensable to the most basic, organic, social responsibility a people can have, which is the responsibility together to decide, in civic response if not in formal elections, what their collective political values really are. ❑

Ronald Dworkin *is professor of jurisprudence at the University of Oxford. Among his many publications are* Taking Rights Seriously *(1977),* Life's Dominion *(1993) and* Freedom's Law *(1996)*

YANG LIAN

Poet without a nation

IN THE introduction to the New Stone Age site of Banpo Village in Xi'an there appear two sentences: 'The cemetery is on the north side of the village. The dead lie with their heads to the west.' Like two gunshots in my ear, they shocked me, left my brain blank. For an instant I didn't know where I was or who I was: corpse or mourner? Both or neither? More than 6,000 years on and thousands of miles away, dislocated in one move. During the 'Cultural Revolution' in a little village near Beijing to which I had been sent down, where I was one of the six who carried the coffin at every funeral, I became very familiar with the cemetery and with their funerary customs: on the north side of the village, and with heads to the west — to an extraordinary extent history had drawn near, had suddenly revealed itself within me.

In space, 'China' is territory; in time, it is tradition. What do these terms mean, precisely? From the 1980s onward I have been assessed in at last three different ways:

— as a 'poet opposed to tradition' — when the poetry began to discover its own language, it was of course bewildering to those whose reading habits had been nurtured by 'Cultural Revolution' slogans;

— as 'a Seeker after Roots — poet pursuing tradition' — poem cycles of mine like *Banpo*, *Dunhuang*, or *In Symmetry with Death* examined histories of the depths of a miserable reality, but because of their titles it was mistakenly assumed that I wanted to 'regress' to a past which had once been exuberant and brilliant:

— as 'a poet who has discarded tradition' — after 1989 I changed from being a Chinese hooligan poet to a Chinese poet who wanders the world on a New Zealand passport, and who has no external proof of 'Chineseness' except his poetry, which is written in Chinese.

POET WITHOUT A NATION

As I said to a Scottish poet who was showing me the ruins of Macbeth's castle, 'I've almost forgotten the feeling of being a poet who lives in his own country.'

But did I ever have 'my own country'? In this world no-one comes from 'China'. I came from 'The People's Republic of China'. 'Chinese' has no other significance for me. It simply points out one of the profundities of existence. Like Chinese nouns which have neither person nor tense, anyone can be reborn in the lines of a poem. And a verb that ignores tenses reveals that the living 'I' was in fact a fossil all along, filled with the terror of knowledge of the world.[1] As for me, if when I was sent down to the countryside I hadn't heard with my own ears the knocking of dead skulls on the coffin boards, then Banpo, the so-called first page of Chinese culture, would have been a mere word, an ancient legend; if it hadn't been for my own work, using metamorphic change to stress the unchanging orientation of the spirit, touching the human condition within me — making a little living tradition of myself — then Qu Yuan, Li Bai, Cao Xueqin and the 'five thousand years' of Chinese civilisation would all be on the outside for me: they would be the past and not the present, they would be knowledge and not thought.

A relationship has to be turned upside down: motherland, mother tongue and tradition are not inherent in nature but are precisely dependent on us; the poet has no need to 'Seek after Roots', for he is the root himself, he is the fountainhead, he is Banpo man moulding the clay to find a voice. A poem — even one written on a computer — is still a Stone Age event in cultural terms. I am not a 'Chinese' poet, not even a poet who writes in 'Chinese'. The limitations and possibilities of the Chinese language have infected my personality and even my eccentricities. I am just a 'Yanglish' poet — my poetry can't be 'translated' into anyone else's public Chinese. (The essential nature of all poetry is this 'non-publicality'.) So the poet dares to say 'Without me, my mother tongue couldn't be as it is.'

There is nothing strange about this. 'China' is smaller by one person. 'Chinese Traditional Culture' is born in a single short poem just newly written. It's not that I am born into a 'motherland' or a 'tradition', but that they are born in my poetry. 'Chineseness' depends on my discovering it again and choosing it again. The 'I', ambiguous, specific, aesthetically-aware, having a temperamental and moral point of view, springs from a unique aesthetic. But a 'motherland' which has physical

YANG LIAN

Country funeral, Vulong village, Yunnan, south west China — Credit: Rhodri Jones/Panos Pictures

properties or is controlled by culture — 'tradition' structured by psychology — is a lowest common denominator that is defined, outlined, inferred and simplified down until it is commensurate with a birth certificate and a residence permit. Then the vastness of its numbers is equivalent to the hollowness of its content, like the show of hands and the applause in the Great Hall of the People in Beijing. In reality this is a necessary aesthetic conflict between refinement and vulgarity. This is also a conflict between contempt for poetry and the abandonment of poetry — let poetry but exist and it will be enough to make the deaf and dumb 'witnesses of history' who stand at the shoulder of government prosecutors slink away in shame.

To open up language is to open up possibilities of thinking and feeling, and this is the profoundest of poetry's themes. It comes by accident, but it has determined the Chinese I use in my poetry. I must then be 'traditional', because of my language, traditional to the point of being unable to endure the name of 'poet of the nation', and having no need of Chinese nationality. What nationality were the people of Banpo? That exquisite polychrome pottery has no need for a parasitic 'source'. It is itself the source and it is the wellspring of a culture. It lets me listen to the first drop of blood circulating in the blind alley of my body — so vivid, so incandescent, 6,000 years on. ❑

Yang Lian *is a poet and critic from Beijing, now living in the UK. A number of his books were banned after 1989. His most recent works are* Non-Person Singular *(parallel text) and the poetic sequence* Where the Sea Stands Still *(Wellsweep Press)*

[1] *Author's Note: The word 'knowledge' in Chinese* (zhidao) *is formed from the two syllables* zhi *'to know' and* dao *'the Tao, the Way, the underlying rational for all phenomena'. Translators Note: there is a pun on* zhidao *in the text which is not translatable. It may also be useful to know that Chinese does not mark tense, person, gender or number: nouns do not decline, and verbs do not conjugate. Verbs are not generally marked for voice, either, and the subject of a sentence is frequently omitted. It is therefore not only possible, but also common poetic practice, to make statements which have a universal resonance precisely because of the absence of these specific grammatical structures.)*

Translated by Brian Holton

Kunming, Yunnan, south west China

IAN BURUMA
God bless America

US imperialism has done more for democratic rights in Asia than well-meaning activists

HUMAN rights have acquired a bad name. The very idea that any rights should be universal is under attack. Universality implies a lack of sensitivity to cultural difference. Some people see the 'human rights ideology' as a form of imperialism. Even if one agrees that, say, the right to be protected from torture or murder should be universally upheld, it is harder to agree about the universality of other rights. Should employment be a universal human right? Or three meals a day, or perhaps two? What about sexual equality? Or the right to choose how to educate one's children? Or to marry a partner of the same sex? These things might be desirable, but are they inalienable human rights? The question of rights is really a political one. Treating it mainly as a matter of moral principle creates problems. One of them is that most moral principles are not universal. And trying to impose them as though they wer, is to enter the project of missionaries.

The modern idea of human rights conceived largely in the West is being criticised from various angles. One line of attack is often heard in parts of southeast and east Asia. Authoritarian leaders in China, Malaysia, Indonesia, Burma and Singapore accuse western human rights advocates of being hypocrites at best, and 'anti-Asian' imperialists at worst. They believe that westerners preaching human rights in non-western countries are hypocritical, because western societies, especially the United States, are themselves in a state of moral collapse. Just think of racism, sexual excess (read AIDS), violent crime, drugs, divorce, selfish individualism, immoral entertainment and so on. So who are these people to come and preach moral principles in societies which (allegedly) do not suffer from these typical symptoms of western decadence?

The fear of western decadence is particularly strong in the more affluent Asian societies, such as Singapore, which are in fact suffering from precisely the same symptoms. Family life in east Asia is under the same pressures as in the West. An increasing number of Singaporean parents are now actually suing their children for refusing to look after them in their old age. Also in Singapore, one non-Muslim marriage out of seven ends in divorce, which is about three times as many as 30 years ago. Drugs are a huge problem in Malaysia. AIDS is a catastrophe in Thailand. The murder rate is higher in Bangkok than most European capitals. Corruption is rife everywhere in Asia. China is largely lawless. And anyone who thinks Hollywood movies are too violent should take a look at Indonesian films.

This makes rather a nonsense of the idea, expressed by the likes of Singapore's Lee Kuan Yew or Malaysia's prime minister Mahathir, that Asia is morally superior. 'Asian values', a vague term at best, are a mixture of Confucian moralism and open nostalgia for the British colonial propaganda that Lee's generation grew up with: discipline; duty; deference to authority, and the idea that Asians are not yet ready for, or indeed are unsuited to, democracy. This last point is of course the most important. Criticism of western human rights policies and the promotion of 'Asian values' are really political points monopolising political authority, and find democratic aspirations among their own people threatening. To say that authoritarian rule is an Asian 'value' is to claim that the political status quo is a natural state of affairs. To protest is to be 'un-Asian', or worse a traitor. The claimed right of Europeans to rule in Asia in the past rested on similar assumptions.

Conservative politicians in the West, whether or not conscious of the colonial provenance of Asian authoritarianism, find much that is attractive in the idea of Asian values. Keen to instil more social discipline, a more punitive justice system, and to cut down on social welfare, as well as curbing sexual freedom in their own societies, they take Lee and Mahathir's propaganda at face value. Otherwise, why would an intelligent man like Conservative former transport secretary David Howell claim that 'Asia may actually be leading the world in moral as well as economic terms?' To say that Asian societies are not morally superior at all is to miss the point. Howell's Asian values are not about Asia, but about his view of modern Britain.

Many observers on the Left are uncomfortable with Asian values too.

The idea that some western values might be superior to Asian ones simply cannot be held to be true. Indeed, the reverse is almost taken for granted by post-colonial, anti-American, pro-Third World leftists. The demons of Hollywood imperialism, western consumerism, Coca-Colonisation etc, loom as large in their minds as in those of many Asian dictators. And yet, Suharto, Lee, Mahathir, or Li Peng are hardly heroes to the European or American Left. And Marxists are by definition universalists. (Marx himself had contempt for Asian cultures.) The way to argue around this problem was nicely illustrated in a report written by Douglas Lummis on a 'Conference on Rethinking Human Rights' held in Kuala Lumpur in 1994 in *AMPO Japan-Asia Quarterly Review*.

Lummis argued that the enemy is not the West, as many Third World

• •

It would make for a more lucid debate if we dropped the language of rights and values, and simply talked about politics

• •

academics think, but the capitalist system that originated in the West. Assertion of human rights is necessary to alleviate the exploitation inherent in the 'liberal capitalist ideology'. But once liberal capitalism is defeated, capitalist Asian values, such as co-operation and solidarity, will reassert themselves. One might well ask what such a pre-capitalist Asian utopia would look like. Mao Zedong's China of the late 1950s comes to mind, when his experiment in mass solidarity during the Great Leap Forward cost about 30 million lives.

Anti-human rights advocates have one more argument up their sleeves, which is largely economic. It is all very well, they say, for rich, post-industrial countries to tell the governments of poor nations to pay their workers more money, improve their working conditions, stop cutting down forests, and build clean factories and democratic institutions. But poor countries need to catch up. This is their Victorian age. They cannot afford to be as soft on people and the environment as richer countries can. And as Lee Kuan Yew loves to point out, democracy is a luxury. To insist on democratic and other human rights is a way for the West to keep the East down. Strong leadership is necessary for economic development.

One might answer this by saying that democracy is not a luxury at all, but the most equitable and effective way to get the best out of people. But apart from that, these criticisms are not entirely spurious. Industrial development in poor countries is inevitably a rougher enterprise than most people in the West would like. Certainly, powerful unions, good wages, clean skies and democratic government are all good things, which must be encouraged, but they are not universal human rights, and they took a long time to be established in the West. In any case, they cannot be imposed on poor countries by western government agencies.

It would make for a more lucid debate if we dropped the language of rights and values, and simply talked about politics. The freedom to elect political representatives, to know what they are doing, to criticise them, and be protected from their whims by law, is the best defence against disastrous policies, which cause human catastrophes. China would undoubtedly be a safer place, both for its own citizens and the outside world, if it were democratically governed. The problem is that the outside world has no effective way to bring it about. US or European (for what that is worth) pressures to improve human rights in China might get a few dissidents out of gaol. And that is good. But they will not change China's political institutions.

It is instructive, though perhaps not comforting to everyone, to look at some of the successes in Asia, as far as democratic change is concerned. In the last 10 years or so, three East Asian countries had non-violent democratic revolutions: the Philippines, South Korea and Taiwan. One could add Thailand at a pinch. And Japan became a functioning democracy after its defeat in World War II. None of these countries has a perfect democracy, to be sure, but all have a more or less free press, free and more or less fair elections and a large degree of legal protection against the use of arbitrary power.

What explains these transformations? Is it culture? Apart from the Philippines and Thailand, all have a Confucian tradition. But to say that Confucianism is especially conducive to democracy is as spurious as to say that it's particularly well suited to authoritarianism. Developmentalists believe that rising affluence leads to democracy. Wealth creates a middle class, which goes on to demand political rights. That would be a fair description of South Korea, but there is nothing automatic about this process, for otherwise rich Malaysia or Singapore should be no less democratic than the Philippines or Thailand.

There is, of course, something all these countries have in common, and that is their close relationship to the United States. Japan was under US occupation; Taiwan and South Korea were under the guardianship of US military forces; Thailand, too, depended for a long time on US aid and security; and the Philippines was a US colony, whose political and business class continued to look to the US for protection. In every case, the democratic changes were started by native elites, supported by the majority of the people, and resisted by local authoritarian regimes. This is where the US made a difference. Well-meaning moralism about human rights would never have got rid of Marcos, Chun Doo Hwan, or martial law in Taiwan. What did the trick was US pressure on client-state regimes to give way. Call this imperialism if you will. But it has done more for Asian liberties than any amount of talk about the superiority of Asian values. ❑

Ian Buruma is a writer and journalist. His latest book is The Missionary and the Libertine: Love and War in East and West *(Faber & Faber 1996)*

---

die tageszeitung

HAPPY BIRTHDAY INDEX

25 years   You have been fighting for the freedom of expression
25 years   You have been the hope of endangered writers, artists and journalists.
You are the source of information not available elsewhere.
For nine years, we have been proud to present *Index on Censorship* to our readers. You have become an institution to them.
We all hope that censorship, the very reason for your work on the magazine, will vanish one day.
But until then we beg you: FIGHT FOR THE RIGHT

...AND PARTY!!!

AUNG SAN SUU KYI

Voice of hope

Burma's opposition leader talks of faith, hope, money and the power of the powerless in Burma

Alan Clements: Daw Suu, what would you say are the main characteristics of the Burmese people — an amazingly diverse culture with over 64 indigenous races and 200 different languages and dialects?

Aung San Suu Kyi: I can't talk as far as the ethnic peoples are concerned, that would be a presumption on my part. I can only talk about the ethnic Burman majority, because that's what I am. There are a great number of ethnic groups in Burma and the Burman are just one of them — the biggest group, we are of Tibeto-Burman stock. I have not studied the cultures of the other ethnic peoples of Burma deeply enough to comment on them, apart from the fact that my mother always taught me to think of them as very close to us, emphasising how loyal they were. She always spoke of them with great respect and warmth.

About the Burmese in Burma, the first thing that comes to mind is the fact that they are Buddhists. But also the fact that not every Burmese is a good Buddhist. Another aspect of the Burmese is that they are a colourful people. I see them in Technicolor, as it were. I think the Burmese do go in not just for colourful clothes but also colourful emotions.

AC: I think many people in the West tend to have a stereotypical notion of southeast Asian countries, especially the less developed nations, as mysterious, alien nations 10,000 miles from our shores. While others often generalise these countries as lands drenched in decades of horror and blood; the wars in Vietnam and Laos, Pol Pot's genocide in Cambodia, Ne Win's 30-odd year brutal dictatorship in your own country and of course, SLORC's ongoing repression. What do you think the common bonds between Burma and western countries are?

Right: Credit: Dean Chapman/Panos Pictures

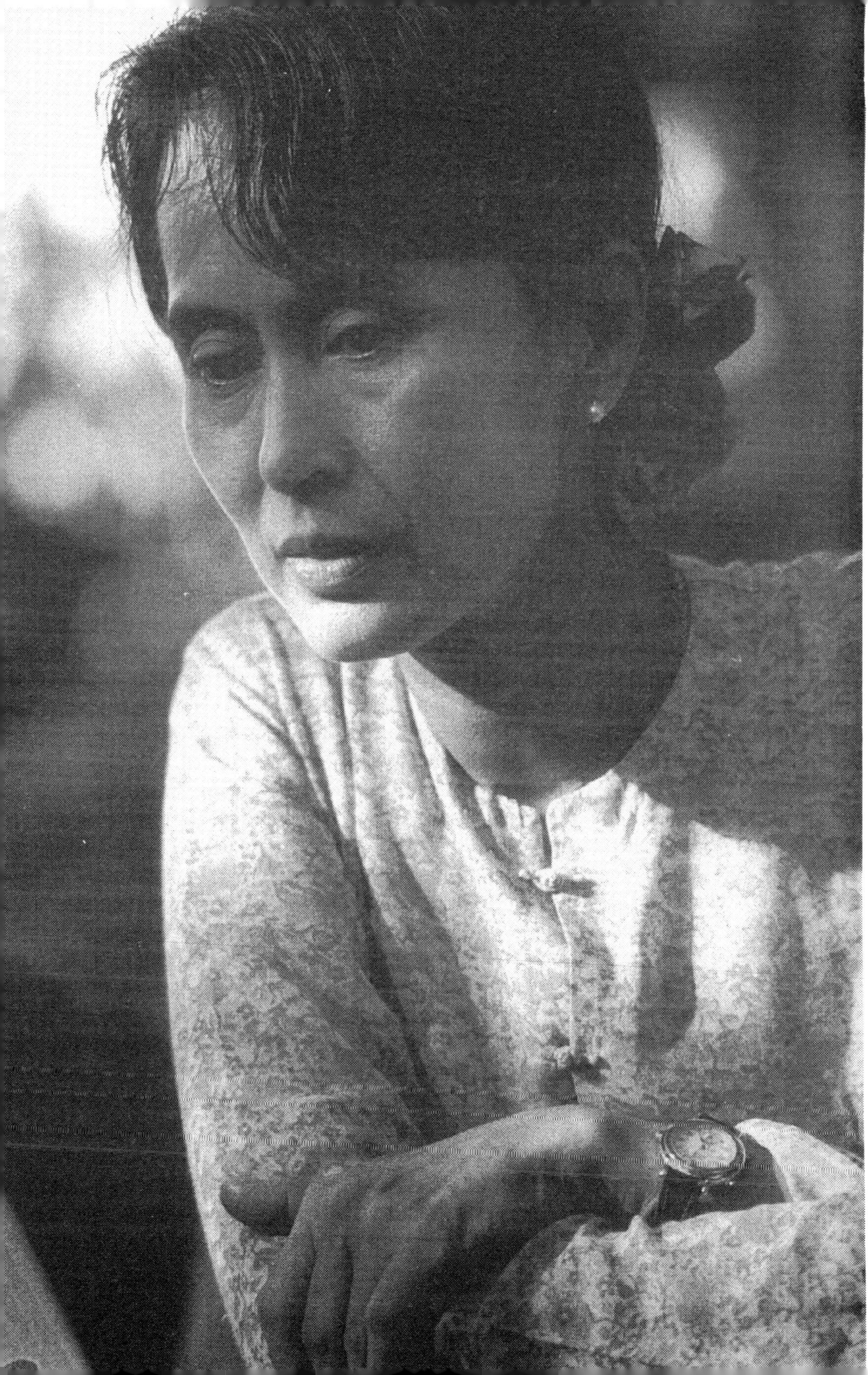

ASSK: Well, our colonial legacy cannot be denied, whether we like it or not. The great majority of existing laws in Burma as well as our educational system were introduced and influenced by the colonial government. The schools, hospitals and railways — all these trappings of colonialism, came to Burma through a western power. Apart from that, I think the Burmese in general are by nature a tolerant race and also very open to other cultures and ideas. But we have been made intolerant by the authoritarian system which has been imposed upon us.

★★★

AC: It's a matter of debate, but politics and religion are usually segregated issues. In Burma today, the large portion of monks and nuns see spiritual freedom and socio-political freedom as separate areas. But, in truth, dharma *and politics are rooted in the same issue — freedom.*

ASSK: Indeed, but this is not unique to Burma. Everywhere you'll find this drive to separate the secular from the spiritual. In other Buddhist countries you'll find the same thing — in Thailand, Sri Lanka, in Mahayana Buddhist countries, in Christian countries, almost everywhere in the world. I think some people find it embarrassing and impractical to think of the spiritual and political life as one. I do not see them as separate. In democracies there is always a drive to separate the spiritual from the secular, but it is not actually required to separate them. Whereas, in many dictatorships, you'll find that there is an official policy to keep politics and religion apart, in case, I suppose, it is used to upset the status quo.

AC: Burma has a long history of monks and nuns being actively engaged in political areas when it concerns the welfare of the people. With the crisis at such a critical moment, do you think that the Sangha *— the order of monks and nuns — can play a greater role in supporting the democracy movement? After all, it's their freedom too.*

ASSK: Well, there are a lot of monks and nuns who have played a very courageous role in our movement for democracy. Of course, I would like to see everybody taking a much more significant role in the movement, not just monks and nuns. After all, there is nothing in democracy that any Buddhist could object to. I think that monks and nuns, like everybody else, have a duty to promote what is good and desirable. And I do think they could be more reflective. In fact, they should help as far as they can.

I do believe in 'engaged Buddhism', to use a modern term.

AC: How might they be more effective?

ASSK: Simply by preaching democratic principles, by encouraging everybody to work for democracy and human rights, and by trying to persuade the authorities to begin dialogue. It would be a great help if every monk and nun in the country were to say, 'What we want to see is dialogue.' After all, that is the way of the Buddha. He encouraged the *Sangha* to talk to each other. He said, 'You can't live like dumb animals. And if you have offended each other, you expiate your sins and offences by confessing them and apologising.'

★★★

AC: President Mandela writes in his autobiography A Long Walk to Freedom *that in 1961 'the days of non-violent struggle were over... We had no choice but to turn to violence.' To substantiate his turn away from non-violence to violence he cited an old African expression, 'The attacks of the wild beast cannot be adverted only with bare hands.' Nevertheless, there were some within the ANC who argued that non-violence was an inviolate principle, not a tactic that should be abandoned when it no longer worked. To this Mr Mandela countered: '[I] believed exactly the opposite... non-violence was a tactic that should be abandoned when it no longer worked... And it was wrong and immoral to subject our people to armed attacks by the state without offering them some kind of alternative.' But, if I am correct, you see non-violent political activism as a moral and spiritual principle and not merely as a political tactic?*

ASSK: No, not exactly. It's also a political tactic. Military coups, which have happened enough in Burma, are violent ways of changing situations and I do not want to encourage and to perpetuate this tradition of bringing about change through violence. Because I'm afraid that if we achieve democracy in this way we will never be able to get rid of the idea that you bring about necessary changes through violence. The very method would be threatening us all the time. Because there are always people who do not agree with democracy. And if we achieve it through violent means, there will be the hard core of those who have always been against the democracy movement who will think, 'It was through violence that they changed the system and if we can develop our own methods of violence which are superior to theirs, we can get back the power.' And we'll go on in this vicious cycle. For me it is as much a political tactic as a spiritual belief, that violence is not the right way. It would simply not assist us in building up a strong democracy.

We have always said that we will never disown those students and others who have taken up violence. We know that their aim is the same as ours. They want democracy and they think the best way to go about it is through armed struggle. And we do not say that we have the monopoly on the right methods of achieving what we want. Also, we cannot guarantee their security. We can't say, 'Follow us in the way of non-violence and you'll be protected,' or that we'll get there without any casualties. That's a promise we can't make. We have chosen the way of non-violence simply because we think it's politically better for the country in the long run to establish that you can bring about change without the use of arms. This has been a clear NLD policy from the beginning.

★★★

AC: The SLORC chairman, General Than Shwe, has been in Bangkok attending the ASEAN [Association of South-East Asian Nations] conference at the invitation of Thailand. Often, such conferences as this one neglect the role of 'human rights' for the sake of economic interests, which generally means self-interest. Take for example the American administration's policy towards China. What do you think of this need of some world leaders to separate money and profits from people and human values?

ASSK: It's a totally artificial separation.

AC: But why do you think so many political leaders insist on this 'artificial' separation as a matter of firm national policy?

ASSK: It's because certain systems which are not what one would call wholly democratic have achieved economic success. There has come about a school of thought that economic success is totally divorced from political freedoms. But, I think, there are other reasons for economic success. Take Singapore for example. I think there are two basic reasons for their economic success. One is that they have had a government which is not corrupt. Nobody can accuse them of corruption. They may not be wholly democratic in the way in which some of us see democracy but they are not corrupt. Secondly, they have put a great value on education and have done everything they can to raise its standard. So I think it's wrong to equate Singapore's economic success to the fact that it's not wholly a democracy. It makes much more sense to link its success to the fact that it has an intelligent, upright government, along with an excellent educational system. I think we're getting our values and equations wrong.

AC: Certain business people and politicians argue that investment in Burma is good because it creates a middle class and, therefore, the most expedient way to usher in democracy. How would you respond to this argument?

ASSK: Investments in Burma during the last seven years [from the time of SLORC taking power] have done nothing to create a stronger middle class. There are a few people who have got very rich, and a rapidly increasing pool of the very poor. The great majority of civil servants, who should normally be part of the middle class, are struggling to get on with their lives. Their salaries are so low compared to the cost of living they have to choose between corruption and starvation.

AC: SLORC presents a grotesquely inaccurate picture of reality in your country to its own people. No-one believes SLORC's newspaper or television reports. The vast majority of the population today rely on your weekend talks for the truth and an analysis of the facts. Are tapes and videos of your talks getting out into the rural areas?

ASSK: I believe so. But people can learn the truth in a variety of ways. For example, everybody was very grateful because the official Burmese media broadcast the whole speech of their ambassador to the United Nations. It gave them a chance to find out what was actually in the resolution *(laughing)*. Otherwise, they would not have known. So truth 'won out' in some way or another.

★★★

AC: We discussed earlier how insecurity was the root psychology of authoritarian regimes — a mistrust of one's own dignity, one's self-worth, and therefore a mistrust of others. I would like to ask you about finding power in vulnerability, rather than seeing it as a weakness. From where does true power originate?

ASSK: The 'power of the powerless' as Vaclav Havel said. I think power comes from within. If you have confidence in what you are doing and you are shored up by the belief that what you are doing is right, that in itself constitutes power, and this power is very important when you are trying to achieve something. If you don't believe in what you are doing, your actions will lack credibility. However hard you try, inconsistencies will appear.

AC: I know that you have a high regard for President Havel. May I ask how he has influenced you as a leader?

ASSK: Well, I've read his writings of course. He has really affected me indirectly, in the sense that it's what he wrote about how it was in Czechoslovakia that influenced me. But what impressed me most about Czechoslovakia was the intellectual honesty that some of the best people maintained. They would rather be plumbers, roadworkers, street-cleaners and bricklayers, than compromise their intellectual integrity by joining a university or the government. They accepted the superiority of the mind over the body and placed the importance of intellectual integrity far above that of material comfort. That has inspired me a great deal, and I think this is a wonderful example of what you can achieve when you try to maintain your spiritual and intellectual integrity. ❑

Aung San Suu Kyi *founded the National League for Democracy in 1988. The following year she was put under house arrest, from where she led her party to a landslide victory in the May 1990 elections, which were annulled by the ruling State Law and Order Council. In 1991, she was awarded the Nobel Peace Prize* **Alan Clements** *is the founder and co-director of the Burma Project USA and one of the world's foremost experts on Burma's democracy movement. He lived in Burma for nearly eight years of which five were spent living as a buddhist monk in Rangoon. His books include* Burma: The Next Killing Fields? *(1991) and the photographic book* Burma's Revolution of the Spirit *(1994)*

© *Excerpted from* The Voice of Hope, Conversations with Alan Clements, *by Aung San Suu Kyi, to be published by Penguin Books (UK) on 29 May, price £7.99*

Right, above: Tribal woman in the village of Ludia, Gujarat/Kutch, India
Credit: Heldur Netocny/Panos Pictures

URVASHI BUTALIA

Indian voices

INDEPENDENT INDIA is 50 years old this year and the nation is back in literature. All over India publishers are gearing up to produce books which look back at half a century of nationhood.

For the state, this is a time to celebrate what it sees as its 'achievements': a reasonable economy, an increase in food production, a functioning democracy. For others — peasants, workers, students, activists, women — a time to look back and ask: has anything actually been achieved? Poverty continues to dog us; ethnic strife is now so common that people seem to have become indifferent; identities have become so polarised on religious issues can we still continue to think of ourselves as a nation? In today's India, the 'nation' is an elusive thing. Other than in TV commercials which celebrating India's plurality and at the odd ceremonial event you hardly get a glimpse of it.

In the early part of this century, the nation, as many Indians rather than outsiders saw it, formed the basis of much writing. Literature at the time was preoccupied with asserting an Indian 'nationness' and writers wrote with the awareness that their work could be, and often would be, pressed into the service of the nation.

With independence came its dark side: Partition. Suddenly the nation became a fragile thing: the sense of community built up over years of living in a kind of social contract disappeared. At the same time, literature, particularly in north and east India and in its languages — Urdu, Punjabi, Hindi, Bengali and English — continued to be dominated by the cataclysmic events of 1947. Nationalism in literature became 'a nationalism of mourning', of valediction: for the peace that was lost, for the sense of community that was shattered.

But much of that has changed today. Over the years, and quite apart from what the Hindu right-wing would have us believe — that there is a common enemy, the Muslim, and that the only real nation is the Hindu nation — it's become clear that the nation is not a unitary concept. It can mean different things to different people: all things to some, nothing to others. And there's some truth in the cliché that India is not one nation, but many nations, or peoples, or communities or all of those. Nor, once again despite the attempts of the right, is literature produced from a single source, a single impetus.

It is this that the rich literature of India reflects in its many languages. And that the languages themselves save from an obsession with the idea of nation. But while it may be possible to say that the nation is too elusive a concept, and literatures in a country as vast and heterogeneous as India simply too diverse, too different to be seen as the 'national allegories' to which one well-known critic consigned all Third World texts, there is an interesting twist to the tale. While it's difficult to pin down the nation in literature — for the nation itself is in question — it's relatively easier to pin down what is anti-nation. Any number of books are taken off the shelves, banned, proscribed, for being 'anti-national' or 'harmful' to the interests of the 'nation'.

Today, the nation is back, but it's a temporary return. No sooner will the fiftieth anniversary be out of the door, than Indian literature will be back to being its vast, heterogeneous, diverse self — if, that is, we look at Indian literature in all its languages and not only at English. ❑

Urvashi Butalia *is a founder of the publishing house Kali for Women, Delhi*

Right: Credit: Stephen Dupont/Panos Pictures

Outsiders

CHINWEIZU

Black redemption

To the memory of General Mohammed Farrah Aidid (1934-1996), valiant defender, in Somalia, of the Black World's right to sovereignty — and to all those who come after

The attitude of the white race is to subjugate, to exploit, and if necessary exterminate the weaker peoples with whom they come in contact —
Marcus Garvey

MY CONSTITUENCY in global matters is the Black World and its prospects under the so-called New World Order that some people are busy constructing.

As matters stand today, the Black World does not have much of a future left. In the fierce, global race war which has been raging since Columbus; in the theatre of that race war where the European World and the Black World have been locked in vicious combat for five centuries, a new and decisive campaign has been quietly launched by the overlords of the Eurocentric Global Order (EGO). After five terrible centuries in which the European World inflicted defeat after defeat on the Black World — first slavery, then colonialism, and then neocolonialism — the overlords have now sentenced the Black World to extermination of the sort inflicted on the Black Tasmanians and the Native Americans.

To make clear what they have decreed for the Black World, and why, we must reach back to the early 1970s, to something called the triage plan, and then forward to a campaign, which became public in the 1990s, to recolonise the Black World and Black Africa in particular.

Back in the days of the Trilateral Commission, an outfit calling itself

The Club of Rome sponsored computer studies of the Earth's resources. The first of these, *Limits to Growth*, drew attention to the fact that there were not enough resources on earth to sustain unlimited economic growth. By the time the debate it triggered on what was to be done had tapered off in the late 1970s, a great solution had been devised. This was the triage plan.

In the course of managing the OPEC oil crisis, and of defeating the Third World campaign for a New International Economic Order, Henry Kissinger, chief US foreign policy adviser at that time, floated the idea of a Fourth World of basket-case economies which would be spun off the global system and consigned to oblivion. That was one version of the triage plan. Actually, Kissinger's version merely proposed to globalise what the USA had done with its American Indian Reservations, what Australia had done with its aboriginal reserves, and what South Africa was then attempting with its Bantustans. Such economic triage, by forcibly leaving a people with grossly inadequate resources for self-sustenance, is a method of slow genocide. Compared to others mooted at the time which proposed mass murder on a horrendous scale, even a few nuclear bombs, Kissinger's proposal was quite mild.

At the heart of the triage plan is the fact that the American Dream cannot be globalised. The Earth just cannot sustain it. It cannot even be realised by a majority of the people now on earth. It was based, even back in the early 1970s, on six per cent of the global population consuming 40 per cent of global resources. Even at that rate, probably superseded by now, by the time a mere 15 per cent of the human population reached the US rate of resource consumption, there would be nothing left for the remaining 85 per cent. The spread of the American Dream requires a drastic depopulation of the globe. If even another 35 per cent were kept alive as helots to mine the ores and grow the crops (as in that slave-owning Athenian democracy which is the European World's ideal), that would still require the extermination of 50 per cent of humanity.

George Bush, that eloquent apostle of the New World Order, has been reported as saying: 'We need Africa, but not with the Africans.' Does it now become clear why Black Africa is a prime target of their population control squads, despite its comparatively very low population density? (Europe is four times more crowded than Black Africa; China six times; India 12 times; and Japan 18 times.) Or is it by chance that Haiti and Central Africa became the epicentres of the AIDS pandemic? Anyone who thinks that triage by epidemic has not begun should think again. For, rather than use the nuclear bomb for the planned extermination, they have started with the AIDS bomb. And bombs of other kinds are on the shelves, ready for employment against those targeted for triage.

In short, the triage plan intends for Blacks exactly what the Nazis attempted on the Jews in Europe, and what the Yankees inflicted on the native Americans, and what the Australians accomplished on the aboriginal Tasmanians: namely, extermination or drastic depopulation.

The conspiracy to recolonise the Black World went public in 1994 when the press in the UK and the USA began debating its pros and cons. The point in colonisation, a century ago, was to have white officials organise the intensive exploitation of Black Africa's resources and labour; the point in recolonisation a century later, is to put white officials in charge of whatever may be required to shove Black Africans into Kissinger's Fourth World, or finally to exterminate them. After all, not even the most stupid of Black rulers can be trusted to execute faithfully a programme that would put him out of business and his race out of existence.

By 1994, most of the groundwork for recolonisation had been laid, and the job of preparing the public mind for it could begin. The media debate flew a kite, tested the waters and, given that there was no general and resounding outcry against the idea, not even from the Black world, and that the trial runs in Somalia (1992) and Haiti (1994) were cheered by the media all over the world, including the media of the Black World, established that there is no public relations obstacle to recolonisation. It can proceed full blast, to loud cheers on all sides, whenever the imperialist powers issue the appropriate orders.

Why are we the chosen targets of triage at this time? Because we have become strategically vulnerable as never before, due to three conditions which have converged for the first time ever. First, their globalised economy does not need Blacks any more, whether as labourers or as consumers, whereas for five centuries it always needed at least our labour. Second, their economy needs the resources from the land we call our own. Third, we are too weak to stop them from permanently seizing our resources by exterminating us. Thus, at the end of the twentieth century we have allowed ourselves to arrive at the same deadly situation as the Native Americans found themselves in during the sixteenth century when more than 90 per cent of them were wiped out by bullets and by deliberately induced epidemics. For example: in Mexico, 24 million out of 25 million (96 per cent) were wiped out; in Hispaniola, today's Haiti and Dominican Republic, over 99 per cent were wiped out. If we do nothing, or not enough, the same will happen to us in the twenty-first century.

The Black World today is in mortal danger. The most serious aspects of that danger, however, are not the intentions of our enemies; rather, they are the Black World's wilful blindness to the signs of that danger, and its unwillingness to even accept its possibility. Two years after the imperialists publicly aired their intention to recolonise Black Africa, and four years after George Bush made the first brazen attempt at recolonisation in Somalia, the Black World's elite shows no sign of taking the matter seriously. In fact, it shows no sign of having noticed the threat at all!

Have Blacks not yet learnt the central lesson of the last 500 years of global history: that if a people sit upon great resources and neglect to build the power to defend themselves, then their goose is cooked whenever the powerful want those resources? For they are expelled, or even killed off, whenever the Whites want whatever land or resources their 'reservations' occupy, witness the case of the Amazon rain forest where their extermination is proceeding despite all the protest it had evoked around the world. Or is it that our Black World elite think that if they ignore the danger it will go away?

To those whose unthinking reaction to the threat is 'It can't happen!', I should address the following questions: if the armies of the White World should invade the Black World tomorrow morning to make good George Bush's desire to have our land without us, what is to stop them? What armies or nuclear weapons do you have that can stop them? And even if you hastily put together armies and volunteers that are heroically determined, where would they get their weapons? And what happens when the arms merchants of the entire Pan-European World, from Vladivostok to Vancouver, refuse to resupply whatever you now have in hand? Where are your steel mills and electronic factories and rubber industries? Where are your factories for guns and tanks and trucks and ships and aircraft and nuclear bombs and ballistic missiles? Who built your barracks and bunkers? Who made the maps your troops will use? Who trained your soldiers and shaped their minds and made their doctrines for them? What do you have or know that the White World does not know about? So how could you possibly prevent them from exterminating you and taking your entire land whenever they choose?

THE first task in responding to the challenge before us is to reappraise our geohistorical situation and clear our minds of all manner of obfuscations, delusions and diversions. I propose to start by focusing on the following doctrines: that to lose sovereignty is to lose everything; that the Black World has been in a Race War with the White World, and for five centuries so far, without acknowledging it; that without industrialisation, the Black World cannot sustain its sovereignty or win the race war; that the Black World's security concerns must focus on the EGO as the systemic source of our strategic insecurity; that no Black state can guarantee its own security, hence a collective security system is imperative.

A people's sovereignty is their most precious possession, even more precious than their land; for without their sovereignty, they cannot hold on to their land; without their sovereignty, they can be deprived even of the opportunity to breathe the free fresh air. Sensible people risk their last ounce of treasure and their last drop of blood to protect or recover their sovereignty; fools part lightly with it. And how incomparably precious it is becomes painfully felt only when dispossession, enslavement and extermination stare its losers in the face. Yet, history records that some threw it away in a fit of delusion, and some signed it away for a mess of porridge, and some bartered it away for temporary advantage in some local rivalry or strife. But once it was lost, they paid bitterly for their folly. African history offers many examples during the European invasion a century ago. To cite just one: in February 1888, in exchange for British friendship, Lobengula, King of the Amandebele, in what is today Zimbabwe, signed away his sovereign right to communicate with any 'foreign State or Power'. Then in October 1888, for 1,000 guns and 100,000 cartridges, plus a monthly payment of £100, he signed away to Cecil Rhodes all the metals and minerals in his country, together with 'full power to do all things that they may deem necessary to win and procure the same, and to hold, collect and enjoy the profits and revenues, if any, derivable from the said metals and minerals.' Before long, he regretted his folly. In the end, his nation had to fight to hold on to the sovereignty he had signed away. When they lost that war, the Amandebele lamented:

> Our country is gone, our cattle have gone, our people are scattered, we have nothing to live for, our women are deserting us; the white man does as he likes with them; we are the slaves of the white man, we are nobody and have no rights or laws of any kind.

Cecil Rhodes in Rhodesia sketch by 'an officer with the Imperial Forces' — Credit: Camera Press

They were to lose much more: their religion, customary liberties, political rights, etc. Not till a century later, in 1980, after another generation had fought a bloody war against the British settlers, did they regain the power to rule themselves. And till this day, they have yet to get back most of the land the White settlers expropriated from them.

All in all, to be without sovereignty is like being roofless in a storm while surrounded by menacing predators. Those who permit their sovereignty to be undermined or blown away have only themselves to blame for whatever horrors befall them.

The Black Race has been embroiled in a Race War with the White Race for much longer than five centuries; but the present phase began in the fifteenth century with the overseas expansion of the Europeans.

To appreciate the point that the Black and the White worlds have been at race war since the fifteenth century, we need to be quite clear and precise on the experiences and processes that are hidden under conventional names like the slave trade, colonialism, neocolonialism, and racism.

When the era is examined, what do we find? The two main features of the so-called Slave Trade were interminable wars and forced labour; the targets of both were the Black Race; and the entire thing was organised by Whites of European stock who were its prime beneficiaries. In its search for labour, Europe took war to the Black Race; Europeans went to Africa as deliberate war provocateurs, committed and suborned war acts and craftily fomented wars in order to stimulate a harvest of war prisoners. These they then carried into captivity across the waters, converted them into chattel-slaves and put them to toil under a system of state and private terrorism. For example, according to E D Morel in *The Black Man's Burden* (1969), 'For a hundred years slaves in Barbados were mutilated, tortured, gibbeted alive and left to starve to death, burnt alive, flung into coppers of boiling sugar, whipped to death.'

For four centuries, from Columbus' arrival in 1492 till the last act of emancipation in the 1890s, the Americas were a vast forced-labour camp for Black prisoners of war, vaster than Siberia with all its Gulags. In the eyes of the operators of this war system, these captives were chattels, things excluded from humanity and from the polity, the legal equals of cattle and pigs and pots and pans. All Blacks were livestock, beasts of burden to be hunted, corralled, marched to market, bought and sold, broken and tamed and stripped of human culture, and then worked to death and replaced by another breathing tool.

The era of so-called colonialism was ushered in by two distinct and antithetical processes: the emancipation of the slaves in the diaspora, and the invasion and conquest of Africa by European powers. With emancipation, the White Race ceased to officially regard the Black Race as chattel, as chattel-in-the-corral and chattel-in-the-wild. All were admitted into humanity, even if in a handicapped or lower status. For the alleged privilege of being tutored in the ways of civilisation, Blacks were subjected to genocide, terrorism, and expropriation, property confiscation, forced labour and taxation. Everywhere, white armies, white terror squads, white bureaucrats, white politicians, white employers and white society sat upon the conquered Black Race.

This so-called colonialism was, in reality, helotism, a Spartan-type despotism maintained by an ambience of raw terror. Whether called Jim Crow or Racial Segregation in the USA, Separate Development or Apartheid in South Africa, *Assimilation* and *Indigenat* in the French colonies, *Assimilado* and *Indigenato* in the Portuguese colonies, *Patronato de Indigenas* in Spanish colonies or Colour Bar in the British colonies, these were merely varieties of the same system of legalised servitude for the Black helots. Black labour, initially obtained by physical force, was subsequently channelled into a legalised system of low wages, or even of starvation wages, for the Black helots. It was a system of immiseration maintained by raw, white terror. It was the helotic phase of the Race War, and should be so recognised.

WORLD War I, the Bolshevik Revolution in Russia, World War II and the Cold War which followed it combined to drastically shorten the period of this helotism. Sensing the weakness of their master, and discovering a new and strong ally in the Soviet Union, the helotised Blacks sought to reverse their recent and thorough defeat. Appraising the new situation, and fearful of losing all in a storm of agitation and insurrection backed by Soviet power, most of the European conquerors made concessions to their restive Blacks.

First of all, the Black helots were admitted to full human status, and accorded human rights in keeping with the UN Charter of 1945. The stateapparatus of each colony was then handed over to a trans-civilised elite of Black politicians and soldiers, who had been carefully bred and culled from among the helots; they were to supervise it on behalf of the White conquerors. In 1960 alone, the great year of freedom, 17 countries in Black

CHINWEIZU

Africa were granted self-rule. Where these political concessions were delayed, the Black Helots took to insurrection, and even to full scale wars of liberation, which they eventually won against Pan-European armies.

Even in the USA, Cold War exigencies obliged the Whites to retreat from overt manifestations of White Supremacy. Thus, in the mid-1960s, after a decade of great agitation, Blacks there were reluctantly readmitted to that full citizenship which had been granted them a century before, at Emancipation, but which had been quickly annulled. And after its Portuguese-ruled neighbours fell to Black liberation armies in 1975, a USA-style retreat from helotism was orchestrated for the unabashedly White Supremacist Republic of South Africa, and Black-majority rule was eventually installed there in 1994. And so it came to pass that Blacks were everywhere installed as administrators of the countries into which the Black World had been carved by white power. This partially reversed the military and political defeats which the Black World had suffered in the helotisation wars of the last decade of the nineteenth century.

However, this Black World counter-offensive had not even been completed, had not even consolidated its very limited gains, when the Pan-European World launched its recolonisation offensive, beginning spectacularly in Somalia in 1992. The five-centuries-old Race War continues. And with their determination to implement extermination through triage, the race war will get even more nasty.

Historically, pre-industrial societies have not withstood assaults from the industrial powers unless they quickly industrialised or acquired a reliable supply of the industrial sinews of war. If it fails to industrialise, how can Africa guarantee the sinews of war with which to deter or defeat recolonisation and extermination whenever the industrial giants launch their planned attack?

Today, it is industrialise or die, not just industrialise or be enslaved; to refuse to industrialise is to refuse to adapt to meet an unprecedented and final danger. Today, more than ever before, the Black World needs its Meiji generation, its Mao generation, its Stalin generation, its Ataturk generation to reconstruct it for industrial power; failing which, it shall perish.

For five centuries, our strategic insecurity has derived from our subordinate integration into the EGO. By constraining us to produce and export raw materials and import manufactures, it keeps us maldeveloped; by holding us in its economic cage and stimulating our appetites while ruthlessly reducing our purchasing power, the EGO sharpens the competition for crumbs within and between our nations and states. We are so engrossed in these inter-personal, inter-ethnic, and inter-locality competitions that we fail to focus on the danger which the EGO poses for us all. Besides, propaganda from the EGO diverts our attention from the EGO's contribution to our plight, and helps to focus our antagonisms on one another. Because it imposes the conditions which generate the tensions under which we live most insecurely, the EGO — including its Global Information System which, through its advertising, movies, news, pornography and propaganda, afflicts us with consumania, importmania, alienation, self-doubt and disorientation, and its UN Political System which insists on eroding our sovereignty — remains the systemic source of our lack of security. Any Black World security concern that does not principally focus on the EGO, and on its multi-dimensional threat to the Black World, is not just obtuse but suicidal.

Only a strongly organised bloc of states, led by a great power (such as the Soviet Bloc used to be) can long withstand the determined hostility of the imperialist overlords of the EGO. Needless to say, no Black state has the resources or capabilities that the Soviet Union had, or that China has. Only the Black World as a whole has resources of an appropriate order of magnitude: a population of some 800 million; a continental-size heartland — sub-Saharan Africa; a diaspora which could become our equivalent of China's Overseas Chinese. However, these potentials still need to be organised. The clear implication of all this is that the Black World must quickly and durably put together a collective security alliance to protect itself and its civilisation, a civilisation 70 centuries old, the oldest on earth. ❑

© *Chinweizu, September 1996*

Chinweizu *is a Nigerian writer and journalist. He is the author of many books, most notably* The West and the Rest of Us *(2nd edition 1987)*

Camp for African refugees, Ceuta, Spain

KENAN MALIK

The perils of pluralism

A re-examination of the terms of engagement between races and cultures, and a plea for equality

THERE are few beliefs more entrenched in the modern liberal imagination than that of the virtues of pluralism and a multicultural society. The degree to which Sarajevo has assumed symbolic significance expresses the measure of attachment to the principles of a multicultural, multiethnic community. Just as in the thirties the struggle for Barcelona during the Spanish Civil War became symbolic of the defence of democracy against fascism, so the siege of Sarajevo has assumed a mythic status as a struggle between pluralism and barbarism. On the other hand there are few crimes which contemporary society regards as more monstrous than that of 'ethnic cleansing', the attempt to eliminate diversity and difference and to create an ethnically and culturally homogenous society. From Bosnia to Rwanda the forcible expulsion of rival ethnic groups has become the measure of the breakdown of civilised values.

Belief in pluralism and the multicultural society is so much woven into the fabric of our lives that we rarely stand back to question some of its assumptions. They are seen as self-evidently good. As the American academic, and former critic of pluralism, Nathan Glazer puts it in the title of a new book, *We are All Multiculturalists Now*. The celebration of difference, the promotion of a diverse society, tolerance for a variety of cultural identities — these are seen by almost everyone as the hallmarks of a decent, liberal, democratic, non-racist society.

I want in this essay to question this easy assumption that pluralism is self-evidently good. I want to show, rather, that the notion of pluralism is a deeply ambiguous one; that the idea of difference has always been at the heart, not of the antiracist, but of the racist agenda; and that the creation of a 'multiculturalist' society has been at the expense of a more equal one.

Even a superficial look at the idea of pluralism reveals how ambiguous a notion it is. Sarajevo may be a symbol of multiculturalism; but it was the assertion of 'difference' that originally led to the break-up of the Yugoslav federation and to a savage civil war. The far right in France has long adroitly exploited the idea of cultural difference to argue against the possibility of Muslims becoming French. The Council of Europe's campaign against racism and xenophobia has adopted a slogan — 'All equal, all different' — that a generation ago was the battle cry of segregationists in the American south and of apologists for apartheid in South Africa.

If such examples reveal the difficulty in drawing a line between respect for difference and contempt for the Other, then the US philosopher Richard Rorty suggests that advocacy of pluralism may be inimical to the pursuit of equality. Pluralism, he observes, places what he calls 'Enlightenment liberals' in a terrible dilemma:

> Their liberalism forces them to call any doubts about human equality a result of irrational bias. Yet their connoisseurship [of pluralism] forces them to realise that most of the globe's inhabitants do not believe in equality, that such a belief is a western eccentricity. Since they think it would be shockingly ethnocentric to say 'So what? We western liberals do believe in it and so much the better for us', they are stuck.

Rorty himself solves the dilemma by arguing that equality is good for 'us' but not necessarily for 'them'. This is in line with the argument of many liberals today who want to redefine equality to fit in with a more pluralistic world. But when respect for others means a refusal to judge others' values or norms, when backward habits, reactionary institutions and illogical beliefs are defended on the grounds that they may not make much sense in our culture but they do in others', then the pursuit of difference has turned into indifference, into a callous disregard for the fate of others on the grounds that they are 'not like us'. Rorty is right to suggest that pluralism and equality make conflicting demands on society. The answer, however, is not to abandon our commitment to equality but to rethink what we mean by pluralism.

The promotion of 'difference', far from being an antiracist principle, has from the start been at the heart of the racial agenda. Ever since the Enlightenment, western thinkers and policy makers have wrestled with the contradiction of societies that express a deep-seated belief in, and respect for, equality and yet are themselves profoundly unequal. Out of this contradiction the ideology of race developed. Racial theory attempted to explain the gulf between an abstract attachment to equality and the reality of social inequality by suggesting that inequality itself was naturally given. Society was unequal because the destiny of every social group was in some way linked to intrinsic qualities that each possessed. For racial theorists the nature of a society was explained by the differences it embodied.

In the nineteenth century, group differences were seen largely as biological in nature — as in the ideology of scientific racism. Today those differences are more often than not seen as cultural. The horrors of Nazism and the Holocaust helped discredit racial science and biological theories of human differences. But if, in the post-war world, racial science was buried, racial thinking was not. The biological arguments for racial superiority were thrown into disrepute and overt expressions of racism were discredited. All the assumptions of racial thinking, however, were maintained intact — in particular the belief that humanity can be divided into discrete groups; that each group should be considered in its own terms; that each is in some way incommensurate with the others; and that the important relationships in society arise not out of commonalties but out of the differences between groups. The form of racial thinking, however, changed. It was cast not in biological terms but in the language of cultural pluralism. At the policy level this led to the pursuit of 'multiculturalism' as a desirable social goal.

The concept of a multicultural society developed in the post-war world largely in response to the impact of mass immigration into western societies. Eleven million workers came to Europe in the 1950s and 1960s, encouraged by an economic boom. In the USA a different kind of mass migration took place — the huge movement of African Americans to the northern cities in the fifties and sixties. In both cases the newcomers found themselves on the margins of society, subject to racism and discrimination, and unable to gain access to levers of power. The ideology of multiculturalism developed as an accommodation to the persistence of inequalities despite the rhetoric of integration, assimilation and equality.

In the United States of the 1960s, for instance, most commentators, both black and white, hoped and expected that African American migrants to the north would eventually integrate into US society, as fully as had European immigrants. The title of a 1966 article by Irving Kristol in the *New York Times* captured that hope: 'The Negro Today is like the Immigrant Yesterday.' Three decades later we can see how sadly misplaced were such claims. Virtually every social statistic — from housing segregation to rates of intermarriage, from infant mortality rates to language use — shows that African Americans live very different lives to the rest of America. The experience even of Hispanic Americans is far closer to that of American whites than it is to that of African Americans.

The failure of the movement for equality has led to the celebration of difference. The black American critic bell hooks observes that 'civil rights reform reinforced the idea that black liberation should be defined by the degree to which black people gained equal access to material opportunities and privileges to whites — jobs, housing, schooling etc.' This strategy could never bring about liberation, argues hooks, because such 'ideas of "freedom" were informed by efforts to imitate the behaviour, lifestyles and most importantly the values and consciousness of white colonisers'. The failure of equality has led radical critics like hooks to declare that equality itself is problematic because African Americans are 'different' from whites.

Politicians and policy-makers have responded to such arguments by reinventing the United States as a 'multicultural' nation. Multiculturalism is premised on the idea that it is a nation composed of many different cultural groups and peoples. But in reality it is the product of the continued exclusion of one group: African Americans. The promotion of multiculturalism is a tacit admission that the barriers that separate blacks and whites cannot be breached and that equality has been abandoned as a social policy goal. 'Multiculturalism', Nathan Glazer has written, 'is the price America is paying for the inability or unwillingness to incorporate into its society African Americans, in the same way and to the same degree it has incorporated so many other groups.' The real price, however, is being paid by African Americans themselves. For in truth America is not multicultural; it is simply unequal. And the promotion of multiculturalism is an acknowledgement of the inevitability of that inequality.

The 'apartness' of black and immigrant communities in western Europe is probably not so great as that of African Americas in the USA. Nevertheless, here too pluralism has become a means to avoid debate about the failure of equality. As black communities have remained excluded from mainstream society, subject to discrimination and often clinging to old habits and lifestyles as a familiar anchor in a hostile world, so such differences have become rationalised not as the negative product of racism but as the positive result of pluralism.

Many young people in Marseilles or East London call themselves Muslim, for instance, less because of religious faith or cultural habits, than because in the face of a hostile, anti-Muslim society, calling oneself Muslim is a way of defending the dignity of one's community. Their Islam

Pluralism has become a means of avoiding debate about the failure of equality... In describing such fractured societies as 'multicultural', we are in danger of celebrating the differences that are imposed by a racist society

is not the free celebration of an identity, but an attempt to negotiate a difficult relationship with a hostile society as best they can. Muslims in London or Paris no more choose their 'difference' than African American youth do in the Bronx or South Central LA — or indeed Jews did in Nazi Germany. As one Muslim activist from Bradford put it, 'Our Islam is constructed by the strength of anti-Muslim hysteria in this country.' In describing such fractured societies as 'multicultural' we are in danger of celebrating the differences that are imposed by a racist society.

It is useful to compare the experience of post-war immigrants — and of African American migrants to northern cities in the USA — with earlier waves of immigration into Europe and America. Between the 1890s and the 1920s there was a large influx of east Europeans into Britain, of Italians and Portuguese into France, and of east and south Europeans into the USA. These newcomers were often met with the same hostility as greeted post-war black immigrants. They too were condemned as alien, as less intelligent, as immoral and promiscuous, as given to violence, drugs and drink.

Yet they eventually became integrated into the host nations, and unlike today no one regarded their presence as presaging the creation of a 'multicultural' society. The contrast between the experience of pre-war and post-war immigration lies less with the immigrants themselves than with the host societies. Three major changes in society have made the pursuit of integration and equality that much more difficult. First, the material capacity of society to provide equality has been eroded. The recessions that have hit western economies since the 1970s has helped entrench the marginalisation of black immigrants and of African American migrants.

Second, the idea of a common culture has weakened. The break-up of the post-war consensus and the end of the Cold War has created a fragile and anxious mood, in which the idea of a coherent national identity has become problematic. Particularly in the USA, the Cold War provided a common external enemy and a sense of mission around which to articulate what it meant to be American. The loss of that has sapped the belief in a common culture to which all belong.

Third, and perhaps most importantly, the notion of equality itself has been transformed. The inability of struggles such as the civil rights movements in the USA to transform the lives of the majority of African Americans has sapped the morale of anti-racists. Campaigning for equality means challenging accepted practices, being willing to march against the grain, to believe in the possibility of social transformation. Conversely, celebrating differences between peoples allows us to accept society as it is — all it says is 'we live in a diverse world, enjoy it'. It allows us to accept the divisions and inequalities that characterise the world today.

The social changes that have swept the world over the past decade have intensified this sense of pessimism. The end of the Cold War, the collapse of the left, the crumbling of the post-war order and the fragmentation of social movements have shattered many of the certainties of the past. In particular they have thrown into doubt our capacity to change the world for the better. In this context the quest for equality has largely been abandoned in favour of the claim to a diverse society. The idea of multiculturalism, like that of race, is an attempt to come to terms with inequalities in a society that professes belief in equality. Whereas racial theorists used to say that social differences were the inevitable product of natural differences and there is nothing we could do about it, multiculturalists argue that they are the product of cultural differences and there is nothing we should do about it. But this is simply to rename inequality.

Equality is not a 'western eccentricity'. It refers to our universal capacity to act as political equals. In an equal society, that capacity can take a myriad of forms, and hence can become the basis of true difference. Indeed, only in an equal society can difference have any meaning, because it is only here that difference can be freely chosen. In an unequal society, however, the pursuit of difference all too often means the entrenchment of already existing inequalities. Inequalities simply become reframed through the discourse of 'difference'. The challenge today is not to embrace 'difference' as a political goal but to transcend the whole language of race and to put the case clearly for equality. ❑

Kenan Malik *is a writer and journalist living in London. His most recent book,* The Meaning of Race *(Macmillan, UK) was published last year*

HARPER'S MAGAZINE

Salutes

INDEX ON CENSORSHIP

For a quarter-century in support of free expression and human rights worldwide

IRENA MARYNIAK

Rights of passage

Since 1989, eastern Europe has become the marshalling yard for all those who seek final refuge in the West. And the community on the 'right' side of the 'green line' that divides Europe as sharply as any wall ever did, is determined to keep them there

THEY come through central and eastern Europe packed into trucks and vans with cargoes of oranges or coal. Some do it with false documents. Others swim or row across rivers, and walk across green borders by night. The numbers are thought to run into thousands a day. Sometimes they drown; sometimes they freeze; sometimes they are caught. And still they keep coming, often buying time by claiming asylum in central Europe en route, before continuing the journey west.

The fall of the Berlin Wall coincided with a rush of movement from the south and since 1989 billions of dollars have gone into controls designed to stem the flow of people who can no longer bear to live in the country to which history consigned them by birth.

In Albania, the desperate are paying mobsters hundreds of dollars to board anything that floats. Derelict, motorless crafts with makeshift paddles and sails made of rubbish bags are reported to have drifted out into the Adriatic, packed with passengers. Over 7,000 people have reached Brindisi in Italy. At least one boat is known to have capsized and sunk. In July 1995 a locked refrigerator-truck trailer found abandoned on the outskirts of Gyor in western Hungary yielded 18 human bodies. All were Sri Lankans who had paid US$800 to a Bulgarian trucker for transport to Germany and Italy; they suffocated when the ventilation system broke down.

'Western countries are quite aware of the growing money being made on this. And of course it looks more moral to be combating trafficking than to be fighting migration,' Philippe Labreveux, the United Nations High Commissioner for Refugees' (UNHCR) representative in Budapest, says. Since Hungary still maintains a reservation whereby only people of European origin may be considered for refugee status, Labreveux is responsible for examining the cases of all non-Europeans. He has probably seen it all, but his manner is disconcertingly lightweight. 'There are no serious sanctions against trafficking in Hungary,' he adds. 'A small fine. And chains of traffickers do work. They must be international organisations with local representatives who negotiate with the police.'

Most of the transported will not be recognised as refugees. Killing, violence and civil war are no passport to refugee status. For that, according to the 1951 Geneva Convention, there must be evidence of persecution by the state. In the eyes of a world still mapped in terms of nations and borders, the umbilical bond with the mother country must be visibly severed before the international community will agree to foster. The Convention offers no protection to those in flight from generalised violence, the internally displaced, or the historically deported. People from a recognised war zone may be given temporary protection — as the 800,000 Bosnians who fled the war in Yugoslavia were. Now arrangements to return them are well in hand.

But where poverty and violence are directly linked to a political system how can any distinction between refugees and 'economic migrants' be made? An administrative nicety can mean the difference between asylum, aid and international protection and being left with no official recognised status or help, in danger of *refoulement* (that chilling Convention term which means 'return').

Some of those who brave the journey will be caught by border guards who are said to have direct access to secret service methods of investigation. They will face a protracted process of identification in a detention centre with bars on windows and doors where they will be locked up at night. And, if they do not manage to disappear in time, they will be sent home. 'The border guards are glad to see these people go,' Ferenc Koszeg of the Hungarian Helsinki Committee says. 'Though if they do allow them to vanish they have to face the protest of the Austrians.'

THERE were four border guards ready and waiting at the detention shelter in Kiskunhalas — a small Hungarian town about half an hour's drive north of the Serbian border. They served Coke and peanuts on a pristine white tablecloth embossed with little hearts.

'The Austrians say 100 people cross from Slovakia and Hungary every night,' they confided amicably after a few tense moments. 'Until 1989, we were the country defending western Europe from migrants. Now it's up to them, and they're doing all they can to protect themselves.' Four hundred extra troops and helicopters after dark, it seems. But surely these people aren't all criminals and thugs, I protest. Sometimes they come from a country which has buckled under to anarchy and civil war. What then? 'If people don't want to go home, if they may be killed, we ask where they want to go,' a border guard says blithely. 'And we make papers for Germany and they go there. Then it's trouble for that country. It's their problem.' Now just a minute. What about the common heritage of Fortress Europe? Just whose side are you on? 'Germany is merely an example,' (the border guard is serene); 'I might, for instance, have said the Congo.' And later, just a little anxiously, 'But you know, when they go illegally, it's their choice. *It's not us.*'

Quite. At the Bicske refugee camp 35 kilometres west of Budapest cars appear regularly to spirit away people who will never return. A chatty young Albanian from Kosovo, called Nasser, says that the former camp director committed suicide following allegations of corruption. 'I think it's still happening,' he adds. 'Some people seem to get away so quickly.' In January Nasser struck lucky and bought a Slovene passport and air tickets to London for himself, his wife and two children. But the passport was stamped 'Lyubliana'. All flights between Lyubliana and Budapest had been suspended and the Hungarian Airline MALEV caught on just as they were about to board the plane. These days western governments are applying sanctions against airlines that carry asylum seekers. So here they were in Bicske: with board, lodging and bare necessities catered for, after a fashion (they have a small room with four beds and a wardrobe), but no future to speak of. Nasser shows me an application form for Canada.

False passports, false identities, erased pasts, uncharted futures, and above all silence. No voice, no representation, no rights, no name. But people who really cannot be identified cannot be returned. 'Stories told to the UNHCR are often a tissue of lies,' Philippe Labreveux throws out impatiently: 'Liberians' and 'Rwandans' from Central Africa, 'Angolans' from the Belgian Congo. The unidentified and the rejected are frequently left to walk the streets, sleep at Budapest's Keleti station or at the City's

RIGHTS OF PASSAGE

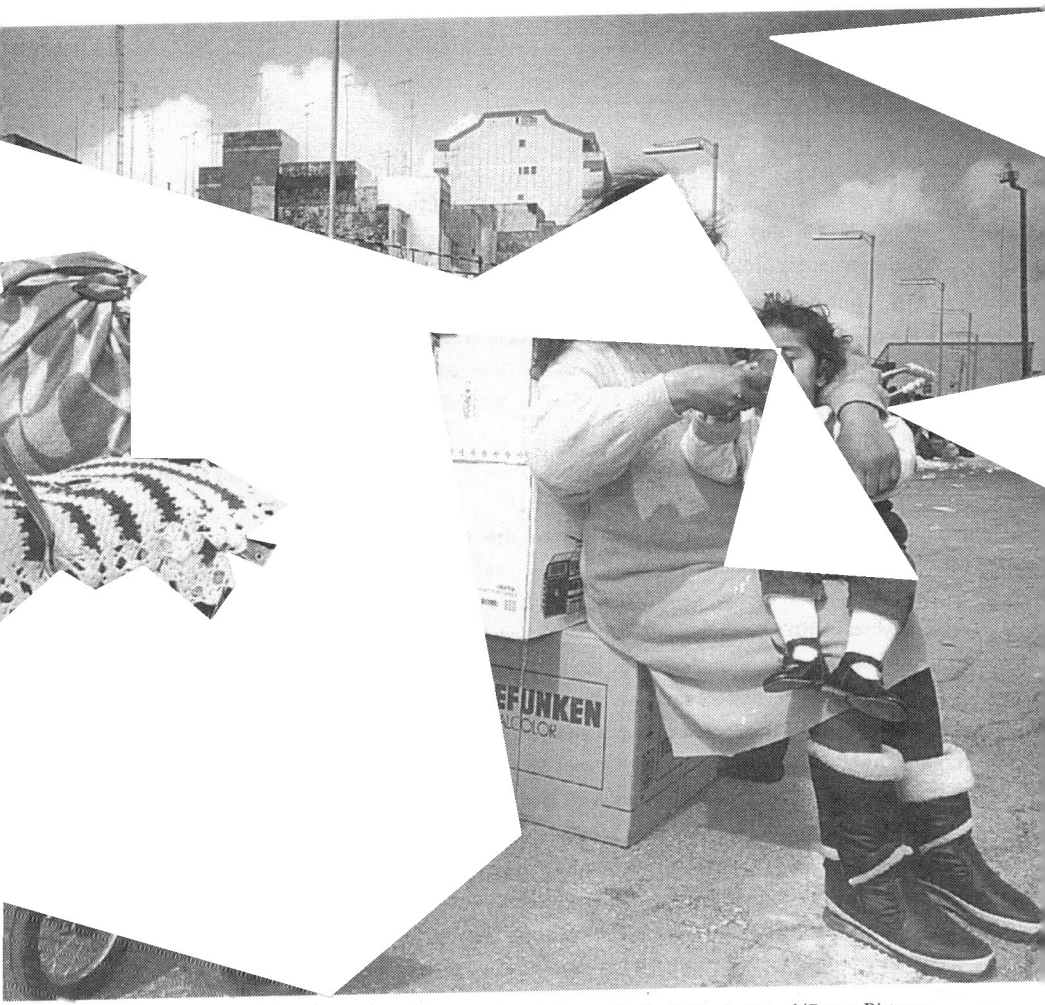

Albanian refugees in Brindisi, Italy — Credit: Melanie Friend/Panos Pictures

IRENA MARYNIAK

Senada's story

Senada is 13. She lives with her mother, sister and brother at the border guards' detention centre in Kiskunhalas

In Croatia people don't even try to understand. They don't have a heart to feel like we feel. Maybe they don't have a heart at all. Or maybe only for their own people. But not for other places or other people. My mum is Orthodox and my father is Muslim, and so are we. People in Croatia don't like that. I don't understand why they all hate us. In school they say: you are Muslim, why are you still here? We are Serbian, our family is in Serbia.

When the soldiers came we had to leave Croatia. My mum didn't have a job because the factory was closed down. Only my father worked and we lived on what he earned. My mother helped a foreign soldier [sic] from UNICEF and so he gave us food and clothes. But when UNICEF went, we had nothing. So my father went to be a soldier in Serbia. But the Croatian soldiers wouldn't let us go together as a family and we were left behind.

Then my mum got very sick. We ate only bread and tea and mum had very little money. She went to the policemen to see if she could get papers to go to Serbia. Her passport was Croatian but we didn't want to wait for a visa for Serbia. So we went by bus to the northern border and walked through to Hungary. The police stopped us at Kethely and then they let us go. We stayed in Tolna, we lived in a house where there was a man who tried to help us. We waited five months for a visa to go to Serbia. Then my mother went to Budapest to try and get the documents, but they wouldn't let her have them.

So we tried to cross into Serbia without. We just went. The policemen stopped us and took us to talk to them and then my mum got angry and shouted and tried to burn her passport. I was more and more afraid. I was shaking but my mum told me not to worry and to be careful. I began to feel better, and then I saw her in handcuffs.

We have been here two months.. It's strange, frightening. We feel gaoled, although we can go out in the day. We joke with the soldiers, because we don't know what to do. We want to go back to my father in Serbia, or maybe to Australia. I'd like to be together with him always, like a family. IM shelter for the homeless in Banya utca which recently opened a small outhouse for 'foreigners' (read 'blacks'). It is about four by seven yards square, with grating on the windows, a concrete floor, and two rooms packed with bunks and mattresses. Thirty-seven young Africans live there. A chair appears. I sit and everyone crowds around.

'We suffer some embarrassment here', 'Dr Bobi' says a little shyly. 'It's a group who call themselves skinheads. They attack, abuse us. We go to the police. The police don't support a black man. We are really embarrassed by this type of thing. In a tram or a bus a white man will stand up and move because a black man is sitting in a chair.'

Someone in a red T-shirt intervenes brusquely: 'We don't have work or money. We live like rats, congested between people, sleeping on floors. There are no job opportunities. Some people here are mechanics, drivers. We have no way of using our skills.'

'You don't eat, you don't sleep,' says 'Eduard', lean and tense. He tells me he is from Rwanda. 'You don't have your health. We are all human. And we have come such a long way.'

Who cares? Since 1994 the number of asylum seekers in the West has fallen because governments have introduced legislation permitting their removal to 'safe third countries': Poland, the Czech Republic or Hungary, for example. Financial incentives are being offered to countries in the east in exchange for further controls including a guarantee to take back those who have passed through on the journey west. All with no assurance that they can seek asylum there. And the restrictions are creeping eastward. The EU is returning people to its eastern and southern neighbours who now implement 'safe third country' policies of their own. Asylum seekers are being bounced from 'safe' country to 'safe' country until, in the end willingly or not, they go home.

'It's no longer a moral or a political matter for the EU, it's about security,' declares Bela Jungbert, director general of the Hungarian Office of Refugee and Migration Affairs, 'We are the main transit route for illegal migration and trafficking in human beings. It is in the interest of the EU to strengthen us and make us a filter from the east against persons trying to enter. And we accept this position. But we need more technical and financial support. We do not have the resources to be more efficient. We don't want to become a buffer zone for rejected asylum seekers at the periphery of the Union. We want to be part of it. We helped to destroy the Iron Curtain and we have no interest in building a new one.'

IRENA MARYNIAK

Not along the green line to the West anyway. And for the moment it is at this crossroads between affluence and the shaky regions of the east and south that Europe sees itself. It is where everyone meets: seasonal workers, suitcase peddlers plying their cutlery and lingerie in stations and bazaars, day shoppers, tourists, refugees, traffickers, yesterday's crooks and today's capitalists. This is it: the corridor of flight from insecurity, poverty and prejudice, or from unwelcome obligations such as military service in Dagestan; the waiting room for the West; Europe's fragile and perennially unpredictable hall of mirrors. ❑

"The perverse human need *not* to be understood is seen as the only way of defining, and defending one's existence. Only when languages rid themselves of 'political contamination' can people recognise that there exists only one language above all, the language of humanity."
— Kim Mehmeti, Skopje

Congratulations to our Dearest Friends and Neighbours at Index!
Liberating language for 25 years — and for 25 years to come

Institute for War & Peace Reporting
33 Islington High Street, London N1 9LH
warreport@iwpr.org.uk

i.w.p.r.

Right: Algerian refugee in Ceuta, Spain — Credit: Stephen Dupont/Panos Pictures

Body politics

WOLE SOYINKA

A call for sanctions

In March 1997 Nigeria's Nobel prize-winning author and 11 other pro-democracy activists were charged with treason and 'waging war against Nigeria' for their alleged involvement in a recent wave of bomb attacks against military targets — further evidence, says Soyinka, of the desperate lengths to which the Abacha regime will go to silence its critics, and a warning to the international community that it's time to get tough

Let me tell you: torture, of the most vile, unimaginable kind, has become institutionalised in Nigeria. Bello Fadile [imprisoned in connection with an alleged coup attempt] was tortured senseless before he broke down and gave evidence against Obasanjo [former Nigerian head of state, imprisoned on the same charge]. Colonel Lawan Gwadabe was equally tortured, in the most brutal and filthily obscene manner. He was hung upside down. He had buckets of excrement poured over him. Electric shocks were applied to him. And then, to break him down, his girlfriend was brought to come and witness the torture. That girl, I understand, was also imprisoned for some time. So we are really dealing with the very dregs of humanity when we think of the people carrying on the so-called art of government in Nigeria at the moment. The main purpose, of course, is to show the entire opposition that nobody is beyond the reach of Abacha. This is the lesson which they are trying to imprint on everyone.

Now, for the first time in Nigeria's history, the families of the regime's opponents are being punished for the alleged activities of their relatives. The family of Colonel Iluyomade [a retired officer now in exile and charged with treason] were all arrested; his wife and children, et cetera. Dapo Olonyomi, the journalist who escaped a few months ago from

Nigeria and won a prize in California for outstanding journalism — his wife was arrested a few days ago. Hostage-taking has become institutionalised. You can't find the target, you find the wife, children, relations. We never saw this even in apartheid South Africa. This is back to Idi Amin.

We have to tell the international community: please, don't make the same mistake as you made in the case of Ken Saro-Wiwa. You are not dealing with a rational being. I don't want to use any more of the epithets I've used for Abacha, because I'm even beginning to get bored with using the same words, and I haven't been back to the dictionary for some time. But in all seriousness, I've got to find a way of penetrating the mind-set of the international community. They still tend to believe that there are certain bounds this character will not cross. I am telling them, I am telling the world: there is absolutely no limit for him. He does not recognise, he does not understand, the meaning of decency, humanity, honesty, truth; he doesn't know what a nation is; he is the original throwback from the 'Slough of Despond'. I have no other way of describing him.

We know that Abacha has a bunch of killers in Nigeria, they are housed in Abuja and they take their orders directly from a Major Mustapha, who takes his orders directly from Abacha. These killers are the ones who flew to Lagos to go and assassinate Mrs Kudirat Abiola. They were trained in North Korea and Libya, and it's a very tight squad: they never come out in the daytime; they only go out at night for their operations, and return either at night or early dawn.

And we know, also, that a couple of embassies outside Nigeria have been given the task of co-ordinating and facilitating the work of some of these killers, when they come outside to operate. So Abacha is not to be taken lightly, but at the same time, he's also handicapped by the fact that a number of government security agencies overseas keep a tab on the movements of his killer squad. I must add this: there has been a secret meeting between Abacha and some African heads of state at which our extradition was discussed. Some countries didn't attend — they didn't see why they should go and waste their time. One told Abacha to go to hell. Another was shifty. But at least two of them [Togo and the Gambia] acceded to Abacha's request that if any of us made the mistake of stepping in those countries, we would be extradited to Nigeria.

Let's begin with what the international community should NOT do, what they should STOP doing. They should begin by stopping to pretend

WOLE SOYINKA

Wole Soyinka in Burlington Arcade, London 1996

A CALL FOR SANCTIONS

that they are looking at some authentic democratic process, and thereby modify their language. They should change their language radically — turn it from a language of 'Oh, we're examining this process that's going on,' change it radically to a REJECTION of the entire process. You see, as long as there is that element of 'critical accommodation', it is giving credibility to something which is rotten from the very foundations.

There has already been an election [on 12 June 1993]. There is a president-elect [Chief Abiola] rotting in jail. The democrats in society say: 'There is one solution and one solution only — an immediate government of national unity headed by the winner of the 12 June 1993 election.' The outside world knows very well that what we predicted is now giving off such signals that only the deaf and the dumb will say they cannot perceive those signals: Abacha is planning to succeed himself! His five creature [political] parties — I keep describing them as 'these five fingers of a rotting, leprous hand' — these five fingers are getting together. In fact it was a condition for the creation of many of them, that when the time comes you call for your own form of unity. You say: 'The only way to unify the country is for us five parties to come together, and consent to one candidate.' And that is happening.

Don Etiebet [leader of one of the new parties] who had the nerve to declare his aspiration to the presidency was grabbed; he was arrested. After a few days in the cooler, I am sure you won't hear anything more of his presidential ambitions. Abacha is buying, bullying or torturing anybody with any suggestion of ambition. This is the ultimate conclusion of his project.

Now we know that the real struggle against him must come from within Nigeria itself. And I assure you that that struggle is going on all the time. It is not terribly well publicised, however. People do not go to the prisons to see how many people have been arrested — arrests that have become so numerous that 'portakabins' are being commandeered from building sites all over Nigeria to hold prisoners. Yes! So, the struggle is on and sacrifices are being made by Nigerians. We have cadres on the ground who go out and campaign against the sham electoral and democratic process of Abacha; who go out and tell the people: 'Don't bother to register; it's a waste of time.' Some of them have been arrested, by the way — I think we have 37 of our members in various prisons right now.

So let the international community stop pretending that they do not know what is going on. They should abandon the language of accommodation and do what the European [and African-Pacific-Caribbean] Joint Assembly recently did — namely, impose sanctions against Nigeria and isolate the Abacha regime totally. Yes, we know that at certain levels, business must be conducted with Nigeria and that there are existing links. But there must be a way of doing the minimal, with a maximum language of condemnation. ❏

Wole Soyinka is Nigeria's foremost novelist, playwright, poet and critic, as well as being an outspoken campaigner for democracy. In 1986 he became the first African writer to win the Nobel Prize for Literature

From an interview by Cameron Duodu

Royal Festival Hall
on the South Bank

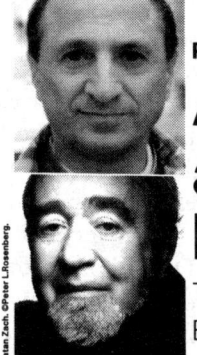

sbc

Tuesday 17 June
Purcell Room RFH3, 7.30pm

Abdullah al-Udhari & Natan Zach

Tickets £6 (£3.50)
Box Office **0171 960 4242**

Twenty-five years ago Arab poet Abdullah al-Udhari and Israeli Natan Zach shared the stage for the first time in a Poetry Society reading. The Royal Festival Hall once again brings together these two astonishing poets - a performance made all the more extraordinary by their contrasting performance styles.

To join our **FREE** Mailing List for Literature Events telephone **0171 921 0906**.

CAROLINE MOOREHEAD
All rights reserved

The worldwide clamour for truth and justice, for human rights for all, has never been louder. But so is the cry of those subjected to the ever-growing range of abuses

IN 1899 the liberal historian Theodor Mommsen dismissed international treaties on human rights as a 'misprint in the history of mankind'. A hundred years later, it is tempting to believe he was right. Human rights are in a mess. As *Index* turns 25, and the Universal Declaration of Human Rights approaches its 50th anniversary, it is far easier to criticise the vast web of international laws and mechanisms for not working than it is to make them work.

Human rights reached its high point this century in 1989. Communism had been defeated and with it the ferocious suppression of Eastern European dissidents: the Berlin wall was down. Latin American dictatorships were gradually being replaced by democratic rule, and an end to apartheid was in sight. At the UN, real progress had been made to persuade governments to agree to the delivery of humanitarian aid to the victims of disasters over and above their own feelings about sovereignty. In its battles to make states recognise that human rights applied even during conflicts, states of emergency were added to the human rights agenda in 1977, 'disappearances' in 1980 and summary executions in 1983. The mood across the human rights world was, if not jubilant, optimistic.

It lasted no more than a few months. All too quickly, it became clear that the end of proxy wars fought between the major powers on battlefields in Asia and Africa did not mean an end to conflicts, that linkage of aid to human rights performance was at best a shaky concept, and that the worst abusers of human rights were not greatly interested in what the West had to say. Since the early 1990s, humanitarian and human

CAROLINE MOOREHEAD

rights concerns have been increasingly linked to wider agendas or military strategies and foreign policy. Massacres flash by, televised, recorded and soon forgotten, with little pause to reflect how another such genocide could be prevented.

In the 30 or so conflicts, all of them internal, currently being fought, it is civilians and not soldiers who make up 95 per cent of the victims. Child soldiers as young as seven fight alongside adults, atrocities are committed on all sides with a barbarity even seasoned observers find sickening, unexploded landmines cripple those who venture into the countryside, while the very western countries most vocal in their support for human rights have turned into major providers of weapons. Rape, like water, has become a weapon of war. Elsewhere, in countries nominally at peace, citizens are being arrested, tortured, 'disappeared' and summarily executed. Censorship — whose role not only in famine but in the violation of all human rights has been documented by *Index* over the last 25 years — silences editors and journalists and now threatens the Internet.

Every year, for the last six years, the European Union has sponsored a motion to censor China at the annual UN Human Rights Commission. This year, France and Germany backed off and China was let off the hook. 'Conditionality' and 'linkage' have lost all credibility as economic ties and strategic importance are cited as reasons for non-interference and only poor states, with few rich pickings or international friends, are censored and subjected to economic pressure.

The impotence of the modern human rights movement was summed up recently by Alex de Waal in the *Times Literary Supplement* writing about the genocide of the Tutsis in Rwanda, which many see as a watershed for human rights. For a while, he argues, the 'second generation' of human rights activists, born of the Cold War and highly professional as lawyers, lobbyists and journalists, was able, in the words of Aryeh Neier, founder of Human Rights Watch, to 'mobilise shame'. But shame is transient and governments soon learnt to keep ahead of their critics, disappear their dissidents and bypass international standards. Even one of the most hopeful of all experiments, the creation of international tribunals to try those accused of genocide in Rwanda and Bosnia has collapsed in what Rakiya Omaar, co-founder of African Rights, calls a 'massive mess': the failure to arrest and bring the guilty to trial, the ineptitude of investigators,

Right: Hutu prisoners accused of genocide, Rwanda — Credit: Seamus Murphy/Panos Pictures

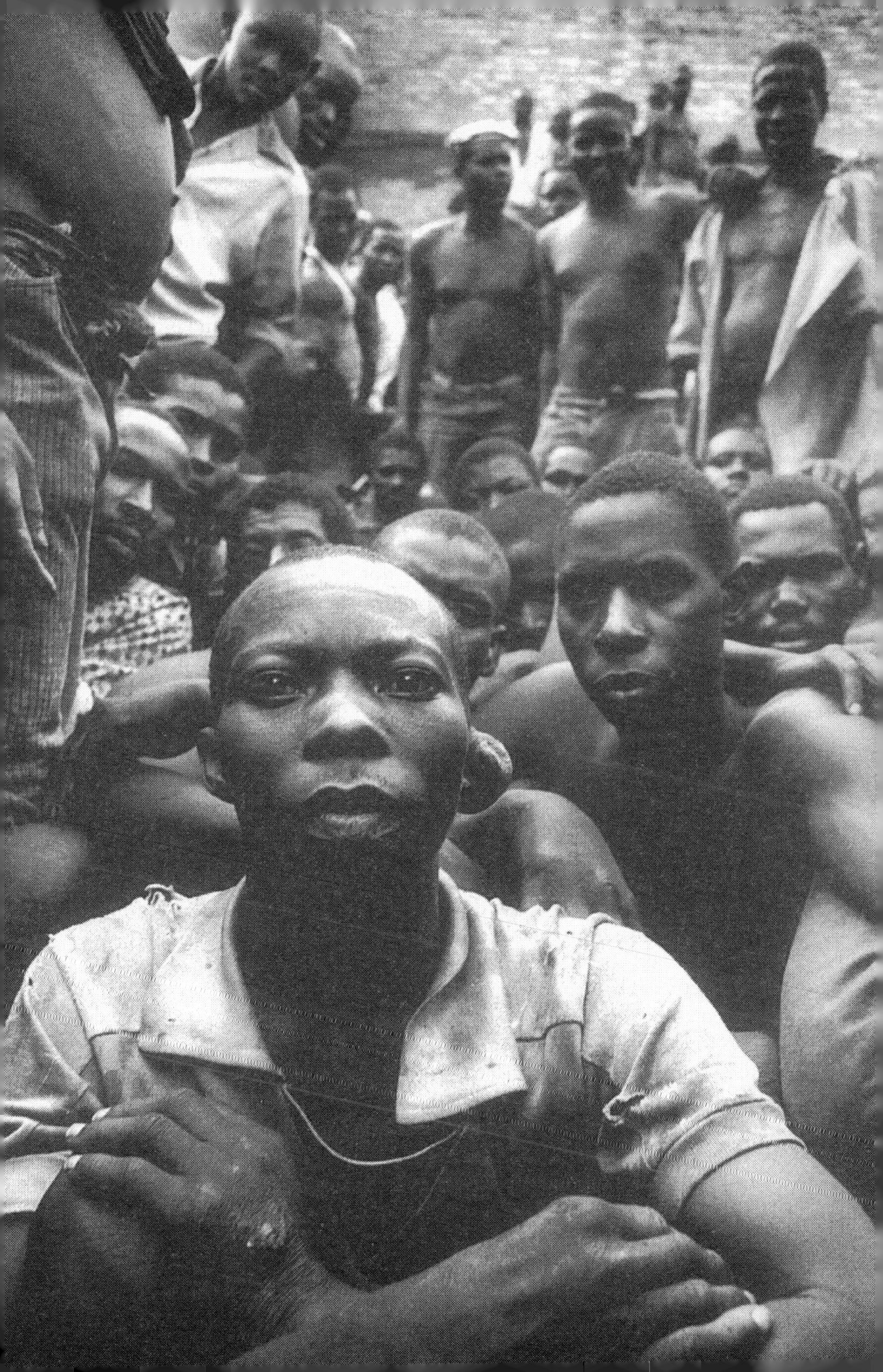

the withdrawal of funds.

The recent history of human rights is marked by swings between those who maintain that major powers like America have a duty to intervene to promote freedom, democracy and self-determination, and those who believe that states should mind their own business. For this last group, human rights are an irritant, getting in the way of promoting and protecting a country's economic interests and security. With the failure, since 1990, to make much progress in human rights, what the *Economist* recently called the 'realists' are again in the ascendant, arguing that economic prosperity must come first, and that the political freedoms will follow.

Paradoxically, these 'realists' may be benefiting from a convergence of the human rights and development lobbies. Against those who call for a narrowing of the definition of what is or is not a 'human right', who argue that one way out of the mess is to take a small number of fundamental and truly universal rights — the right not to be enslaved, tortured or massacred, say, the right to a fair trial and to freedom of information — and enforce these with all the legal machinery and international weight and pressure possible, there are moves to try to honour broader commitments. At the 1993 UN Vienna conference on human rights a 'right to development' was agreed. Since then there has been growing talk of promoting the neglected rights to education, health and clean water, enshrined in the Covenant on Social and Economic Rights in 1966 and now featuring in Oxfam's 'right to a sustainable livelihood'. By opening the door to a whole range of such rights, is there not a danger that all will be so diluted as to make them easier to ignore? Wars of starvation cannot be reconciled with human rights, but to say that everyone has a 'right' to food has very little meaning, and it is noticeable that international human rights bodies have been unable to translate this right into entitlements and obligations. Perhaps the time has come to make human rights a tighter, more strictly defined area, sharply distinct from humanitarian concerns and confined to precise and narrow violations the international community refuses to tolerate, and where it is prepared to act, and to return to it some of the immediacy of earlier days, as Amnesty International are now doing so successfully with their 'urgent action' campaign.

What people fear today is the prospect of 'horror fatigue' becoming so overwhelming that it dulls the sense of outrage that atrocities ought to provoke. Yet among the disappointments, there are reasons to feel pleased. The founders of *Index*, discussing the appalling difficulties faced by dissidents throughout the Soviet bloc 25 years ago, could never have foreseen a world in which non-governmental organisations, in their thousands, thrived in places where they were once systematically crushed, in which the clamour for truth and justice has produced real, if limited, successes, in which new technology brings instant news of violations, in which the relatives of the 'disappeared' everywhere from Turkey to Guatemala make common cause. In 25 years, human rights has found a voice, however incoherent. For this alone, history is proving Mommsen wrong. ❏

Caroline Moorehead is a writer and broadcaster specialising in human rights. She is currently writing a history of the International Committee of the Red Cross

Congratulations on 25 years of articles defending freedom, many of which we have been proud to share with our readers in the U.S.

WORLD PRESS
Review

NEWS AND VIEWS FROM AROUND THE WORLD

New York City   worldpress@worldpress.org

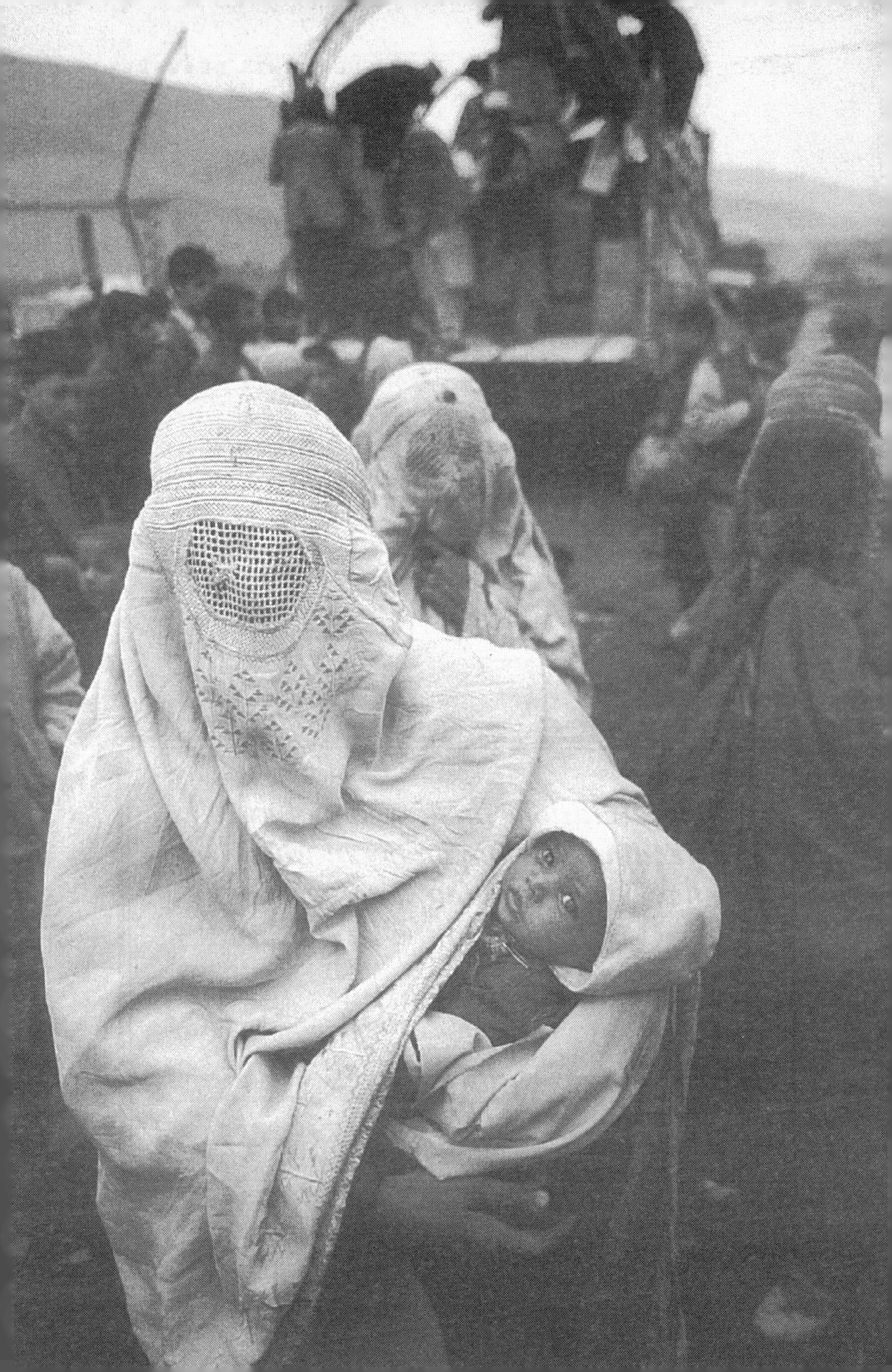

MICHAEL IGNATIEFF

Varieties of experience

UMBERTO ECO takes us to the moral core of *Index*'s mandate when he writes, 'there are universal ideas about constraints: nobody wants anyone to stop them speaking, seeing, listening...' Because this is the late twentieth century — and scepticism is our second nature — we close in on that word which makes such large claims — 'universal' — and begin imagining societies in which the silence into which most people are cast is *not* experienced as a constraint: societies where it is essential to a woman's dignity to remain silent, societies where the code of family honour assigns the right of speech to the patriarch alone; societies where some great creed, secular or religious, teaches individuals to disregard or quell their inner disquiet or discontent, or so indoctrinates them that they feel no inner rebellion at their indoctrination at all. Only those societies which allow the emergence of a certain kind of individuated self feel the particular suffocation, the thwarted sense of injustice, which Umberto Eco beautifully describes. This self need not be a secular, western, disenchanted, rights-oriented liberal self. The modern self is wonderfully varied and it is capable of making complex compromises between its particular individuality and the religions, traditions, ethnicity, geography and language — the collective forces — which forge it into a social being. But for them to feel the constraint of which Eco speaks — which gives rise to the longing for freedom of speech — they must feel that they have a voice of their own. Eco speaks of the 'conviction that the other is within us'. Whatever else this may mean, it should also include the idea that there is some space for self-expression between the individual and the social, between private experience and public belief. It has become an

Left: Women of Afghanistan — Credit: Martin Adler/Panos Pictures

anthropological truism that there are many societies in which this basic sense of the self is absent. Nor is this fact rightly described as an absence, as if these societies were missing something which thwarts or stunts the individuals who live in it. The very absence of a gulf between self and society may be turned into a moral virtue. In some highly patriarchal and religious societies, women learn to think of their silence and segregation from the public realm as a defining feature of their dignity and distinctiveness as women; and if they feel the loss of a public role, they feel the compensation of having authority within the private domain.

Nor is it the case that only so-called 'patriarchal', 'primitive' or 'premodern' societies do away with the self on which a modern rights culture depends. The West is just recovering from two mightily ambitious attempts — Nazi and Communist — to transcend the 'bourgeois' self and to abolish the rights culture which it made possible. It is only since 1989, and the demise of the competing rights culture of the Communist archipelago, that we can speak of a single free speech culture in the modern world. Given our history, modernity offers no guarantees about the perpetual health or diffusion of this culture.

It's possible, in other words, that freedom of speech is neither 'universal' nor 'natural' in the terms that Umberto Eco uses. His spirited and eloquent dialogue with Cardinal Martini is an attempt to ground a secular ethics in something as solid and dignified as the Christian story. But human nature may be too plastic, too malleable and too potentially vicious a thing, and the varieties of conceivable human society too various, for it to be possible to found an ethics on facts about us as a species.

The interesting question is what kind of mess this leaves us in. Anyone who values systematic consistency and ultimate reasons for moral action may think we are in a considerable mess indeed. But that puts a higher value on consistency and certainty than we need in daily life. If we only acted when we were certain that we were right, that our values were universal and were grounded in true facts, we'd never act at all.

If moral perfectionism is in fact an alibi for inaction, then what kinds of arguments should we use to justify moral practices like intervening on behalf of people's right to free speech in other cultures and contexts? The philosopher, Richard Rorty, argues that when we intervene to defend someone's human rights, or, in *Index*'s case, someone's right to free speech, we do so because we are moved by 'sad and sentimental stories'. In other words, arguments have nothing much to do with moral action. Rorty leaves modern human rights culture hanging in a void, sustained by nothing more than sentimental political correctness.

Given that the world presents us with an infinity of sentimental stories, begging for our identification and involvement, we need more than sentiment if we are to decide which stories to make our own. There is one argument, one moral consideration, which has to be cleared up before any form of moral intervention in someone else's life or culture can be undertaken. If you take up someone's cause, you have to be fairly certain that they want you to do so; moreover, that your values — freedom of speech and human rights — are theirs too. Indeed, the demand for moral action, for intervention, must come from them, from their needs, from their sense of what is right and wrong. They must be the ones who define the limits and extent of your impingement on their ways of life and ways of thinking. The ultimate rationale for *Index* is that victims have made its language their own, and their demand for its meanings is spreading around the world. But this demand for moral intervention should not obscure the very real differences of cultural value which remain.

If the essential fact about the human situation is that our values conflict — that cultures and societies place significantly different accents on the rights of individuals *vis-à-vis* the collectivity — then moral intervention has no choice but to become a highly complex experience of intercultural translation, in which each side tries to negotiate its way to a shared understanding which may change each other's values but does not violate each other's moral identities. To give a controversial example of what I mean, Afghan women under Taliban rule may seek the assistance of western human rights activists to gain the right to walk freely in the streets and to meet western journalists unsupervised by their husbands. They are not necessarily seeking to abandon Muslim ideas about a separate sphere for women; they are not necessarily challenging the idea of separate education for their daughters. They want it both ways: to be good Muslim women and rights-bearing creatures at the same time. And there is no reason why they cannot be both. It is a fallacy, symmetrically entertained by Islamic fundamentalists and some western activists alike, that western rights are a package: buy one and you must buy all, and no negotiation about the price. In reality, a human rights politics which makes moral sense is one which tries to expand, rather than contract, the choices which both individuals and societies are free to make about the kind of private and public life they desire.

MICHAEL IGNATIEFF

This is not a moral concession imposed upon the West by our guilty history of imperialism. It is simply the recognition of incorrigible value conflict within our *own* tradition. It may contribute to our moral modesty and increase our understanding of the Other, both at home and abroad, if we abandoned the attempt to find a non-contradictory and incontestable basis for a secular ethics in the facts of the body. This project — so necessary in the struggle of secularism to rescue itself from the charge of nihilism, so necessary to its emancipation from the overwhelming cultural prestige of Christian metaphysic — is intended to give us a common human language with what is Other to the western tradition. But the body doesn't end arguments between cultures: it begins it. What is pure suffering in one culture may be ecstasy in other; what is humiliation in one may be only humbling in another. We share a body, it is true; but we do not live inside it in the same frame of mind. What matters then is not that we agree on ethical substance, but that we agree a procedure, a set of rules in which to thrash out our arguments. The procedure commits us, whatever our cultural tradition, to a moral minimum: to attempt, as far as we can, to enter into the moral world of the Other, to appreciate the very distance which separates the Other from us, and to treat moral dialogue as an exercise in mutual persuasion rather than a display of force or cultural prestige. While this may sound like wanting to conduct the moral conversation on terms dictated by western liberal toleration, it is not. If toleration is a value, it is a 'thin' one: it is better understood as a procedure. It is not the value which trumps all others; it is the one which makes non-murderous moral argument possible. As a human rights organisation, in a radically pluralist world, *Index*'s purpose is not to make one value win out over others, but to do its small part in creating a moral world in which the right to speak for oneself becomes the condition for allowing those who speak antagonistic moral languages to actually hear each other. ❑

© *Michael Ignatieff*

Michael Ignatieff *is a writer and broadcaster. He has recently finished a biography of Isaiah Berlin and is working on a history of the moral imagination in the twentieth century*

MA JIAN

Darkness & light

HE climbed out of the grave, lay on the bamboo-leaf-covered slope. A foul stench lingered on his stomach. With one hand he clutched his chest, then he raised his hand, waved it wildly in the air. He watched the paperbark tree, its skin peeling off and falling layer by layer; her skin, her shapely neck, her behind round and smooth as the moon, a girl's foot...that summer.

She rummaged through the clothes on his stall. She folded her skirt round her knees as she crouched down: those sandals...he put a stool in place for her, her feet close to him, he helped her put them on, inhaled, smelt the odour of sweat from her skirt and the soles of her feet, a sour dampish smell. Sunlight steamed on the concrete road. He felt his forehead and eyelids suddenly convulse — she was looking at him.

He seemed to have woken up, or was still in a daze. He knew there was blood on his hands now: a woman's blood, hers. He knew she lay nearby, in her coffin. Just now, he had burst open the coffin lid, probably with a chisel, or with that pick.

Delivery lorries from the suburbs were beginning to drone along the highway into the city. He felt he should go back. Tomorrow he'd still have to put some bangles on the stall, sew phoney labels onto that parcel of skirts. There was a ruby ring that he'd never put on sale, stolen when his granddad was still alive. Right now he really wanted to hold it in his hand, look at its facets and corners, see that redness, transparent as water. He sat up, looked around. From the thicket a winding road was visible, narrow, and meandering intermittently off into the distance. The hairy bamboo in the graveyard was all twisted and untidy, and no grass grew under it. Some graves were piled with paper money. Behind him two wreaths hung on a headstone, paper flowers cankered by the assaults of the rain, the few leaves of silver paper left on the flame giving off a reluctant light in the gloom of the graveyard. It came to him that an intellectual was buried there. Labelled a rightist just after he'd graduated from university. Seems he'd just come back from overseas as well. Come Sunday he could always be seen at Nanling bus station, where the long-distance buses went to the city, always in the dress suit he'd brought back from overseas, his leather shoes gleaming. He'd never join the scramble to get on. He'd wait for the women dragging their ducks and chickens aboard and the pedlars shouldering their carrying-poles, then once they'd poured on to the bus he'd step carefully on. When he and his father had prised that coffin open they got hardly anything. The gold tooth was fake, and that was a hard thing for his father. He had invited its owner to drink tea a couple of times just to size up the gold tooth, and had told jokes all afternoon. He said it was a genuine foreign gold tooth, too. The watch was mouldy as well, and his clothes were badly torn after they'd dragged them off. My father cursed me for a halfwit, but I'd clearly seen his wife buy a Mao suit from the 'Plan for Prosperity' department store, and she'd bought a jade ring for herself at my stall.

He touched the bamboo leaves: soft and soggy. Behind the hill the cement factory's machines went still. In an instant the graveyard grew frighteningly quiet. His ears suddenly started to ring: this sound always came when he'd had too much to drink, or when he was exhausted after a night of robbing graves.

She tried on the sandals, moving her toes a little. Noiselessly, the sunlight on the concrete road drilled deep into his throat, down his windpipe, scorching his lungs. She lived out by the intersection of the city road and the Yangchun County road. When he was little he'd often bump into her on his way to school in the county town: a girl so little suited to country life. Red schoolbag, legs pressed tight together as she walked. The hearse that took bodies to be buried in Nanling wound its roundabout way along the twisting highway to the village. Even the chickens and the dogs had to sidle along the edge of the street then. When mother was alive, the family stall mainly sold things for paying respect to the dead, like wreaths, incense, paper money, and spirit tablets. Sometimes mother would make silk flowers, or papercuts of Our Lady of Compassion and the Wandering Ghosts which she'd put on sale. The family's costumes for Virgin Boys & Girls, Demons Large & Small, and Yama, Lord of the Dead were only rented out when there was a big funeral procession. The year he was nine he was in one. He put on his Virgin Boy costume apart from the other village children to stand among the ranks in the funeral procession, rouge on his cheeks and a red dot on his brow. He remembered her. Her mother had tried to do her hair in two pigtails sticking up on top of her head, but her hair was so fine they wouldn't stand up until her mother had tied them in with black silk ribbons. She cried, and her mother gave her a silk butterfly. The funeral procession stretched from the little North Well outside the village all the way to the graveyard. He remembered the paper horse! Big as a real horse it was, its tongue wagged in time to its bearers' steps, and at the graveside it fizzed as it burned, its bamboo skeleton twisting and turning in the flames.

The year they repaired the road they brought in a lot of sand, so he dug holes in the sandhill as she stood by and watched. They dug together. Four little hands digging away like fury until the holes were too deep for their hands to touch the bottom. That day she didn't come back. While he waited for her he covered the holes with paper, waiting to be near her, to smell her, to see her little red face damp with sweat, to look in her eyes, look far into them.

He knew she was an only child, a high-school graduate. A good many of the people in the shops on the street knew her, knew she loved to buy rag dolls.

She passed the stall and he followed her, came here — to this graveyard. He lay down, watched her rock a eucalyptus tree, shaking down the raindrops. She smiled, jumped, leaned against the tree. It was getting dark. He longed for darkness. This was a place where he wouldn't be dazzled by headlights, and where he wouldn't be disturbed by passers-by taking a shortcut. He knew every rut and hollow here. At 13 his father had taken him grave robbing, him shaking with fear, and his father had given him a beating. He was clumsy and awkward then, always falling down, his hands always grazed or pricked by thorns. The smell of the corpses made him feel sick, too. He'd got to know this graveyard well these nine years, and could creep silently in and out in the dark.

He thought of that drizzly afternoon; how come it wasn't dark? He had nearly got round behind her. He heard her softly croon a poem to herself. He stretched out behind a headstone, his groin swollen and throbbing. He'd often done this kind of thing. He'd stopped a good few women as they'd crossed the road after coming off shift at the cement factory. He was strong. He could throttle them and stop their mouths in one swift movement.

He watched her touch her rain-wet hair as she walked towards him.

MA JIAN

He saw her fold her skirt as she crouched down — he watched. Blood surged in his eyeballs spasms between his thighs pressing pressing pressing down on her her her her — he hadn't moved, hadn't shifted an inch.

He slowly remembered the banks of the stream some 50 metres below where they'd buried the girl who killed herself with insecticide, rotted away to foul water in these last few years. He tightened his jaw, the back of his neck rigid. No-one knew why she died. That evening, he hadn't let her go until the machines started up for the early shift at the cement factory. She'd got to her knees, hands convulsively gripping the waistband of her trousers, shoes and even socks gone in the struggle, scraped and mud-stained, stray grass stuck to her hair and her belly. He'd dug open the grave, found her skin was even fairer than it had been the night before last. He'd peeled off her new clothes, thrown away a photo album of hers with all the other things her relatives and friends and workmates had given her, and he'd lain on her corpse for half the night, only burying the coffin again when he couldn't stand the smell of insecticide any longer.

He climbed up and staggered to his mother's grave. Here was where he used to hide when he was small and he'd run here to cry after father had beaten him. The grave mound was lower now and already it was impossible to make out what was written on the headstone. He pulled out some weeds to let it show. He was sweating, his trousers and waistcoat soaked through. A cool breeze blew by, rustling the dry bamboo leaves on the ground.

Night. Empty, deserted. Scraps of silk paper from wreaths blew about the forks of empty trees. Unknown creatures scuttled out of the long grass behind the graves to howl mournfully by the stream. Another breeze blew hurriedly between the graves, and he moved: mother. A southern woman you'd see anywhere in the countryside: mouth slightly open, clear untroubled forehead. He turned away (not in the least afraid). Mother came from behind the headstone, touched his head, and he felt hot tears trickle down the nape of his neck into his collar. His eyes were watering, he couldn't open them. He didn't know if this was real, mother's hand was wet. And she was sobbing, too, sobbing on account of him, just like when he was lying ill in bed. She sat there sobbing just like this: he had a carbuncle on his neck, and a fever.

Every day, mother lifted him in her arms, tied him on her back in a bedsheet, went to the hospital to have the pus drained. Day after day they

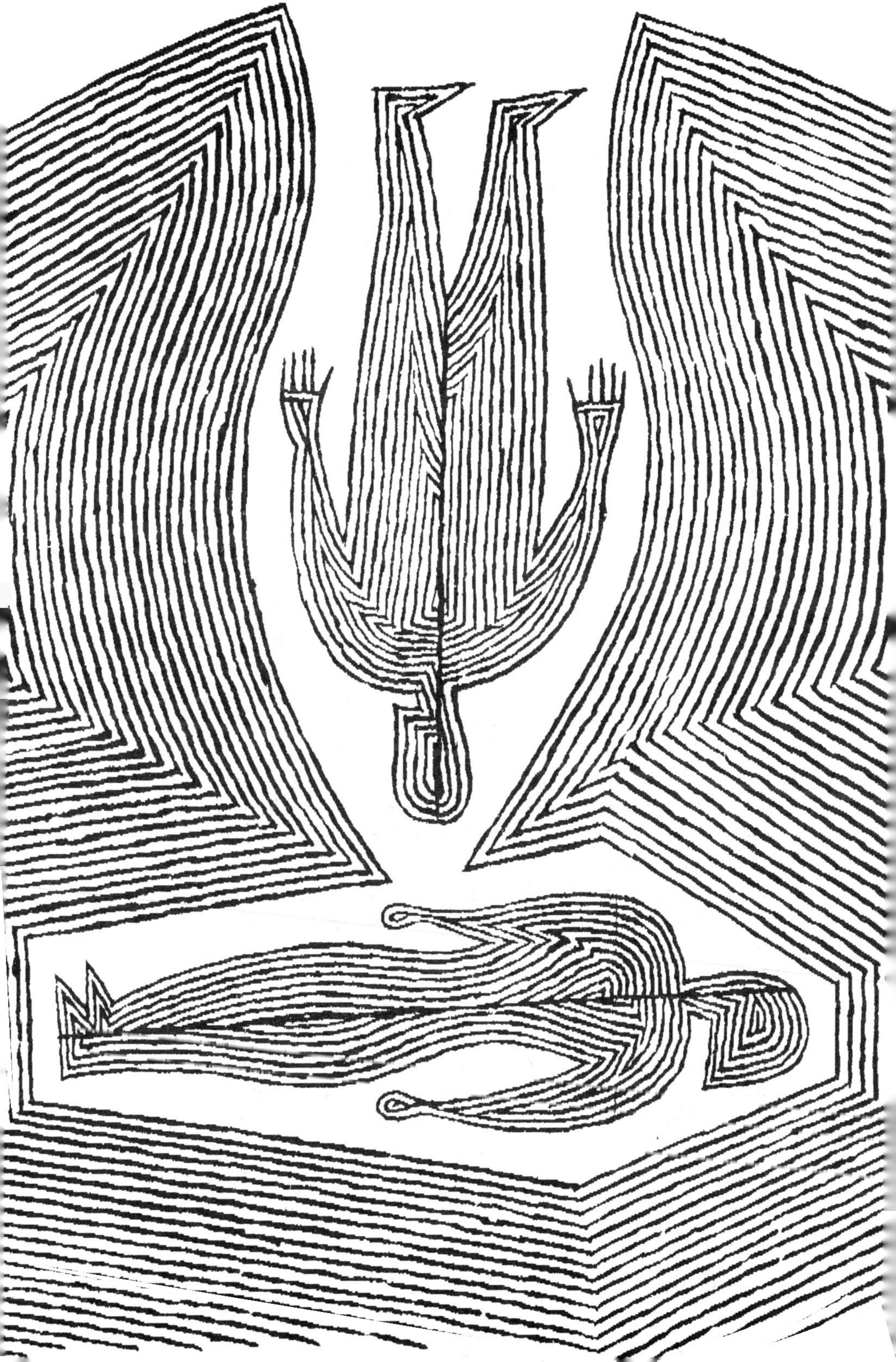

climbed the slope east of the graveyard. He couldn't lift his head, had stabbing pains in his eyes when he looked at anything, but he remembered it all now: her neck running with sweat, her damp hair, her clothes soaked in sweat and the warm smell of her body. On the red earth of that dry road to the county town she softly hummed him folk songs, chewed biscuits until they were moist enough, and fed him.

A little older, it was only when mother passed away that he realised an illness like that could kill someone: mother had given blood for him then.

He looked again at a stretch of lake, was standing on the water, slowly sinking, the water was cold, though he felt hot, still sinking down. Slowly he felt the water soak into his body, flow through his veins. He was a hollow tube, water splashing against him and through him. His flesh felt as if it was peeling away like plaster from an old wall, he had lost awareness of all his organs. He couldn't move, but knew he had swollen up, turned into a stone or a pillar, until he was so big he couldn't tell where he ended. This immense object rolled forward, pressing down on him, he cried out, and then — mother's hand landed on his shoulder. Every bone in his body was blazing with pain. Mother's hand caressed his throat, his spine, the top of his head, his brow. He experienced pain the like of which he'd never felt before. He wanted to grab hold of something. His body seemed still to be in the water. The water was breathable, buoyant, sweet — childhood (something inconceivable to him), the feeling of suckling at mother's breast surging back through his bones. Her milk warm in his mouth, warm in his belly, warm as he pissed it out. He saw how he looked when he was little: black hair, little hand grabbing the breast, little cock peeking out through his open fly. He didn't dare say it was him for sure — the voice wasn't right, for a start. He was 14 or 15 when his voice broke, became gruff and hoarse. More, he could never have laughed like that. Or never have laughed out loud like that. But the child's smell was his. He carefully sniffed the imaginary baby, was even more positive that this was his smell when he was little — that milky smell all babies have. He heaved a sigh of relief, laughed unnaturally. He saw his little paper boat float off down the little stream, go bobbing away on the lake: a rainy day, him splashing and splashing as he played in the water, raising his head, opening his mouth to drink in the rain. A toy he'd loved: mother made a giraffe from scraps of cloth, but it had no eyes. He saw the wooden pencil case he took to school too, he wanted to open it, look at his pencils, he remembered he had a pencil with a red rubber on its tip. He couldn't get it open, his heart locked up tight, he pressed with both hands on the lid, forced it, and it opened: there were no pencils, she lay inside like she'd been just now, lying in the coffin — staring at him, no blood on her mouth now, calmly staring at him.

Those eyes, he couldn't avoid them. He knew her name: Fang Jing. He never called her name when she was alive, never thought to, so grown up but never called anyone's name out. He spoke it quietly first, and only produced a forced and awkward sound he hated. The sounds his tongue made were hardly formed, and he wondered if he hadn't just howled. He said it again, clearly this time, and it was in a man's voice.

And then he was shaken by the rebuke he cried out.

'I've done done done done some some something!

'I should have come sooner — ohhh — sooner sooner sooner sooner...' His voice choked off suddenly. He was howling dry tears as his hands dug viciously at the mud.

HE'D sobered up a bit. He realised he was going there again. 'Should go back there.' His feet seemed to have left the ground, and he moved there in a dull haze, clouds of insects buzzing around his head.

He leaned against a hairy bamboo, wanted to calm down, then wanted to think about something for a bit. A light that brought with it the distant drumming of horses' hooves picked out the graveyard, and he was seeing himself, that self that had been hiding inside his body all along, that low-down, mean, unfeeling, filthy, unsmiling self, insatiable greed in its eyes. He thought, this is the other side of that smiling face father shows to the customers at their stall. He examined himself in detail: mother's forehead, chin even a little bit attractive. All the rest like father, especially the eyebrows and the eyes — grave-robber's eyes: numb. Eyes that can pick any object out in the dark, but blank as an owl's eyes in daylight.

He clung to the bamboo to stop himself sliding to the ground. He was afraid of his father, afraid of those gruesome eyes. Once he was a bit older he found ways of making himself more cruel and unfeeling, to free himself from the fear in his heart. He was a big strong lad nowadays, but was afraid of him still. He hardly ever said anything to his son, just hints at what he should do: one look from father's eyes and he knew exactly what action he should take, how to do things by willpower alone. The most he ever spoke was after coming back from robbing a grave: he'd take his coat off, put it away, and wash his hands in hot spirits, then he'd

spread his finds out in the lamplight and he'd often say:
'This line of work's been handed down through the family: I've brought you up on things like these.' Then he would always raise his eyes and give him a look.

'It's not stealing when we take things from those dead folks there. They can't go on living, and, anyway, they had a good enough time when they were alive — did they take so much with them for it just to rot away? Eh?'

'See on this pick here — that's the marks of your granddad's use. If him and the others hadn't been digging up Fan Yingyuan's grave, he wouldn't have stopped that bullet.'

Coffins today aren't the same as in the old days. Even father couldn't use these piles of hand-me-down ironmongery. He just used the pick: sandalwood shaft, heavy and strong, twin heads, one a duckbill shape, the other like a three-sided awl, and between them, set in the socket where the shaft was fixed, a curved iron spike, its head filed into the shape of a claw-hammer to prise out the bigger coffin-nails.

Father needed less than the time it takes to smoke two pipes to open a grave. He taught him to first put the dry topsoil aside then dig down from the south side of the grave mound. (Silver, gold and valuables are usually put by the corpse's head.) Wet earth was put by on a sheet of sailcloth to be pulled away in one go when they filled in the grave again. Nowadays he could grab hold of any tool, knock on the coffin boards and know if it was rebated or nailed on. He could fish things out of the coffin using just an iron hook. He was stronger than his father. He could open a corpse's mouth without pliers, snap off gold and silver teeth. He knew this kilometre-wide graveyard as well as he knew his own stall — who was buried where (except for the ones that died long ago), and what quality of coffin they had. As father walked the streets during the day selling clothing and jewellery — fake or genuine — that he'd stolen from graves, he would quietly find out who in each family had died or was soon going to die. And he'd suggest people really should buy grave goods for the dead. He'd tell the deceased's family that the dead go off to live somewhere else, so they have to take plenty of the things they'll need — especially gold and silver jewellery. He had described their life in detail so many times (as though he'd been there himself): the old people are waiting there, and as soon as you arrive you have to kowtow to pay your respects. Those who die young will marry and have children.

Sinners will see Yama, Lord of the Dead, and if they haven't got enough valuables they'll be boiled in oil: since they can't die of that, they'll be torn in 18 pieces afterwards by horses and carts; those who've acquired merit in this world must take presents to the Jade Emperor of the Southern Skies, and also present Our Lady of Compassion with a silver bracelet. If they've no grave goods the dead come back every night to wail by the front door. He had some 'True Stories' he'd been telling for half his life, all of them about dissatisfied ghosts who come back home to have it out with their families. He'd curse cremation for an Abomination to God and an Affront to Reason, and concrete coffins for preventing the dead ascending to Heaven.

THE cement factory's machines started up. He knew this was the day shift coming on, it was five am now and the sky showed no sign of brightening. Fireflies blundered into his face and flew off. He found himself at the spot where she had crooned a poem. The ground was more level here, the graves more scattered, less crowded together. A few stalks of dry grass left over from summer poked through the litter of bamboo leaves — echoing around the graveyard, her voice — the slightly husky voice of a young girl, crooning something? Just then — suddenly he was aware of lines stored away in his mind:

> if I can't hang on
> my love
> forgive me
> this is the first shower of summer...
>
> love gives shy gifts
> won't say its name
> snatches away the shadows
> scatters shivers of delight amongst the dust
> catch it
> or be forever wrong,...

These lines he didn't understand them, couldn't even remember them again. It was as if some aroma had flitted through his mind, opening it up in an instant, then flying suddenly away, leaving only the deserted cage that was his self.

He saw Fang Jing standing there, her legs crossed, rain falling on her face, ears sticking out of her soaking black hair. He had a premonition that something was about to happen in his body: he was eaten alive by a lust that longed for torture. He wanted to hide from himself, leave this stinking body.

He dragged himself off to dawdle round the graveyard again.

He went past Fang Jing's grave several times, knowing each time that he was close by. He stopped, stopped there — saw the grave he'd opened, the coffin lid smashed to bits, one end of it flung away, like the great mouth of some wild beast facing down the sky.

Beside her grave was a carved stone tomb fallen into dust now (the ruby ring had been stolen there), its hexagonal headstone sticking laboriously up out of the earth, seeming to sway in the wind. He saw again how mother cuddled him — his chubby little head nestling in her bosom. He cried for mummy, clutched her legs, she lowered her head, looked coldly at him, and he was afraid: it was Fang Jing's face, unsmiling, mouth open, clotted in her mouth a tongue bitten to pulp. He stood up suddenly, looked around: the dead stood on every grave, pressing in on him, the farther away ones flew towards him through the air, the girl who'd killed herself came before him, her eyes wordlessly fixed on his, a foul stench assailed his nostrils, his stomach churned. As well as the 'Rightist' with the gold tooth stretching out his hand to scratch at his throat, he felt an infinity of hands sticking in his flesh, tearing it off strip by strip, he felt no pain, felt himself disintegrating, disappearing. He saw his own skeleton, nothing left on the bones but hair. He felt himself relax, tried to stand up. He was standing up.

He tried to think back to how tonight began. But in his brain there was only an disordered chain of images jumping about.

He'd been drinking, it was spilt all over him, he'd wandered into the graveyard in a daze. He walked in, heard hoarse cries from her grave, was so frightened he dashed ahead, ran into a tree trunk. He sobered up, walked back shaking with fear, and the voice was gone. He thought he'd had too much to drink. He stripped off his coat, started shovelling earth. He thought of the daytime, how he'd stood in the crowd looking at Fang Jing's body — her expression as it had been in life, as if she was still crooning poems, he'd seen some that had been gassed who'd looked like that, calm, not like they were going to rot. He saw how the coffin lid was nailed down, and even then he was figuring out how to open it, how to

DARKNESS & LIGHT

undo her trousers. He smashed the lid open — she wasn't as calm as she'd been in the daytime — her eyes were protruding, blood from her mouth had run all over her chest, her body had twisted terribly before she'd suffocated, and she was all scratched and bloody between her breasts. The voice he'd heard just now was real.

He'd completely sobered up. There was a chill all about him.

The hand-me-down pick lay on a pile of fresh earth. He lifted it up, held it in his hand.

It was March, and the time when spring is strong in the air. An infinity of lives were growing and creeping underground. He thought of the mahogany tree at the house. Every year at this time mother let him climb it to pick the young shoots, and he'd frightened mother by going to jump down. Mother had answered by promising to sew him something nice. Where was the giraffe now? He could smell Fang Jing's scent as she tried on the sandals. When she bent down to look at them he could see her rounded breasts...

He arranged the corpse's limbs nicely, smoothed out her torn clothes, covered up her scratched and bloody breasts. He took off his clothes, covered her face, and strand by strand he straightened her dishevelled hair for her.

THEY didn't find the bodies until three days afterwards. His father got a rope round his son's neck, pulled him out of the coffin, and dug a grave nearby. Nanling Village saw nothing of his father after that.

Each spring there's always a bad smell there, spreading out from a low-lying piece of ground. Dust falls right and left from the weeds, and clouds of bluebottles drone in circles above it. ❏

Ma Jian is a writer and photographer from Beijing where his work was banned, now living in Hong Kong

Translated by Brian Holton
Illustration by Jeff Fisher

• *Quasimodo*, published in our last issue (2/1997) has now been published in Abandoned Wine: Chinese Writing Today 2, published by Wellsweep Press, London (+ 44 171 267 3525)

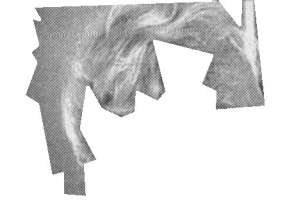

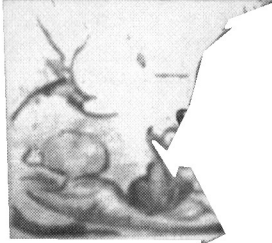

Above: Index's *founder, the late Sir Stephen Spender, with Pavel Litvinov, who sent the plea for support from Russian dissidents which led to the foundation of* Index *25 years ago*

To Russia with love

This summer, when *Index* is celebrating its 25th anniversary, a Russian-language sister journal, *Dos'e na tsenzuru*, will be launched in Moscow. Published by the Glasnost Defence Foundation (GDF) in association with *Index*, *Dos'e* will report on issues of free expression and media freedom and take the essential debates on democracy and human rights to readers in the Russian-speaking world.

Each quarterly issue will include articles translated from *Index*, providing an international dimension to the debate, as well as articles and reports from local writers and journalists. A special series of reports from Transcaucasia and Central Asia is being prepared with *Index's* eastern Europe editor, Irena Maryniak.

This partnership represents an important and fitting milestone in *Index's* history. Twenty-five years ago the first issue of *Index* appeared, in response to an appeal from dissidents in Russia. At the time a publication of this kind was unthinkable in the Soviet Union. *Index* provided a forum for dissident voices and supported them from afar. Now *Index*, through its partnership with the GDF, will support those leading the democratic debate on the ground. *Dos'e* appears with a sense of optimism and purpose at a turning point in history.

Financial support for *Dos'e* has come from the European Commission's TACIS Democracy Programme and the Open Society Institute. Funding for the Transcaucasia and Central Asia reports comes from the Netherlands Foreign Ministry. For more information please contact:

Glasnost Defence Foundation
4-1 Etazh, Kom 432
Zubovskii b-r., d.4
Moscow 119021
Russia
Tel: +7 095 201 4420 or

Index on Censorship
33 Islington High Street
London N1 9LH
UK
Tel: + 44 171 278 2313